FAR AWAY AND LONG AGO

W. H. HUDSON

FOREWORD

HUDSON is, of the writers of our time, the rarest spirit, and has the clearest gift of conveying the nature of that spirit. Writers are to their readers little new worlds to be explored; and each traveller in the realms of literature must needs have a favourite hunting ground, which, in his good will —or perhaps merely in his egoism—he could wish others to share with him.

The great and abiding misfortunes of most of us writers are twofold: we are, as worlds, rather common tramping ground for our readers, rather tame territory; and as guides and dragomans thereto we are too superficial, lacking clear intimacy of expression; in fact—like guide or dragoman— we cannot let folk into the real secrets, or show them the spirit of the land.

Now Hudson, whether in a pure romance like *Green Mansions*, or in that romantic piece of realism *The Purple Land*, or in books like *Idle Days in Patagonia, Afoot in England, The Land's End, Adventures among Birds, A Shepherd's Life, Far Away and Long Ago*, and all his other nomadic records of communings with men, birds, beasts, and Nature, has a supreme gift of disclosing not only the thing he sees but the spirit of his vision. Without apparent effort he takes you with him into a rare, free, natural world, and always you are refreshed, stimulated, enlarged, by going there.

He is, of course, a distinguished naturalist, probably the most acute, broad-minded, and understanding of all observers of Nature. And this, in an age of specialism, which loves to put men into pigeon-holes and label them, has been a misfortune to the reading public, who seeing the label Naturalist, pass on and reach down the nearest novel. Hudson has indeed the gifts and knowledge of a Naturalist, but that is a mere fraction of his value and interest. A really great writer such as this is no more to be circum-

vii

FOREWORD

scribed by a single word than America by the part of it called New York. The expert knowledge which Hudson has of Nature gives to all his work backbone and surety of fibre, and to his sense of beauty an intimate actuality. But his real eminence and extraordinary attraction lie in his spirit and philosophy. We feel from his writings that he is nearer to Nature than other men, and yet more truly civilized. The competitive, towny culture, the queer up-to-date commercial knowingness with which we are so busy coating ourselves, simply will not stick to him. A passage in his *Hampshire Days* describes him better than I can: 'The blue sky, the brown soil beneath, the grass, the trees, the animals, the wind, the rain, and stars are never strange to me; for I am in, and of, and am one with, them; and my flesh and the soil are one, and the heat in my blood and in the sunshine are one, and the winds and the tempests and my passions are one. I feel the "strangeness" only with regard to my fellow-men, especially in towns, where they exist in conditions unnatural to me, but congenial to them. . . . In such moments we sometimes feel a kinship with, and are strangely drawn to, the dead, who were not as these; the long, long dead, the men who knew not life in towns, and felt no strangeness in sun and wind and rain.' This unspoiled unity with Nature pervades all his writings; they are remote from the fret and dust and pettiness of town life; they are large, direct, free. It is not quite simplicity, for the mind of this writer is subtle and fastidious, sensitive to each motion of natural and human life; but his sensitiveness is somehow different from, almost inimical to, that of us others, who sit indoors and dip our pens in shades of feeling. Hudson's fancy is akin to the flight of the birds that are his special loves—it never seems to have entered a house, but since birth to have been roaming the air, in rain and sun, or visiting the trees and the grass. I not only disbelieve utterly, but intensely dislike, the doctrine of metempsychosis, which, if I understand it aright, seems the negation of the creative impulse, an apotheosis of staleness—nothing quite new in the world, never anything quite new—not even the soul of a baby; and so I am not prepared to entertain the whim that a bird was one of his remote incarnations; still, in sweep of wing, quickness of

FOREWORD ix

eye, and natural sweet strength of song he is not unlike a super-bird—which is a horrid image.

Somewhere Hudson says: 'The sense of the beautiful is God's best gift to the human soul.' So it is; and to pass that gift on to others in such great measure must surely have been happiness to him.

Do we realize how far our town life and culture have got away from things that really matter, how instead of making civilization our handmaid to freedom we have set her heel on our necks, and under it bite dust all the time? Hudson, whether he knows it or not, is the chief standard-bearer of another faith. Thus he spake in *The Purple Land*: 'Ah, yes, we are all vainly seeking after happiness in the wrong way. It was with us once and ours, but we despised it, for it was only the old common happiness which Nature gives to all her children, and we went away from it in search of another grander kind of happiness which some dreamer— Bacon or another—assured us we should find. We had only to conquer Nature, find out her secrets, make her our obedient slave, then the Earth would be Eden, and every man Adam and every woman Eve. We are still marching bravely on, conquering Nature, but how weary and sad we are getting! The old joy in life and gaiety of heart have vanished, though we do sometimes pause for a few moments in our long forced march to watch the labours of some pale mechanician, seeking after perpetual motion, and indulge in a little dry, cackling laugh at his expense.' And again: 'For here the religion that languishes in crowded cities or steals shame-faced to hide itself in dim churches, flourishes greatly, filling the soul with a solemn joy. Face to face with Nature on the vast hills at eventide, who does not feel himself near to the Unseen?

> Out of his heart God shall not pass,
> His image stamped is on every grass.'

All Hudson's books breathe this spirit of revolt against our enslavement by towns and machinery, and are true oases in an Age so dreadfully resigned to the 'pale mechanician.'

But Hudson is not, as Tolstoi was, a conscious prophet; his spirit is freer, more wilful, whimsical—almost perverse—

* 956

FOREWORD

and far more steeped in love of beauty. At any one who called him a prophet he would have stamped his foot; but his voice is prophetic, for all that, crying in a wilderness, out of which, at the call, will spring up roses here and there, and the sweet-smelling grass. I would that every man, woman, and child in England were made to read him. He is a tonic, a deep refreshing drink, with a strange and wonderful flavour; he is a mine of new interests, and ways of thought instinctively right. As a simple narrator he is well-nigh unsurpassed; as a stylist he has few, if any, living equals. And in all his work there is an indefinable freedom from any thought of after-benefit—even from the desire that we should read him. He puts down what he sees and feels, out of sheer love of the thing seen, and the emotion felt; the smell of the lamp has not touched a single page that he ever wrote. That alone is a marvel to us who know that to write well, even to write clearly, is a woundy business, long to learn, hard to learn, and no gift of the angels. Style should not obtrude between a writer and his reader; it should be servant, not master. To use words so true and simple, that they oppose no obstacle to the flow of thought and feeling from mind to mind, and yet by juxtaposition of word-sounds set up in the recipient continuing emotion or gratification—this is the essence of style; and Hudson's writing has pre-eminently this double quality. From almost any page of his books an example might be taken. Here is one no better than a thousand others, a description of two little girls on a beach: 'They were dressed in black frocks and scarlet blouses, which set off their beautiful small dark faces; their eyes sparkled like black diamonds, and their loose hair was a wonder to see, a black mist or cloud about their heads and necks composed of threads fine as gossamer, blacker than jet and shining like spun glass—hair that looked as if no comb or brush could ever tame its beautiful wildness. And in spirit they were what they seemed; such a wild, joyous, frolicsome spirit, with such grace and fleetness, one does not look for in human beings, but only in birds or in some small bird-like volatile mammal—a squirrel or a spider-monkey of the tropical forest, or the chinchilla of the desolate mountain slopes; the swiftest, wildest, loveliest, most

FOREWORD   xi

airy, and most vocal of small beasties.' Or this, as the
quintessence of a sly remark: 'After that Manuel got on
to his horse and rode away. It was black and rainy, but
he had never needed moon or lantern to find what he sought
by night, whether his own house, or a fat cow—also his
own, perhaps.' So one might go on quoting felicities from
this writer. He seems to touch every string with fresh
and uninked fingers; and the secret of his power lies, I
suspect, in the fact that his words 'Life being more than
all else to me . . .' are so utterly true.

I do not descant on his love for simple folk and simple
things, his championship of the weak, and the revolt
against the cagings and cruelties of life, whether to men or
birds or beasts, that springs out of him as if against his will;
because, having spoken of him as one with a vital philosophy or faith, I would draw no red herrings across the
main trail of his worth to the world. His work is a vision
of natural beauty and of human life as it might be, quickened
and sweetened by the sun and the wind and the rain, and
by fellowship with all the other forms of life—a vision
given to us, who are more in want of it than any generation
has ever been. A very great writer; and—to my thinking
—the most valuable our Age has possessed.

JOHN GALSWORTHY.

The following is a list of the chief works by W. H. Hudson,
with the dates of their first publication in book form:

The Purple Land that England Lost, 1885; *A Crystal Age*, 1887;
Argentine Ornithology, 1888–9 (this was issued in collaboration
with P. L. Sclater, and all Hudson's own work was later collected
into one volume—*Birds of La Plata*, see below); *The Naturalist
in La Plata*, 1892; *Fan*, 1892 (issued under the pseudonym of
'Henry Harford'); *Idle Days in Patagonia*, 1893; *Birds in a
Village*, 1893 (this was enlarged and extensively revised as *Birds
in Town and Village*, see below); *British Birds*, 1895; *Birds in
London*, 1898; *Nature in Downland*, 1900; *Birds and Man*, 1901;
El Ombú, 1902 (this collection was reissued in 1909 under the
title *South American Sketches*); *Hampshire Days*, 1903; *Green
Mansions*, 1904; *A Little Boy Lost*, 1905; *The Land's End*, 1908;
Afoot in England, 1909; *A Shepherd's Life*, 1910; *Adventures*

xii FOREWORD

Among Birds, 1913; *Far Away and Long Ago*, 1918; *Birds in Town and Village*, 1919 (see above); *The Book of a Naturalist*, 1919; *Dead Man's Plack* and *An Old Thorn*, 1920; *Birds of La Plata*, 1920 (see above); *A Traveller in Little Things*, 1921; *A Hind in Richmond Park*, 1922.

The Collected Edition of Hudson's works was issued in 1923 in twenty-four volumes. It contains, so far as is practicable, everything that Hudson wrote for publication. The minor works of Hudson consist of a story called *Ralph Herne* that appeared serially in 1888 in *Youth*, a weekly publication; a dozen or so pamphlets issued by the Royal Society for the Protection of Birds; one or two other pamphlets, and a small number of miscellaneous contributions to periodicals.

CONTENTS

PAGE

I. EARLIEST MEMORIES

Preamble—The house where I was born—The singular ombú tree—A tree without a name—The plain—The ghost of a murdered slave—Our playmate, the old sheep-dog—A first riding-lesson—The cattle: an evening scene—My mother—Captain Scott—The hermit and his awful penance 1

II. MY NEW HOME

We quit our old home—A winter day journey—Aspect of the country—Our new home—A prisoner in the barn —The plantation—A paradise of rats—An evening scene —The people of the house—A beggar on horseback— Mr Trigg our schoolmaster—His double nature—Impersonates an old woman—Reading Dickens—Mr Trigg degenerates—Once more a homeless wanderer on the great plain 15

III. DEATH OF AN OLD DOG

The old dog Caesar—His powerful personality—Last days and end—The old dog's burial—The fact of death is brought home to me—A child's mental anguish—My mother comforts me—Limitations of the child's mind —Fear of death—Witnessing the slaughter of cattle— —A man in the moat—Margarita, the nursery-maid— Her beauty and lovableness—Her death—I refuse to see her dead 28

IV. THE PLANTATION

Living with trees—Winter violets—The house is made habitable—Red willow—Scissor-tail and carrion-hawk —Lombardy poplars—Black acacia—Other trees—The fosse or moat—Rats—A trial of strength with an armadillo—Opossums living with a snake—Alfalfa field and

xiii

xiv CONTENTS

PAGE

butterflies—Cane brake—Weeds and fennel—Peach trees
in blossom—Paroquets—Singing of a field finch—Concert-singing in birds—Old John—Cow-birds' singing—
Arrival of summer migrants 39

V. ASPECTS OF THE PLAIN

Appearance of a green level land—Cardoon and giant thistles
—Villages of the *vizcacha*, a large burrowing rodent—
Groves and plantations seen like islands on the wide
level plains—Trees planted by the early colonists—
Decline of the colonists from an agricultural to a pastoral people—Houses as part of the landscape—Flesh
diet of the gauchos—Summer change in the aspect of
the plain—The water-like mirage—The giant thistle
and a 'thistle year'—Fear of fires—An incident at a
fire—The *pampero*, or south-west wind, and the fall of
the thistles—Thistle-down and thistle-seed as food for
animals—A great *pampero* storm—Big hailstones—
Damage caused by hail—Zango, an old horse, killed—
Zango and his master 54

VI. SOME BIRD ADVENTURES

Visit to a river on the pampas—A first long walk—Water-
fowl—My first sight of flamingoes—A great dove visitation—Strange tameness of the birds—Vain attempts
at putting salt on their tails—An ethical question:
When is a lie not a lie?—The *carancho*, a vulture-eagle
—Our pair of *caranchos*—Their nest in a peach tree—I am
ambitious to take their eggs—The birds' crimes—I am
driven off by the birds—The nest pulled down . . 66

VII. MY FIRST VISIT TO BUENOS AYRES

Happiest time—First visit to the capital—Old and New
Buenos Ayres—Vivid impressions—Solitary walk—How
I learnt to go alone—Lost—The house we stayed at and
the sea-like river—Rough and narrow streets—Rows
of posts—Carts and noise—A great church festival—
Young men in black and scarlet—River scenes—Washerwomen and their language—Their word-fights with
young fashionables—Night watchmen—A young gentleman's pastime—A fishing dog—A fine gentleman seen
stoning little birds—A glimpse of Don Eusebio, the
Dictator's fool 79

CONTENTS

xv

PAGE

VIII. THE TYRANT'S FALL AND WHAT FOLLOWED

The portraits in our drawing-room—The Dictator Rosas who was like an Englishman—The strange face of his wife, Encarnacion—The traitor Urquiza—The Minister of War, his peacocks and his son—Home again from the city — The war deprives us of our playmate — Natalia, our shepherd's wife—Her son, Medardo—The Alcalde, our grand old man—Battle of Monte Caseros —The defeated army—Demands for fresh horses—In peril—My father's shining defects—His pleasure in a thunderstorm—A childlike trust in his fellow-men— Soldiers turn upon their officer—A refugee given up and murdered—Our Alcalde again—On cutting throats— Ferocity and cynicism—Native blood-lust and its effect on a boy's mind—Feeling about Rosas—A bird poem or tale—Vain search for lost poem and story of its authorship—The Dictator's daughter—Time, the old god .   92

IX. OUR NEIGHBOURS AT THE POPLARS

Homes on the great green plain—Making the acquaintance of our neighbours—The attraction of birds—Los Alamos and the old lady of the house—Her treatment of St Anthony—The strange Barboza family—The man of blood—Great fighters—Barboza as a singer—A great quarrel but no fight—A cattle-marking—Doña Lucía del Ombú—A feast—Barboza sings and is insulted by El Rengo—Refuses to fight—The two kinds of fighters —A poor little angel on horseback—My feeling for Anjelita—Boys unable to express sympathy—A quarrel with a friend—Enduring image of a little girl . .   114

X. OUR NEAREST ENGLISH NEIGHBOUR

Casa Antigua, our nearest English neighbour's house—Old Lombardy poplars—Cardoon thistle or wild artichoke —Mr Royd, an English sheep-farmer—Making sheep's-milk cheeses under difficulties—Mr Royd's native wife —The negro servants—The two daughters: a striking contrast—The white blue-eyed child and her dusky playmate—A happy family—Our visits to Casa Antigua —Gorgeous dinners—Estanislao and his love of wild life—The Royds' return visits—A home-made carriage —The gaucho's primitive conveyance—The happy home broken up   127

xvi CONTENTS

PAGE

XI. A BREEDER OF PIEBALDS

La Tapera, a native estancia—Don Gregorio Gandara—
His grotesque appearance and strange laugh—Gandara's wife and her habits and pets—My dislike of
hairless dogs—Gandara's daughters—A pet ostrich—In
the peach orchard—Gandara's herds of piebald brood
mares—His masterful temper—His own saddle-horses
—Creating a sensation at gaucho gatherings—The
younger daughter's lovers—Her marriage at our house
—The priest and the wedding breakfast—Demetria
forsaken by her husband 135

XII. THE HEAD OF A DECAYED HOUSE

The Estancia Cañada Seca—Low lands and floods—Don
Anastacio, a gaucho exquisite—A greatly respected man
—Poor relations—Don Anastacio a pig-fancier—Narrow
escape from a pig—Charm of the low green lands—The
flower called *mácachina*—A sweet-tasting bulb—Beauty
of the green flower-sprinkled turf—A haunt of the
golden plover—The *bolas*—My plover-hunting experience—Rebuked by a gaucho—A green spot, our playground in summer and lake in winter—The venomous
toad-like *Ceratophrys*—Vocal performance of the toad-
like creature—We make war on them—The great lake
battle and its results 144

XIII. A PATRIARCH OF THE PAMPAS

The grand old man of the plains—Don Evaristo Peñalva,
the Patriarch—My first sight of his estancia house—
Don Evaristo described—A husband of six wives—
How he was esteemed and loved by every one—On
leaving home I lose sight of Don Evaristo—I meet him
again after seven years—His failing health—His old
first wife and her daughter, Cipriana—The tragedy of
Cipriana—Don Evaristo dies and I lose sight of the
family 155

XIV. THE DOVECOTE

A favourite climbing tree—The desire to fly—Soaring birds
—A peregrine falcon—The dovecote and pigeon-pies
—The falcon's depredations—A splendid aerial feat—
A secret enemy of the dovecote—A short-eared owl in
a loft—My father and birds—A strange flower—The
owls' nesting-place—Great owl visitations . . . 164

CONTENTS   xvii

PAGE

XV. SERPENT AND CHILD

My pleasure in bird life—Mammals at our new home—
Snakes and how children are taught to regard them
—A colony of snakes in the house—Their hissing confabulations—Finding serpent sloughs—A serpent's
saviour—A brief history of our English neighbours,
the Blakes 177

XVI. A SERPENT MYSTERY

A new feeling about snakes—Common snakes of the country
—A barren weedy patch—Discovery of a large black
snake—Watching for its reappearance—Seen going to
its den—The desire to see it again—A vain search—
Watching a bat—The black serpent reappears at my
feet—Emotions and conjectures—Melanism—My baby
sister and a strange snake—The mystery solved . . 185

XVII. A BOY'S ANIMISM

The animistic faculty and its survival in us—A boy's animism and its persistence—Impossibility of seeing our
past exactly as it was—Serge Aksakoff's history of his
childhood—The child's delight in nature purely physical
—First intimations of animism in the child—How it
affected me—Feeling with regard to flowers—A flower
and my mother—History of a flower—Animism with
regard to trees—Locust trees by moonlight—Animism
and nature-worship—Animistic emotion not uncommon
—Cowper and the Yardley oak—The religionist's fear
of nature—Pantheistic Christianity—Survival of nature-
worship in England—The feeling for nature—Wordsworth's pantheism and animistic emotion in poetry . 194

XVIII. THE NEW SCHOOLMASTER

Mr Trigg recalled—His successor—Father O'Keefe—His
mild rule and love of angling — My brother is assisted
in his studies by the priest—Happy fishing afternoons
—The priest leaves us—How he had been working out
his own salvation—We run wild once more—My brother's
plan for a journal to be called *The Tin Box*—Our imperious editor's exactions—My little brother revolts
—*The Tin Box* smashed up—The loss it was to me . 205

xviii   CONTENTS

                                                            PAGE
                        XIX. BROTHERS

Our third and last schoolmaster—His many accomplishments—His weakness and final breakdown—My important brother—Four brothers, unlike in everything
except the voice—A strange meeting—Jack the killer,
his life and character—A terrible fight—My brother
seeks instructions from Jack—The gaucho's way of
fighting and Jack's contrasted—Our sham fight with
knives—A wound, and the result—My feeling about
Jack and his eyes—Bird-lore—My two elder brothers'
practical joke   215

                  XX. BIRDING IN THE MARSHES

Visiting the marshes—*Pajonales* and *juncales*—Abundant
bird life—A coots' metropolis—Frightening the coots
—Grebe and painted snipe colonies—The haunt of the
social marsh-hawk—The beautiful jacana and its eggs
—The colony of marsh-troupials—The bird's music—
The aquatic plant *durasmillo*—The triupial's nest and
eggs—Recalling a beauty that has vanished—Our games
with gaucho boys—I am injured by a bad boy—The
shepherd's advice—Getting my revenge in a treacherous
manner—Was it right or wrong?—The game of hunting
the ostrich   226

                XXI. WILD-FOWLING ADVENTURES

My sporting brother and the armoury—I attend him on
his shooting expeditions—Adventure with golden plover
—A morning after wild duck—Our punishment—I learn
to shoot—My first gun—My first wild duck—My ducking
tactics—My gun's infirmities—Duck-shooting with a
blunderbuss—Ammunition runs out—An adventure with
rosy-bill duck—Coarse gunpowder and home-made shot
—The war danger comes our way—We prepare to
defend the house—The danger over and my brother
leaves home   236

                    XXII. BOYHOOD'S END

The book—The Saladero, or killing-grounds, and their smell
—Walls built of bullock's skulls—A pestilential city—
River water and *aljibe* water—Days of lassitude—
Novel scenes—Home again—Typhus—My first day
out—Birthday reflections—What I asked of life—
A boy's mind—A brother's resolution—End of our
thousand and one nights—A reading spell—My boy-
hood ends in disaster   248

CONTENTS

XXIII. A DARKENED LIFE

A severe illness—Case pronounced hopeless—How it affected me—Religious doubts and a mind distressed—Lawless thoughts—Conversation with an old gaucho about religion—George Combe and the desire for immortality . 262

XXIV. LOSS AND GAIN

The soul's loneliness—My mother and her death—A mother's love for her son—Her character—Anecdotes——A mystery and a revelation—The autumnal migration of birds—Moonlight vigils—My absent brother's return—He introduces me to Darwin's works—A new philosophy of life—Conclusion 272

INDEX 291

CHAPTER I

EARLIEST MEMORIES

Preamble—The house where I was born—The singular ombú tree
— A tree without a name — The plain — The ghost of a
murdered slave—Our playmate, the old sheep-dog—A first
riding-lesson—The cattle: an evening scene—My mother—
Captain Scott—The hermit and his awful penance.

IT was never my intention to write an autobiography.
Since I took to writing in my middle years I have, from
time to time, related some incident of my boyhood, and
these are contained in various chapters in *The Naturalist
in La Plata, Birds and Man, Adventures among Birds*,
and other works, also in two or three magazine articles:
all this material would have been kept back if I had
contemplated such a book as this. When my friends
have asked me in recent years why I did not write a
history of my early life on the pampas, my answer was
that I had already told all that was worth telling in
these books. And I really believed it was so; for when
a person endeavours to recall his early life in its entirety
he finds it is not possible: he is like one who ascends a
hill to survey the prospect before him on a day of heavy
cloud and shadow, who sees at a distance, now here,
now there, some feature in the landscape—hill or wood
or tower or spire—touched and made conspicuous by
a transitory sunbeam while all else remains in obscurity.
The scenes, people, events we are able by an effort to
call up do not present themselves in order; there is no
order, no sequence or regular progression—nothing, in
fact, but isolated spots or patches, brightly illumined
and vividly seen, in the midst of a wide shrouded mental
landscape.

2   FAR AWAY AND LONG AGO

It is easy to fall into the delusion that the few things thus distinctly remembered and visualized are precisely those which were most important in our life, and on that account were saved by memory while all the rest has been permanently blotted out. That is indeed how our memory serves and fools us; for at some period of a man's life—at all events of some lives—in some rare state of the mind, it is all at once revealed to him as by a miracle that nothing is ever blotted out.

It was through falling into some such state as that, during which I had a wonderfully clear and continuous vision of the past, that I was tempted—forced I may say—to write this account of my early years. I will relate the occasion, as I imagine that the reader who is a psychologist will find as much to interest him in this incident as in anything else contained in the book.

I was feeling weak and depressed when I came down from London one November evening to the south coast; the sea, the clear sky, the bright colours of the after-glow kept me too long on the front in an east wind in that low condition, with the result that I was laid up for six weeks with a very serious illness. Yet when it was over I looked back on those six weeks as a happy time! Never had I thought so little of physical pain. Never had I felt confinement less—I who feel, when I am out of sight of living, growing grass, and out of sound of birds' voices and all rural sounds, that I am not properly alive!

On the second day of my illness, during an interval of comparative ease, I fell into recollections of my childhood, and at once I had that far, that forgotten past with me again as I had never previously had it. It was not like that mental condition, known to most persons, when some sight or sound or, more frequently, the perfume of some flower, associated with our early life, restores the past suddenly and so vividly that it is

EARLIEST MEMORIES

almost an illusion. That is an intensely emotional condition and vanishes as quickly as it comes. This was different. To return to the simile and metaphor used at the beginning, it was as if the cloud shadows and haze had passed away and the entire wide prospect beneath me made clearly visible. Over it all my eyes could range at will, choosing this or that point to dwell upon, to examine it in all its details; or in the case of some person known to me as a child, to follow his life till it ended or passed from sight; then to return to the same point again to repeat the process with other lives and resume my rambles in the old familiar haunts.

What a happiness it would be, I thought, in spite of discomfort and pain and danger, if this vision would continue! It was not to be expected: nevertheless it did not vanish, and on the second day I set myself to try and save it from the oblivion which would presently cover it again. Propped up with pillows I began with pencil and writing-pad to put it down in some sort of order, and went on with it at intervals during the whole six weeks of my confinement, and in this way produced the first rough draft of the book.

And all this time I never ceased wondering at my own mental state; I thought of it when, quickly tired, my trembling fingers dropped the pencil; or when I woke from uneasy sleep to find the vision still before me, inviting, insistently calling to me, to resume my childish rambles and adventures of long ago in that strange world where I first saw the light.

It was to me a marvellous experience; to be here, propped up with pillows in a dimly lighted room, the night-nurse idly dozing by the fire; the sound of the everlasting wind in my ears, howling outside and dashing the rain like hailstones against the window-panes; to be awake to all this, feverish and ill and sore, conscious of my danger too, and at the same time to be thousands

4 FAR AWAY AND LONG AGO

of miles away, out in the sun and wind, rejoicing in other sights and sounds, happy again with that ancient long-lost and now recovered happiness!

During the three years that have passed since I had that strange experience, I have from time to time, when in the mood, gone back to the book and have had to cut it down a good deal and to reshape it, as in the first draft it would have made too long and formless a history.

The house where I was born, on the South American pampas, was quaintly named *Los Veinte-cinco Ombues*, which means 'The Twenty-five Ombú Trees,' there being just twenty-five of these indigenous trees—gigantic in size, and standing wide apart in a row about four hundred yards long. The ombú is a very singular tree indeed, and being the only representative of tree-vegetation, natural to the soil, on those great level plains, and having also many curious superstitions connected with it, it is a romance in itself. It belongs to the rare Phytolacca family, and has an immense girth—forty or fifty feet in some cases; at the same time the wood is so soft and spongy that it can be cut into with a knife, and is utterly unfit for firewood, for when cut up it refuses to dry, but simply rots away like a ripe water-melon. It also grows slowly, and its leaves, which are large, glossy, and deep green, like laurel leaves, are poisonous; and

· because of its uselessness it will probably become extinct, like the graceful pampas grass in the same region. In this exceedingly practical age men quickly lay the axe at the root of things which, in their view, only cumber the ground; but before other trees had been planted the antiquated and grand-looking ombú had its uses; it served as a gigantic landmark to the traveller on the great monotonous plains, and also afforded refreshing shade to man and horse in summer; while the native doctor or herbalist would sometimes pluck a leaf for

EARLIEST MEMORIES 5

a patient requiring a very violent remedy for his disorder. Our trees were about a century old and very large, and, as they stood on an elevation, they could be easily seen at a distance of ten miles. At noon in summer the cattle and sheep, of which we had a large number, used to rest in their shade; one large tree also afforded us children a splendid play-house, and we used to carry up a number of planks to construct safe bridges from branch to branch, and at noon, when our elders were sleeping their siesta, we would have our arboreal games unmolested.

Besides the famous twenty-five, there was one other tree of a different species, growing close to the house, and this was known all over the neighbourhood as 'The Tree,' this proud name having been bestowed on it because it was the only one of the kind known in that part of the country; our native neighbours always affirmed that it was the only one in the world. It was a fine large old tree, with a white bark, long smooth white thorns, and dark-green undeciduous foliage. Its blossoming time was in November—a month about as hot as an English July—and it would then become covered with tassels of minute wax-like flowers, pale straw-colour, and of a wonderful fragrance, which the soft summer wind would carry for miles on its wings. And in this way our neighbours would discover that the flowering season had come to the tree they so much admired, and they would come to beg for a branch to take home with them to perfume their lowly houses.

The pampas are, in most places, level as a billiard-table; just where we lived, however, the country happened to be undulating, and our house stood on the summit of one of the highest elevations. Before the house stretched a great grassy plain, level to the horizon, while at the back it sloped abruptly down to a broad, deep stream, which emptied itself in the river Plata,

6   FAR AWAY AND LONG AGO

about six miles to the east. This stream, with its three ancient red willow trees growing on the banks, was a source of endless pleasure to us. Whenever we went down to play on the banks, the fresh penetrating scent of the moist earth had a strangely exhilarating effect, making us wild with joy. I am able now to recall these sensations, and believe that the sense of smell, which seems to diminish as we grow older, until it becomes something scarcely worthy of being called a sense, is nearly as keen in little children as in the inferior animals, and, when they live with nature, contributes as much to their pleasure as sight or hearing. I have often observed that small children, when brought on to low, moist ground from a high level, give loose to a sudden spontaneous gladness, running, shouting, and rolling over the grass just like dogs, and I have no doubt that the fresh smell of the earth is the cause of their joyous excitement.

Our house was a long low structure, built of brick, and, being very old, naturally had the reputation of being haunted. A former proprietor, half a century before I was born, once had among his slaves a very handsome young negro, who, on account of his beauty and amiability, was a special favourite with his mistress. Her preference filled his poor silly brains with dreams and aspirations, and, deceived by her gracious manner, he one day ventured to approach her in the absence of his master and told her his feelings. She could not forgive so terrible an insult to her pride, and when her husband returned went to him, white with indignation, and told him how this miserable slave had abused their kindness. The husband had an implacable heart, and at his command the offender was suspended by the wrists to a low, horizontal branch of 'The Tree,' and there, in sight of his master and mistress, he was scourged to death by his fellow-slaves. His battered

EARLIEST MEMORIES · 7

body was then taken down and buried in a deep hollow
at some little distance from the last of the long row of
ombú trees. It was the ghost of this poor black, whose
punishment had been so much heavier than his offence
deserved, that was supposed to haunt the place. It was
not, however, a conventional ghost, stalking about in a
white sheet; those who had seen it averred that it invariably rose up from the spot where the body had been
buried, like a pale, luminous exhalation from the earth,
and, assuming a human shape, floated slowly towards
the house, and roamed about the great trees, or, seating
itself on an old projecting root, would remain motionless
for hours in a dejected attitude. I never saw it.

Our constant companion and playmate in those days
was a dog, whose portrait has never faded from remem-
brance, for he was a dog with features and a personality
which impressed themselves deeply on the mind. He
came to us in a rather mysterious manner. One
summer evening the shepherd was galloping round the
flock, and trying by means of much shouting to induce
the lazy sheep to move homewards. A strange-looking
lame dog suddenly appeared on the scene, as if it had
dropped from the clouds, and limping briskly after the
astonished and frightened sheep, drove them straight
home and into the fold; and, after thus earning his
supper and showing what stuff was in him, he established
himself at the house, where he was well received. He
was a good-sized animal, with a very long body, a smooth
black coat, tan feet, muzzle, and 'spectacles,' and a face
of extraordinary length, which gave him a profoundly
wise baboon-like expression. One of his hind legs had
been broken or otherwise injured, so that he limped and
shuffled along in a peculiar lop-sided fashion; he had no
tail, and his ears had been cropped close to his head:
altogether he was like an old soldier returned from
the wars, where he had received many hard knocks,

8 FAR AWAY AND LONG AGO

besides having had sundry portions of his anatomy shot away.

No name to fit this singular canine visitor could be found, although he responded readily enough to the word *pechicho*, which is used to call any unnamed pup by, like 'pussy' for a cat. So it came to pass that this word *pechicho*—equivalent to 'doggie' in English— stuck to him for only name until the end of the chapter; and the end was that, after spending some years with us, he mysteriously disappeared.

He very soon proved to us that he understood children as well as sheep; at all events he would allow them to tease and pull him about most unmercifully, and actually appeared to enjoy it. Our first riding- lessons were taken on his back; but old Pechicho eventu- ally made one mistake, after which he was relieved from the labour of carrying us. When I was about four years old, my two elder brothers, in the character of riding- masters, set me on his back, and, in order to test my capacity for sticking on under difficulties, they rushed away, calling him. The old dog, infected with the pretended excitement, bounded after them, and I was thrown and had my leg broken, for, as the poet says:

> Children, they are very little,
> And their bones are very brittle.

Luckily their little brittle bones quickly solder, and it did not take me long to recover from the effects of this mishap.

No doubt my canine steed was as much troubled as any one at the accident. I seem to see the wise old fellow now, sitting in that curious one-sided fashion he had acquired so as to rest his lame leg, his mouth opened to a kind of immense smile, and his brown benevolent eyes regarding us with just such an expres- sion as one sees in a faithful old negress nursing a flock

EARLIEST MEMORIES 9

of troublesome white children—so proud and happy to be in charge of the little ones of a superior race!

All that I remember of my early life at this place comes between the ages of three or four and five; a period which, to the eye of memory, appears like a wide plain blurred over with a low-lying mist, with here and there a group of trees, a house, a hill, or other large object, standing out in the clear air with marvellous distinctness. The picture that most often presents itself is of the cattle coming home in the evening; the green quiet plain extending away from the gate to the horizon; the western sky flushed with sunset hues, and the herd of four or five hundred cattle trotting homewards with loud lowings and bellowings, raising a great cloud of dust with their hoofs, while behind gallop the herdsmen urging them on with wild cries. Another picture is of my mother at the close of the day, when we children, after our supper of bread and milk, join in a last grand frolic on the green before the house. I see her sitting out of doors watching our sport with a smile, her book lying in her lap, and the last rays of the setting sun shining on her face.

When I think of her I remember with gratitude that our parents seldom or never punished us, and never, unless we went too far in our domestic dissensions or tricks, even chided us. This, I am convinced, is the right attitude for parents to observe, modestly to admit that nature is wiser than they are, and to let their little ones follow, as far as possible, the bent of their own minds, or whatever it is they have in place of minds. It is the attitude of the sensible hen towards her ducklings, when she has had frequent experience of their incongruous ways, and is satisfied that they know best what is good for them; though, of course, their ways seem peculiar to her, and she can never entirely sympathize with their fancy for going into water. I need not be

FAR AWAY AND LONG AGO

told that the hen is after all only stepmother to her ducklings, since I am contending that the civilized woman—the artificial product of our self-imposed conditions—cannot have the same relation to her offspring as the uncivilized woman really has to hers. The comparison, therefore, holds good, the mother with us being practically stepmother to children of another race; and if she is sensible, and amenable to nature's teaching, she will attribute their seemingly unsuitable ways and appetites to the right cause, and not to a hypothetical perversity or inherent depravity of heart, about which many authors will have spoken to her in many books:

> But though they wrote it all by rote
> They did not write it right.

Of all the people outside of the domestic circle known to me in those days, two individuals only are distinctly remembered. They were certainly painted by memory in very strong unfading colours, so that now they seem to stand like living men in a company of pale phantom forms. This is probably due to the circumstance that they were considerably more grotesque in appearance than the others, like old Pechicho among our dogs—all now forgotten save him.

One was an Englishman named Captain Scott, who used to visit us occasionally for a week's shooting or fishing, for he was a great sportsman. We were all extremely fond of him, for he was one of those simple men that love and sympathize with children; besides that, he used to come to us from some distant wonderful place where sugar-plums were made, and to our healthy appetites, unaccustomed to sweets of any description, these things tasted like an angelic kind of food. He was an immense man, with a great round face of a purplish-red colour, like the sun setting in glory, and surrounded with a fringe of silvery-white hair and

EARLIEST MEMORIES 11

whiskers, standing out like the petals round the disk of a sunflower. It was always a great time when Captain Scott arrived, and while he alighted from his horse we would surround him with loud demonstrations of welcome, eager for the treasures which made his pockets bulge out on all sides. When he went out gunning he always remembered to shoot a hawk or some strangely painted bird for us; it was even better when he went fishing, for then he took us with him, and while he stood motionless on the bank, rod in hand, looking, in the light-blue suit he always wore, like a vast blue pillar crowned with that broad red face, we romped on the sward, and revelled in the dank fragrance of the earth and rushes.

I have not the faintest notion of who Captain Scott was, or of what he was ever captain, or whether residence in a warm climate or hard drinking had dyed his broad countenance with that deep magenta red, nor of how and when he finished his earthly career; for when we moved away the huge purple-faced strange-looking man dropped for ever out of our lives; yet in my mind how beautiful his gigantic image looks! And to this day I bless his memory for all the sweets he gave me, in a land where sweets were scarce, and for his friendliness to me when I was a very small boy.

The second well-remembered individual was also only an occasional visitor at our house, and was known all over the surrounding country as the Hermit, for his name was never discovered. He was perpetually on the move, visiting in turn every house within a radius of forty or fifty miles; and once about every seven or eight weeks he called on us to receive a few articles of food—enough for the day's consumption. Money he always refused with gestures of intense disgust, and he would also decline cooked meat and broken bread. When hard biscuits were given him, he would carefully

12   FAR AWAY AND LONG AGO

examine them, and if one was found chipped or cracked he would return it, pointing out the defect, and ask for a sound one in return. He had a small, sun-parched face, and silvery long hair; but his features were fine, his teeth white and even, his eyes clear grey and keen as a falcon's. There was always a set expression of deep mental anguish on his face, intensified with perhaps a touch of insanity, which made it painful to look at him. As he never accepted money or anything but food, he of course made his own garments—and what garments they were! Many years ago I used to see, strolling about St James's Park, a huge hairy gentleman, with a bludgeon in his hand, and clothed with a bear's skin to which the head and paws were attached. It may be that this eccentric individual is remembered by some of my readers, but I assure them that he was quite a St James's Park dandy compared with my hermit. He wore a pair of gigantic shoes, about a foot broad at the toes, made out of thick cow-hide with the hair on; and on his head was a tall rimless cow-hide hat shaped like an inverted flower-pot. His bodily covering was, however, the most extraordinary: the outer garment, if garment it can be called, resembled a very large mattress in size and shape, with the ticking made of innumerable pieces of raw hide sewn together. It was about a foot in thickness and stuffed with sticks, stones, hard lumps of clay, rams' horns, bleached bones, and other hard heavy objects; it was fastened round him with straps of hide, and reached nearly to the ground. The figure he made in this covering was most horribly uncouth and grotesque, and his periodical visits used to throw us into a great state of excitement. And as if this awful burden with which he had saddled himself —enough to have crushed down any two ordinary men —was not sufficient, he had weighted the heavy stick used to support his steps with a great ball at the end,

EARLIEST MEMORIES

also with a large circular bell-shaped object surrounding the middle. On arriving at the house, where the dogs would become frantic with terror and rage at sight of him, he would stand resting himself for eight or ten minutes; then in a strange language, which might have been Hebrew or Sanscrit, for there was no person learned enough in the country to understand it, he would make a long speech or prayer in a clear ringing voice, intoning his words in a monotonous sing-song. His speech done, he would beg, in broken Spanish, for the usual charity; and, after receiving it, he would commence another address, possibly invoking blessings of all kinds on the donor, and lasting an unconscionable time. Then, bidding a ceremonious farewell, he would take his departure.

From the sound of certain oft-recurring expressions in his recitations we children called him 'Constair Lo-vair'; perhaps some clever pundit will be able to tell me what these words mean—the only fragment saved of the hermit's mysterious language. It was commonly reported that he had at one period of his life committed some terrible crime, and that, pursued by the phantoms of remorse, he had fled to this distant region, where he would never be met and denounced by any former companion, and had adopted his singular mode of life by way of penance. This was, of course, mere conjecture, for nothing could be extracted from him. When closely questioned or otherwise interfered with, then old Constair Lo-vair would show that his long cruel penance had not yet banished the devil from his heart. A terrible wrath would disfigure his countenance and kindle his eyes with demoniac fire; and in sharp ringing tones, that wounded like strokes, he would pour forth a torrent of words in his unknown language, doubtless invoking every imaginable curse on his tormentor.

FAR AWAY AND LONG AGO

For upwards of twenty years after I as a small child made his acquaintance he continued faithfully pursuing his dreary rounds, exposed to cold and rain in winter and to the more trying heats of summer; until at last he was discovered lying dead on the plain, wasted by old age and famine to a mere skeleton, and even in death still crushed down with that awful burden he had carried for so many years. Thus, consistent to the end, and with his secret untold to any sympathetic human soul, perished poor old Constair Lo-vair, the strangest of all strange beings I have met with in my journey through life.

CHAPTER II

MY NEW HOME

We quit our old home—A winter day journey—Aspect of the country—Our new home—A prisoner in the barn—The plantation—A paradise of rats—An evening scene—The people of the house—A beggar on horseback—Mr Trigg our schoolmaster—His double nature—Impersonates an old woman—Reading Dickens—Mr Trigg degenerates—Once more a homeless wanderer on the great plain.

THE incidents and impressions recorded in the preceding chapter relate, as I have said, to the last year or two of my five years of life in the place of my birth. Further back my memory refuses to take me. Some wonderful persons go back to their second or even their first year; I can't, and could only tell from hearsay what I was and did up to the age of three. According to all accounts, the clouds of glory I brought into the world—a habit of smiling at everything I looked at and at every person that approached me—ceased to be visibly trailed at about that age; I only remember myself as a common little boy—just a little wild animal running about on its hind legs, amazingly interested in the world in which it found itself.

Here, then, I begin, aged five, at an early hour on a bright, cold morning in June—midwinter in that southern country of great plains or pampas; impatiently waiting for the loading and harnessing to be finished; then the being lifted to the top with the other little ones—at that time we were five; finally, the grand moment when the start was actually made with cries and much noise of stamping and snorting of horses and rattling of chains. I remember a good deal of that long journey, which began at sunrise and ended between the lights some

15

16   FAR AWAY AND LONG AGO

time after sunset; for it was my very first, and I was going out into the unknown. I remember how, at the foot of the slope at the top of which the old home stood, we plunged into the river, and there was more noise and shouting and excitement until the straining animals brought us safely out on the other side. Gazing back, the low roof of the house was lost to view before long, but the trees—the row of twenty-five giant ombú trees which gave the place its name—were visible, blue in the distance, until we were many miles on our way.

The undulating country had been left behind; before us and on both sides the land, far as one could see, was absolutely flat, everywhere green with the winter grass, but flowerless at that season, and with the gleam of water over the whole expanse. It had been a season of great rains, and much of the flat country had been turned into shallow lakes. That was all there was to see, except the herds of cattle and horses and an occasional horseman galloping over the plain, and the sight at long distances of a grove or small plantation of trees, marking the site of an estancia, or sheep and cattle farm, these groves appearing like islands on the sea-like flat country. At length this monotonous landscape faded and vanished quite away, and the lowing of cattle and tremulous bleating of sheep died out of hearing, so that the last leagues were a blank to me, and I only came back to my senses when it was dark and they lifted me down, so stiff with cold and drowsy that I could hardly stand on my feet.

Next morning I found myself in a new and strange world. The house to my childish eyes appeared of vast size: it consisted of a long range of rooms on the ground, built of brick, with brick floors and roof thatched with rushes. The rooms at one end, fronting the road, formed a store, where the people of the surrounding

MY NEW HOME 17

country came to buy and sell, and what they brought
to sell was 'the produce of the country'—hides and
wool and tallow in bladders, horsehair in sacks, and
native cheeses. In return they could purchase anything they wanted—knives, spurs, rings for horse-gear,
clothing, yerba maté, and sugar; tobacco, castor-oil, salt
and pepper, and oil and vinegar, and such furniture as
they required—iron pots, spits for roasting, cane chairs,
and coffins. A little distance from the house were
the kitchen, bakery, dairy, huge barns for storing the
produce, and wood-piles big as houses, the wood being
nothing but stalks of the cardoon thistle or wild artichoke, which burn like paper, so that immense quantities
had to be collected to supply fuel for a large establishment.

Two of the smallest of us were handed over to the
care of a sharp little native boy, aged about nine or ten
years, who was told to take us out of the way and keep
us amused. The first place he took us to was the great
barn, the door of which stood open; it was nearly empty
just then, and was the biggest interior I had ever seen;
how big it really was I don't know, but it seemed to
me about as big as Olympia, or the Agricultural Hall,
or the Crystal Palace would be to any ordinary little
London boy. No sooner were we in this vast place
than we saw a strange and startling thing—a man,
sitting or crouching on the floor, his hands before him,
the wrists tied together, his body bound with thongs of
raw hide to a big post which stood in the centre of the
floor and supported the beam of the loft above. He
was a young man, not more than twenty perhaps, with
black hair and a smooth, pale, sallow face. His eyes
were cast down, and he paid no attention to us, standing
there staring at him, and he appeared to be suffering
or ill. After a few moments I shrank away to the door
and asked our conductor in a frightened whisper why

he was tied up to a post there. Our native boy seemed
to be quite pleased at the effect on us, and answered
cheerfully that he was a murderer—he had committed
a murder somewhere, and had been caught last evening,
but as it was too late to take him to the lock-up at the
village, which was a long distance away, they had
brought him here as the most convenient place, and tied
him in the barn to keep him safe. Later on they would
come and take him away.

Murder was a common word in those days, but I had
not at that time grasped its meaning; I had seen no
murder done, nor any person killed in a fight; I only
knew that it must be something wicked and horrible.
Nevertheless, the shock I had received passed away in
the course of that first morning in a new world; but
what I had seen in the barn was not forgotten: the
image of that young man tied to the post, his bent head
and downward gaze, and ghastly face shaded by
lank black hair, is as plain to me now as if I had seen
him but yesterday.

A little back from the buildings were gardens and
several acres of plantation—both shade and fruit trees.
Viewed from the outside, it all looked like an immense
poplar grove, on account of the double rows of tall
Lombardy poplar trees at the borders. The whole
ground, including the buildings, was surrounded by an
immense ditch or moat.

Up till now I had lived without trees, with the exception of those twenty-five I have spoken of, which formed
a landmark for all the country round; so that this great
number—hundreds and thousands—of trees was a marvel
and delight. But the plantation and what it was to
me will form the subject of a chapter by itself. It was
a paradise of rats, as I very soon discovered. Our little
native guide and instructor was full of the subject, and
promised to let us see the rats with our own eyes as

MY NEW HOME 19

soon as the sun went down; that would finish the day of strange sights with the strangest of all.

Accordingly, when the time came he led us to a spot beyond the barns and wood-piles, where all the offal of slaughtered animals, bones, and unconsumed meats from the kitchen, and rubbish from a wasteful, disorderly establishment, were cast out each day. Here we all sat down in a row on a log among the dead weeds on the border of the evil-smelling place, and he told us to be very still and speak no word; for, said he, unless we move or make a sound the rats will not heed us; they will regard us as so many wooden images. And so it proved, for very soon after the sun had gone down we began to see rats stealing out of the wood-pile and from the dead weeds on every side, all converging to that one spot where a generous table was spread for them and for the brown carrion hawks that came by day. Big, old, grey rats with long, scaly tails, others smaller, and smaller still, the least of all being little bigger than mice, until the whole place swarmed with them, all busily hunting for food, feeding, squealing, fighting, and biting. I had not known that the whole world contained so many rats as I now saw congregated before me.

Suddenly our guide jumped up and loudly clapped his hands, which produced a curious effect—a short, sharp little shriek of terror from the busy multitude, followed by absolute stillness, every rat frozen to stone, which lasted for a second or two; then a swift scuttling away in all directions, vanishing with a rustling sound through the dead grass and wood.

It had been a fine spectacle, and we enjoyed it amazingly; it raised *Mus decumanus* to a beast of immense importance in my mind. Soon he became even more important in an unpleasant way when it was discovered that rats were abundant indoors as well

20 FAR AWAY AND LONG AGO

as out. The various noises they made at night were terrifying; they would run over our beds and sometimes we would wake up to find that one had got in between the sheets and was trying frantically to get out. Then we would yell, and half the house would be roused and imagine some dreadful thing. But when they found out the cause, they would only laugh at and rebuke us for being such poor little cowards.

But what an astonishing place was this to which we had come! The great house and many buildings and the people in it, the fosse, the trees that enchanted me, the dirt and disorder, vile rats and fleas and pests of all sorts! The place had been for some years in the hands of a Spanish or native family—indolent, careless, happy-go-lucky people. The husband and wife were never in harmony or agreement about anything for five minutes together, and by and by he would go away to the capital 'on business,' which would keep him from home for weeks, and even months, at a stretch. And she, with three light-headed, grown-up daughters, would be left to run the establishment with half a dozen hired men and women to assist her. I remember her well, as she stayed on a few days in order to hand over the place to us—an excessively fat, inactive woman, who sat most of the day in an easy-chair, surrounded by her pets—lap-dogs, Amazon parrots, and several shrieking paroquets.

Before many days she left, with all her noisy crowd of dogs and birds and daughters, and of the events of the succeeding days and weeks nothing remains in memory except one exceedingly vivid impression—my first sight of a beggar on horseback. It was by no means an uncommon sight in those days when, as the gauchos were accustomed to say, a man without a horse was a man without legs; but it was new to me when one morning I saw a tall man on a tall horse ride up to our

MY NEW HOME

gate, accompanied by a boy of nine or ten on a pony.
I was struck with the man's singular appearance, sitting
upright and stiff in his saddle, staring straight before
him. He had long grey hair and beard, and wore a
tall straw hat shaped like an inverted flower-pot, with
a narrow brim—a form of hat which had lately gone out
of fashion among the natives but was still used by a
few. Over his clothes he wore a red cloak or poncho,
and heavy iron spurs on his feet, which were cased in
the *botas de potro*, or long stockings made of a colt's
untanned hide.

Arrived at the gate he shouted *Ave Maria purissima*
in a loud voice, then proceeded to give an account of
himself, informing us that he was a blind man and
obliged to subsist on the charity of his neighbours.
They in their turn, he said, in providing him with all
he required were only doing good to themselves, seeing
that those who showed the greatest compassion towards
their afflicted fellow-creatures were regarded with special
favour by the Powers above.

After delivering himself of all this and much more as
if preaching a sermon, he was assisted from his horse
and led by the hand to the front door, after which the
boy drew back and, folding his arms across his breast,
stared haughtily at us children and the others who had
congregated at the spot. Evidently he was proud of
his position as page or squire or groom of the important
person in the tall straw hat, red cloak, and iron
spurs, who galloped about the land collecting tribute
from the people and talking loftily about the Powers
above.

Asked what he required at our hands the beggar
replied that he wanted yerba maté, sugar, bread, and
some hard biscuits, also cut tobacco and paper for
cigarettes and some leaf tobacco for cigars. When all
these things had been given him, he was asked (not

*B 956

22   FAR AWAY AND LONG AGO

ironically) if there was anything else we could supply
him with, and he replied, Yes, he was still in want of
rice, flour, and farina, an onion or two, a head or two of
garlic, also salt, pepper, and pimento, or red pepper.
And when he had received all these comestibles and felt
them safely packed in his saddle-bags, he returned
thanks, bade good-bye in the most dignified manner,
and was led back by the haughty little boy to his
tall horse.

We had been settled some months in our new home,
and I was just about half-way through my sixth year,
when one morning at breakfast we children were informed to our utter dismay that we could no longer be
permitted to run absolutely wild; that a schoolmaster
had been engaged who would live in the house and would
have us in the schoolroom during the morning and part
of the afternoon.

Our hearts were heavy in us that day, while we waited
apprehensively for the appearance of the man who
would exercise such a tremendous power over us and
would stand between us and our parents, especially our
mother, who had ever been our shield and refuge from
all pains and troubles.   Up till now they had acted on
the principle that children were best left to themselves,
that the more liberty they had the better it was for
them.   Now it almost looked as if they were turning
against us; but we knew that it could not be so—we
knew that every slightest pain or grief that touched us
was felt more keenly by our mother than by ourselves,
and we were compelled to believe her when she told
us that she, too, lamented the restraint that would be
put upon us, but knew that it would be for our ultimate
good.

And on that very afternoon the feared man arrived,
Mr Trigg by name, an Englishman, a short, stoutish,

MY NEW HOME

almost fat little man, with grey hair, clean-shaved sunburnt face, a crooked nose which had been broken or
was born so, clever mobile mouth, and blue-grey eyes
with a humorous twinkle in them and crow's-feet at the
corners. Only to us youngsters, as we soon discovered,
that humorous face and the twinkling eyes were capable
of a terrible sternness. He was loved, I think, by adults
generally, and regarded with feelings of an opposite
nature by children. For he was a schoolmaster who
hated and despised teaching as much as children in the
wild hated to be taught. He followed teaching because
all work was excessively irksome to him, yet he had to
do something for a living, and this was the easiest thing
he could find to do. How such a man ever came to be
so far from home in a half-civilized country was a
mystery, but there he was, a bachelor and homeless man
after twenty or thirty years on the pampas, with little
or no money in his pocket, and no belongings except
his horse—he never owned more than one at a time—
and its cumbrous native saddle, and the saddle-bags in
which he kept his wardrobe and whatever he possessed
besides. He didn't own a box. On his horse, with his
saddle-bags behind him, he would journey about the
land, visiting all the English, Scotch, and Irish settlers,
who were mostly sheep-farmers, but religiously avoiding
the houses of the natives. With the natives he could
not affiliate, and not properly knowing and incapable of
understanding them, he regarded them with secret dislike and suspicion. And by and by he would find a
house where there were children old enough to be taught
their letters, and Mr Trigg would be hired by the month,
like a shepherd or cowherd, to teach them, living with
the family. He would go on very well for a time, his
failings being condoned for the sake of the little ones;
but by and by there would be a falling-out, and Mr
Trigg would saddle his horse, buckle on the saddle-bags,

24   FAR AWAY AND LONG AGO

and ride forth over the wide plain in quest of a new home. With us he made an unusually long stay; he liked good living and comforts generally, and at the same time he was interested in the things of the mind, which had no place in the lives of the British settlers of that period; and now he found himself in a very comfortable house, where there were books to read and people to converse with who were not quite like the rude sheep- and cattle-farmers he had been accustomed to live with. He was on his best behaviour, and no doubt strove hard and not unsuccessfully to get the better of his weak- nesses. He was looked on as a great acquisition, and made much of; in the schoolroom he was a tyrant, and having been forbidden to punish us by striking, he restrained himself when to thrash us would have been an immense relief to him. But pinching was not striking, and he would pinch our ears until they almost bled. It was a poor punishment and gave him little satisfaction, but it had to serve. Out of school his temper would change as by magic. He was then the life of the house, a delightful talker with an inexhaustible fund of good stories, a good reader, mimic, and actor as well.

One afternoon we had a call from a quaint old Scotch dame, in a queer dress, sunbonnet, and spectacles, who introduced herself as the wife of Sandy Maclachlan, a sheep-farmer who lived about twenty-five miles away. It wasn't right, she said, that such near neighbours should not know one another, so she had ridden those few leagues to find out what we were like. Established at the tea-table, she poured out a torrent of talk in broadest Scotch, in her high-pitched cracked old- woman's voice, and gave us an intimate domestic history of all the British residents of the district. It was all about what delightful people they were, and how even their little weaknesses—their love of the bottle, their

MY NEW HOME 25

meannesses, their greed and low cunning—only served
to make them more charming. Never was there such
a funny old dame or one more given to gossip and scandal-
mongering! Then she took herself off, and presently
we children, still under her spell, stole out to watch her
departure from the gate. But she was not there—she
had vanished unaccountably; and by and by what was
our astonishment and disgust to hear that the old
Scotch body was none other than our own Mr Trigg!
That our needle-sharp eyes, concentrated for an hour
on her face, had failed to detect the master who was so
painfully familiar to us seemed like a miracle.

Mr Trigg confessed that play-acting was one of the
things he had done before quitting his country; but it
was only one of a dozen or twenty vocations which he
had taken up at various times, only to drop them again
as soon as he made the discovery that they one and all
entailed months and even years of hard work if he was
ever to fulfil his ambitious desire of doing and being
something great in the world. As a reader he certainly
was great, and every evening, when the evenings were
long, he would give a two hours' reading to the household. Dickens was then the most popular writer in the
world, and he usually read Dickens, to the delight of his
listeners. Here he could display his histrionic qualities
to the full. He impersonated every character in the
book, endowing him with voice, gestures, manner, and
expression that fitted him perfectly. It was more like
a play than a reading.

'What should we do without Mr Trigg?' our elders
were accustomed to say; but we little ones, remembering
that it would not be the beneficent countenance of Mr
Pickwick that would look on us in the schoolroom on
the following morning, only wished that Mr Trigg was
far, far away.

Perhaps they made too much of him: at all events he

26   FAR AWAY AND LONG AGO

fell into the habit of going away every Saturday morning
and not returning until the following Monday. His
week-end visit was always to some English or Scotch
neighbour, a sheep-farmer, ten or fifteen or twenty
miles distant, where the bottle or demijohn of white
Brazilian rum was always on the table. It was the
British exile's only substitute for his dear lost whisky
in that far country. At home there was only tea and
coffee to drink. From these outings he would return on
Monday morning, quite sober and almost too dignified in
manner, but with inflamed eyes and (in the schoolroom)
the temper of a devil. On one of these occasions,
something—our stupidity perhaps, or an exceptionally
bad headache—tried him beyond endurance, and taking
down his *revenque*, or native horse-whip made of raw
hide, from the wall, he began laying about him with
such extraordinary fury that the room was quickly in
an uproar. Then all at once my mother appeared on
the scene, and the tempest was stilled, though the
master, with the whip in his uplifted hand, still stood,
glaring with rage at us. She stood silent a moment or
two, her face very white, then spoke: 'Children, you
may go and play now. School is over'; then, lest the
full purport of her words should not be understood, she
added: 'Your schoolmaster is going to leave us.'

It was an unspeakable relief, a joyful moment; yet
on that very day, and on the next before he rode away,
I, even I who had been unjustly and cruelly struck
with a horsewhip, felt my little heart heavy in me when
I saw the change in his face—the dark, still, brooding
look, and knew that the thought of his fall and the loss
of his home was exceedingly bitter to him. Doubtless
my mother noticed it, too, and shed a few compassionate tears for the poor man, once more homeless on the
great plain. But he could not be kept after that in-
sane outbreak. To strike their children was to my

MY NEW HOME 27

parents a crime; it changed their nature and degraded them, and Mr Trigg could not be forgiven.

Mr Trigg, as I have said before, was a long time with us, and the happy deliverance I have related did not occur until I was near the end of my eighth year. At the present stage of my story I am not yet six, and the incident related in the following chapter, in which Mr Trigg figures, occurred when I was within a couple of months of completing my sixth year.

CHAPTER III

DEATH OF AN OLD DOG

The old dog Caesar—His powerful personality—Last days and
end—The old dog's burial—The fact of death is brought home
to me—A child's mental anguish—My mother comforts me—
Limitations of the child's mind—Fear of death—Witnessing
the slaughter of cattle—A man in the moat—Margarita, the
nursery-maid—Her beauty and lovableness—Her death—
I refuse to see her dead.

WHEN recalling the impressions and experiences of that
most eventful sixth year, the one incident which looks
biggest in memory, at all events in the last half of that
year, is the death of Caesar. There is nothing in the
past I can remember so well: it was indeed the most
important event of my childhood—the first thing in a
young life which brought the eternal note of sadness in.

It was in the early spring, about the middle of August,
and I can even remember that it was windy weather
and bitterly cold for the time of year, when the old dog
was approaching his end.

Caesar was an old valued dog, although of no superior
breed: he was just an ordinary dog of the country,
short-haired, with long legs and a blunt muzzle. The
ordinary dog or native cur was about the size of a
Scotch collie; Caesar was quite a third larger, and it
was said of him that he was as much above all other
dogs of the house, numbering about twelve or fourteen,
in intelligence and courage as in size. Naturally, he
was the leader and master of the whole pack, and when
he got up with an awful growl, baring his big teeth, and
hurled himself on the others to chastise them for quarrel-
ling or any other infringement of dog law, they took it
lying down. He was a black dog, now in his old age

28

DEATH OF AN OLD DOG 29

sprinkled with white hairs all over his body, the face and legs having gone quite grey. Caesar in a rage, or on guard at night, or when driving cattle in from the plains, was a terrible being; with us children he was mild-tempered and patient, allowing us to ride on his back, just like old Pechicho the sheep-dog, described in the first chapter. Now, in his decline, he grew irritable and surly, and ceased to be our playmate. The last two or three months of his life were very sad, and when it troubled us to see him so gaunt, with his big ribs protruding from his sides, to watch his twitchings when he dozed, groaning and wheezing the while, and marked, too, how painfully he struggled to get up on his feet, we wanted to know why it was so—why we could not give him something to make him well. For answer they would open his great mouth to show us his teeth—the big blunt canines and old molars worn down to stumps. Old age was what ailed him—he was thirteen years old, and that did verily seem to me a great age, for I was not half that, yet it seemed to me that I had been a very, very long time in the world.

No one dreamed of such a thing as putting an end to him—no hint of such a thing was ever spoken. It was not the custom in that country to shoot an old dog because he was past work. I remember his last day, and how often we came to look at him and tried to comfort him with warm rugs and the offer of food and drink where he was lying in a sheltered place, no longer able to stand up. And that night he died: we knew it as soon as we were up in the morning. Then, after breakfast, during which we had been very solemn and quiet, our schoolmaster said: 'We must bury him to-day —at twelve o'clock, when I am free, will be the best time; the boys can come with me, and old John can bring his spade.' This announcement greatly excited us, for we had never seen a dog buried, and

30   FAR AWAY AND LONG AGO

had never even heard of such a thing having ever
been done.

About noon that day old Caesar, dead and stiff, was
taken by one of the workmen to a green open spot
among the old peach trees, where his grave had already
been dug. We followed our schoolmaster and watched
while the body was lowered and the red earth shovelled
in. The grave was deep, and Mr Trigg assisted in filling
it, puffing very much over the task and stopping at
intervals to mop his face with his coloured cotton
handkerchief.

Then, when all was done, while we were still standing
silently around, it came into Mr Trigg's mind to improve
the occasion. Assuming his schoolroom expression he
looked round at us and said solemnly: 'That's the end.
Every dog has his day and so has every man; and the
end is the same for both. We die like old Caesar, and
are put into the ground and have the earth shovelled
over us.'

Now these simple, common words affected me more
than any other words I have heard in my life. They
pierced me to the heart. I had heard something terrible
—too terrible to think of, incredible—and yet—and yet
if it was not so, why had he said it? Was it because
he hated us, just because we were children and he had
to teach us our lessons, and wanted to torture us?
Alas! no, I could not believe that! Was this, then, the
horrible fate that awaited us all? I had heard of death
—I knew there was such a thing; I knew that all animals
had to die, also that some men died. For how could
any one, even a child in its sixth year, overlook such a
fact, especially in the country of my birth—a land of
battle, murder, and sudden death? I had not forgotten
the young man tied to the post in the barn who had
killed someone, and would perhaps, I had been told, be
killed himself as a punishment. I knew, in fact, that

DEATH OF AN OLD DOG 31

there was good and evil in the world, good and bad men, and the bad men—murderers, thieves, and liars—would all have to die, just like animals; but that there was any life after death I did not know. All the others, myself and my own people included, were good and would never taste death. How it came about that I had got no further in my system or philosophy. of life I cannot say; I can only suppose that my mother had not yet begun to give me instruction in such matters on account of my tender years, or else that she had done so and that I had understood it in my own way. Yet, as I discovered later, she was a religious woman, and from infancy I had been taught to kneel and say a little prayer each evening: 'Now I lay me down to sleep, I pray the Lord my soul to keep'; but who the Lord was or what my soul was I had no idea. It was just a pretty little way of saying in rhyme that I was going to bed. My world was a purely material one, and a most wonderful world it was, but how I came to be in it I didn't know; I only knew (or imagined) that I would be in it always, seeing new and strange things every day, and never, never get tired of it. In literature it is only in Vaughan, Traherne, and other mystics that I find any adequate expression of that perpetual rapturous delight in nature and my own existence which I experienced at that period.

And now these never-to-be-forgotten words spoken over the grave of our old dog had come to awaken me from that beautiful dream of perpetual joy!

When I recall this event I am less astonished at my ignorance than at the intensity of the feeling I experienced, the terrible darkness it brought on so young a mind. The child's mind we think, and in fact know, is like that of the lower animals; or if higher than the animal mind, it is not so high as that of the simplest savage. He cannot concentrate his thought—he cannot

32   FAR AWAY AND LONG AGO

think at all; his consciousness is in its dawn; he revels
in colours, in odours, is thrilled by touch and taste and
sound, and is like a well-nourished pup or kitten at play
on a green turf in the sunshine. This being so, one
would have thought that the pain of the revelation I had
received would have quickly vanished—that the vivid
impressions of external things would have blotted it
out and restored the harmony. But it was not so; the
pain continued and increased until it was no longer to
be borne; then I sought my mother, first watching until
she was alone in her room. Yet when with her I feared
to speak lest with a word she should confirm the dreadful
tidings. Looking down, she all at once became alarmed
at the sight of my face, and began to question me.
Then, struggling against my tears, I told her of the
words which had been spoken at the old dog's burial,
and asked her if it was true, if I—if she—if all of us
had to die and be buried in the ground? She replied
that it was not wholly true; it was only true in a way,
since our bodies had to die and be buried in the earth,
but we had an immortal part which could not die. It
was true that old Caesar had been a good faithful dog,
and felt and understood things almost like a human
being, and most persons believed that when a dog died
he died wholly and had no after-life. We could not
know that; some very great, good men had thought
differently; they believed that the animals, like us,
would live again. That was also her belief—her strong
hope; but we could not know for certain, because it
had been hidden from us. For ourselves, we knew that
we could not really die, because God Himself, who made
us and all things, had told us so, and His promise of
eternal life had been handed down to us in His Book
—in the Bible.

To all this and much more I listened trembling, with
a fearful interest, and when I had once grasped the idea

DEATH OF AN OLD DOG 33

that death when it came to me, as it must, would leave
me alive after all—that, as she explained, the part of
me that really mattered, the myself, the I am I, which
knew and considered things, would never perish, I
experienced a sudden immense relief. When I went
out from her side again I wanted to run and jump for
joy and cleave the air like a bird. For I had been in
prison and had suffered torture, and was now free again
—death would not destroy me!

There was another result of my having unburdened
my heart to my mother. She had been startled at the
poignancy of the feeling I had displayed, and, greatly
blaming herself for having left me too long in that
ignorant state, began to give me religious instruction.
It was too early, since at that age it was not possible
for me to rise to the conception of an immaterial world.
That power, I imagine, comes later to the normal child
at the age of ten or twelve. To tell him when he is
five or six or seven that God is in all places at once and
sees all things, only produces the idea of a wonderfully
active and quick-sighted person, with eyes like a bird's,
able to see what is going on all round. A short time
ago I read an anecdote of a little girl who, on being put
to bed by her mother, was told not to be afraid in the
dark, since God would be there to watch and guard her
while she slept. Then, taking the candle, the mother
went downstairs; but presently her little girl came down
too, in her nightdress, and, when questioned, replied:
'I 'm going to stay down here in the light, mummy, and
you can go up to my room and sit with God.' My own
idea of God at that time was no higher. I would lie
awake thinking of Him there in the room, puzzling over
the question as to how He could attend to all His
numerous affairs and spend so much time looking after
me. Lying with my eyes open, I could see nothing in
the dark; still, I knew He was there, because I had been

34   FAR AWAY AND LONG AGO

told so, and this troubled me. But no sooner would I close my eyes than His image would appear standing at a distance of three or four feet from the head of the bed, in the form of a column five feet high or so and about four feet in circumference. The colour was blue, but varied in depth and intensity; on some nights it was sky-blue, but usually of a deeper shade, a pure, soft, beautiful blue like that of the morning-glory or wild geranium.

It would not surprise me to find that many persons have some such material image or presentiment of the spiritual entities they are taught to believe in at too tender an age. Recently, in comparing childish memories with a friend, he told me that he too always saw God as a blue object, but of no definite shape.

That blue column haunted me at night for many months; I don't think it quite vanished, ceasing to be anything but a memory, until I was seven—a date far ahead of where we are now.

To return to that second blissful revelation which came to me from my mother. Happy as it made me to know that death would not put an end to my existence, my state after the first joyful relief was not one of perfect happiness. All she said to comfort and make me brave had produced its effect—I knew now that death was but a change to an even greater bliss than I could have in this life. How could I, not yet six, think otherwise than as she had told me to think, or have a doubt? A mother is more to her child than any other being, human or divine, can ever be to him in his subsequent life. He is as dependent on her as any fledgeling in the nest on its parent—even more, since she warms his callow mind or soul as well as body.

Notwithstanding all this, the fear of death came back to me in a little while, and for a long time disquieted me, especially when the fact of death was brought

DEATH OF AN OLD DOG 35

sharply before me. These reminders were only too frequent; there was seldom a day on which I did not see something killed. When the killing was instantaneous, as when a bird was shot and dropped dead like a stone, I was not disturbed; it was nothing but a strange, exciting spectacle, but failed to bring the fact of death home to me. It was chiefly when cattle were slaughtered that the terror returned in its full force. And no wonder! The native manner of killing a cow or bullock at that time was peculiarly painful. Occasionally it would be slaughtered out of sight on the plain, and the hide and flesh brought in by the men, but, as a rule, the beast would be driven up close to the house to save trouble. One of the two or three mounted men engaged in the operation would throw his lasso over the horns, and, galloping off, pull the rope taut; a second man would then drop from his horse, and running up to the animal behind, pluck out his big knife and with two lightning-quick blows sever the tendons of both hind legs. Instantly the beast would go down on his haunches, and the same man, knife in hand, would flit round to its front or side, and, watching his opportunity, presently thrust the long blade into its throat just above the chest, driving it in to the hilt and working it round; then when it was withdrawn a great torrent of blood would pour out from the tortured beast, still standing on his fore-legs, bellowing all the time with agony. At this point the slaughterer would often leap lightly on to its back, stick his spurs in its sides, and, using the flat of his long knife as a whip, pretend to be riding a race, yelling with fiendish glee. The bellowing would subside into deep, awful, sob-like sounds and chokings; then the rider, seeing the animal about to collapse, would fling himself nimbly off. The beast down, they would all run to it, and throwing themselves on its quivering side as on a couch, begin making and lighting their cigarettes.

36   FAR AWAY AND LONG AGO

Slaughtering a cow was grand sport for them, and
the more active and dangerous the animal, the more
prolonged the fight, the better they liked it; they were
as joyfully excited as at a fight with knives or an ostrich
hunt. To me it was an awful object-lesson, and held
me fascinated with horror. For this was death! The
crimson torrents of blood, the deep, human-like cries,
made the beast appear like some huge, powerful man
caught in a snare by small, weak, but cunning adversaries, who tortured him for their delight and mocked
him in his agony.

There were other occurrences about that time to keep
the thoughts and fear of death alive. One day a traveller
came to the gate, and, after unsaddling his horse, went
about sixty or seventy yards away to a shady spot,
where he sat down on the green slope of the fosse to
cool himself. He had been riding many hours in a
burning sun, and wanted cooling. He attracted everybody's attention on his arrival by his appearance:
middle-aged, with good features and curly brown hair
and beard, but huge—one of the biggest men I had
ever seen; his weight could not have been under about
seventeen stone. Sitting or reclining on the grass, he
fell asleep, and rolling down the slope fell with a tremendous splash into the water, which was about six
feet deep. So loud was the splash that it was heard by
some of the men at work in the barn, and running out
to ascertain the cause, they found out what had happened. The man had gone under and did not rise; with
a good deal of trouble he was raised up and drawn with
ropes to the top of the bank.

I gazed on him lying motionless, to all appearances
stone dead—the huge, ox-like man I had seen less than
an hour ago, when he had excited our wonder at his great
size and strength, and now still in death—dead as old
Caesar under the ground with the grass growing over

DEATH OF AN OLD DOG 37

him! Meanwhile the men who had hauled him out were busy with him, turning him over and rubbing his body, and after about twelve or fifteen minutes there was a gasp and signs of returning life, and by and by he opened his eyes. The dead man was alive again; yet the shock to me was just as great and the effect as lasting as if he had been truly dead.

Another instance which will bring me down to the end of my sixth year and the conclusion of this sad chapter. At this time we had a girl in the house, whose sweet face is one of a little group of half a dozen which I remember most vividly. She was a niece of our shepherd's wife, an Argentine woman married to an Englishman, and came to us to look after the smaller children. She was nineteen years old, a pale, slim, pretty girl, with large dark eyes and abundant black hair. Margarita had the sweetest smile imaginable, the softest voice and gentlest manner, and was so much loved by everybody in the house that she was like one of the family. Unhappily she was consumptive, and after a few months had to be sent back to her aunt. Their little place was only half a mile or so from the house, and every day my mother visited her, doing all that was possible with such skill and remedies as she possessed to give her ease, and providing her with delicacies. The girl did not want a priest to visit her and prepare her for death; she worshipped her mistress, and wished to be of the same faith, and in the end she died a pervert or convert, according to this or that person's point of view.

The day after her death we children were taken to see our beloved Margarita for the last time; but when we arrived at the door, and the others following my mother went in, I alone hung back. They came out and tried to persuade me to enter, even to pull me in, and described her appearance to excite my curiosity.

38 FAR AWAY AND LONG AGO

She was lying all in white, with her black hair combed out and loose, on her white bed, with our flowers on her breast and at her sides, and looked very, very beautiful. It was all in vain. To look on Margarita dead was more than I could bear. I was told that only her body of clay was dead—the beautiful body we had come to say good-bye to; that her soul—she herself, our loved Margarita—was alive and happy, far, far happier than any person could ever be on this earth; that when her end was near she had smiled very sweetly, and assured them that all fear of death had left her—that God was taking her to Himself. Even this was not enough to make me face the awful sight of Margarita dead; the very thought of it was an intolerable weight on my heart; but it was not grief that gave me this sensation, much as I grieved; it was solely my fear of death.

CHAPTER IV

THE PLANTATION

Living with trees—Winter violets—The house is made habitable
— Red willow — Scissor-tail and carrion-hawk — Lombardy
poplars—Black acacia—Other trees—The fosse or moat—
Rats—A trial of strength with an armadillo—Opossums living
with a snake—Alfalfa field and butterflies—Cane brake—
Weeds and fennel—Peach trees in blossom—Paroquets—
Singing of a field finch—Concert-singing in birds—Old John
—Cow-birds' singing—Arrival of summer migrants.

I REMEMBER—better than any orchard, grove, or wood
I have ever entered or seen, do I remember that shady
oasis of trees at my new home on the illimitable grassy
plain.   Up till now I had never lived with trees excepting those twenty-five I have told about and that other
one which was called *el arbol* because it was the only
tree of its kind in all the land.   Here there were
hundreds, thousands of trees, and to my childish unaccustomed eyes it was like a great unexplored forest.
There were no pines, firs, nor eucalyptus (unknown in
the country then), nor evergreens of any kind; the trees
being all deciduous were leafless now in midwinter,
but even so it was to me a wonderful experience to be
among them, to feel and smell their rough moist bark
stained green with moss, and to look up at the blue
sky through the network of interlacing twigs.   And
spring with foliage and blossom would be with us by
and by, in a month or two; even now in midwinter
there was a foretaste of it, and it came to us first as a
delicious fragrance in the air at one spot beside a row of
old Lombardy poplars—an odour that to the child is
like wine that maketh the heart glad to the adult.
Here at the roots of the poplars there was a bed or carpet

40   FAR AWAY AND LONG AGO

of round leaves which we knew well, and putting the clusters apart with our hands, lo! there were the violets already open—the dim, purple-blue, hidden violets, the earliest, sweetest, of all flowers the most loved by children in that land, and doubtless in many other lands.

There was more than time enough for us small children to feast on violets and run wild in our forest; since for several weeks we were encouraged to live out of doors as far away as we could keep from the house where we were not wanted. For just then great alterations were being made to render it habitable: new rooms were being added on to the old building, wooden flooring laid over the old bricks and tiles, and the half-rotten thatch, a haunt of rats and the home of centipedes and of many other hibernating creeping things, was being stripped off to be replaced by a clean healthy wooden roof. For me it was no hardship to be sent away to make my playground in that wooded wonderland. The trees, both fruit and shade, were of many kinds, and belonged to two widely separated periods. The first were the old trees planted by some tree-loving owner a century or more before our time, and the second the others which had been put in a generation or two later to fill up some gaps and vacant places and for the sake of a greater variety.

The biggest of the old trees, which I shall describe first, was a red willow growing by itself within forty yards of the house. This is a native tree, and derives its specific name *rubra*, as well as its vernacular name, from the reddish colour of the rough bark. It grows to a great size, like the black poplar, but has long narrow leaves like those of the weeping willow. In summer 1 was never tired of watching this tree, since high up in one of the branches, which in those days seemed to me 'so close against the sky,' a scissor-tail tyrant-bird always had its nest, and this high open exposed nest

THE PLANTATION 41

was a constant attraction to the common brown carrion-hawk, called *chimango*—a hawk with the carrion-crow's habit of perpetually loitering about in search of eggs and fledgelings.

The scissor-tail is one of the most courageous of that hawk-hating, violent-tempered tyrant-bird family, and every time a *chimango* appeared, which was about forty times a day, he would sally out to attack him in mid-air with amazing fury. The marauder driven off, he would return to the tree to utter his triumphant rattling castanet-like notes and (no doubt) to receive the congratulations of his mate; then to settle down again to watch the sky for the appearance of the next *chimango*.

A second red willow was the next largest tree in the plantation, but of this willow I shall have more to say in a later chapter.

The tall Lombardy poplars were the most numerous of the older trees, and grew in double rows, forming walks or avenues, on three sides of the entire enclosed ground. There was also a cross-row of poplars dividing the gardens and buildings from the plantation, and these were the favourite nesting-trees of two of our best-loved birds—the beautiful little goldfinch or Argentine siskin, and the bird called firewood-gatherer by the natives on account of the enormous collection of sticks which formed the nest.

Between the border poplar walk and the fosse outside there grew a single row of trees of a very different kind —the black acacia, a rare and singular tree, and of all our trees this one made the strongest and sharpest impression on my mind as well as flesh, pricking its image in me, so to speak. It had probably been planted originally by the early first planter, and, I imagine, experimentally, as a possible improvement on the wide-spreading disorderly aloe, a favourite with the first settlers; but it is a wild lawless plant and had refused

42 FAR AWAY AND LONG AGO

to make a proper hedge. Some of these acacias had remained small and were like old scraggy bushes, some were dwarfish trees, while others had sprung up like the fabled bean-stalk and were as tall as the poplars that grew side by side with them. These tall specimens had slender boles and threw out their slender horizontal branches of great length on all sides, from the roots to the crown, the branches and the bole itself being armed with thorns two to four inches long, hard as iron, black or chocolate-brown, polished and sharp as needles; and to make itself more formidable every long thorn had two smaller thorns growing out of it near the base, so that it was in shape like a round tapering dagger with a cross-guard to the handle. It was a terrible tree to climb, yet, when a little older, I had to climb it a thousand times, since there were certain birds which would make their nests in it, often as high up as they could, and some of these were birds that laid beautiful eggs, such as those of the Guira cuckoo, the size of pullets' eggs, of the purest turquoise blue flecked with snowy white.

Among our old or ancient trees the peach was the favourite of the whole house on account of the fruit it gave us in February and March, also later, in April and May, when what we called our winter peach ripened. Peach, quince, and cherry were the three favourite fruit trees in the colonial times, and all three were found in some of the *quintas* or orchards of the old estancia houses. We had a score of quince trees, with thick gnarled trunks and old twisted branches like rams' horns, but the peach trees numbered about four to five hundred and grew well apart from one another, and were certainly the largest I have ever seen. Their size was equal to that of the oldest and largest cherry trees one sees in certain favoured spots in southern England, where they grow not in close formation but wide apart

THE PLANTATION 43

with ample room for the branches to spread on all sides.

The trees planted by a later generation, both shade and fruit, were more varied. The most abundant was the mulberry, of which there were many hundreds, mostly in rows, forming walks, and albeit of the same species as our English mulberry they differed from it in the great size and roughness of the leaves and in producing fruit of a much smaller size. The taste of the fruit was also less luscious and it was rarely eaten by our elders. We small children feasted on it, but it was mostly for the birds. The mulberry was looked on as a shade, not a fruit tree, and the other two most important shade trees, in number, were the *Acacia blanca* or false acacia, and the paradise tree or pride of China. Besides these there was a row of eight or ten ailanthus trees, or tree of heaven as it is sometimes called, with tall white smooth trunk crowned with a cluster of palm-like foliage. There was also a modern orchard, containing pear, apple, plum, and cherry trees.

The entire plantation, the buildings included, comprising an area of eight or nine acres, was surrounded by an immense ditch or fosse about twelve feet deep and twenty to thirty feet wide. It was undoubtedly very old and had grown in width owing to the crumbling away of the earth at the sides. This in time would have filled and almost obliterated it, but at intervals of two or three years, at a time when it was dry, quantities of earth were dug up from the bottom and thrown on the mound inside. It was in appearance something like a prehistoric earthwork. In winter as a rule it became full of water and was a favourite haunt, especially at night, of flocks of teal, also duck of a few other kinds—widgeon, pin-tail, and shoveller. In summer it gradually dried up, but a few pools of muddy water usually remained through all the hot season and

44   FAR AWAY AND LONG AGO

were haunted by the solitary or summer snipe, one of the many species of sandpiper and birds of that family which bred in the northern hemisphere and wintered with us when it was our summer. Once the water had gone down in the moat, long grass and herbage would spring up and flourish on its sloping sides, and the rats and other small beasties would return and riddle it with innumerable burrows.

The rats were killed down from time to time with the 'smoking machine,' which pumped the fumes of sulphur, bad tobacco, and other deadly substances into their holes and suffocated them; and I recall two curious incidents during these crusades. One day I was standing on the mound at the side of the moat or fosse some forty yards from where the men were at work, when an armadillo bolted from his earth and running to the very spot where I was standing began vigorously digging to escape by burying himself in the soil. Neither men nor dogs had seen him, and I at once determined to capture him unaided by any one and imagined it would prove a very easy task. Accordingly I laid hold of his black bone-cased tail with both hands and began tugging to get him off the ground, but couldn't move him. He went on digging furiously, getting deeper and deeper into the earth, and I soon found that instead of my pulling him out he was pulling me in after him. It hurt my small-boy pride to think that an animal no bigger than a cat was going to beat me in a trial of strength, and this made me hold on more tenaciously than ever and tug and strain more violently, until not to lose him I had to go flat down on the ground. But it was all for nothing: first my hands, then my aching arms were carried down into the earth, and I was forced to release my hold and get up to rid myself of the mould he had been throwing up into my face and all over my head, neck, and shoulders.

THE PLANTATION 45

In the other case, one of my elder brothers, seeing the dogs sniffing and scratching at a large burrow, took a spade and dug a couple of feet into the soil and found an adult black-and-white opossum with eight or nine half-grown young lying together in a nest of dry grass, and, wonderful to tell, a large venomous snake coiled up amongst them. The snake was the dreaded *vivora de la cruz*, as the gauchos call it, a pit-viper of the same family as the fer-de-lance, the bush-master, and the rattlesnake. It was about three feet long, very thick in proportion, and with broad head and blunt tail. It came forth hissing and striking blindly right and left when the dogs pulled the opossums out, but was killed with a blow of the spade without injuring the dogs.

This was the first *serpent with a cross* I had seen, and the sight of the thick blunt body of a greenish-grey colour blotched with dull black, and the broad flat head with its stony-white lidless eyes, gave me a thrill of horror. In after years I became familiar with it and could even venture to pick it up without harm to myself, just as now in England I pick up the less dangerous adder when I come upon one. The wonder to us was that this extremely irascible and venomous serpent should be living in a nest with a large family of opossums, for it must be borne in mind that the opossum is a rapacious and an exceedingly savage-tempered beast.

This then was the world in which I moved and had my being, within the limits of the old rat-haunted fosse among the enchanted trees. But it was not the trees only that made it so fascinating, it had open spaces and other forms of vegetation which were exceedingly attractive too.

There was a field of alfalfa about half an acre in size, which flowered three times a year, and during the flowering time it drew the butterflies from all the surrounding plain with its luscious bean-like fragrance,

c 95⁶

46   FAR AWAY AND LONG AGO

until the field was full of them, red, black, yellow, and white butterflies, fluttering in flocks round every blue spike.

Canes, too, in a large patch or 'brake' as we called it, grew at another spot; a graceful plant about twenty-five feet high, in appearance unlike the bamboo, as the long pointed leaves were of a glaucous blue-green colour. The canes were valuable to us as they served as fishing-rods when we were old enough for that sport, and were also used as lances when we rode forth to engage in mimic battles on the plain. But they also had an economic value, as they were used by the natives when making their thatched roofs as a substitute for the bamboo cane, which cost much more as it had to be imported from other countries. Accordingly at the end of the summer, after the cane had flowered, they were all cut down, stripped of their leaves, and taken away in bundles, and we were then deprived till the following season of the pleasure of hunting for the tallest and straightest canes to cut them down and strip off leaves and bark to make beautiful green polished rods for our sports.

There were other open spaces covered with a vegetation almost as interesting as the canes and the trees: this was where what were called 'weeds' were allowed to flourish. Here were the thorn-apple, chenopodium, sow-thistle, wild mustard, red-weed, viper's bugloss, and others, both native and introduced, in dense thickets five or six feet high. It was difficult to push one's way through these thickets, and one was always in dread of treading on a snake. At another spot fennel flourished by itself, as if it had some mysterious power, perhaps its peculiar smell, of keeping other plants at a proper distance. It formed quite a thicket, and grew to a height of ten or twelve feet. This spot was a favourite haunt of mine, as it was in a waste place at the furthest

THE PLANTATION 47

point from the house, a wild solitary spot where I could spend long hours by myself watching the birds. But I also loved the fennel for itself, its beautiful green feathery foliage and the smell of it, also the taste, so that whenever I visited that secluded spot I would rub the crushed leaves in my palms and chew the small twigs for their peculiar fennel flavour.

Winter made a great change in the plantation, since it not only stripped the trees of their leaves but swept away all that rank herbage, the fennel included, allowing the grass to grow again. The large luxuriantly growing annuals also disappeared from the garden and all about the house, the big four-o'clock bushes with deep red stems and wealth of crimson blossoms, and the morning-glory convolvulus with its great blue trumpets, climbing over and covering every available place with its hop-like mass of leaves and abundant blooms. My life in the plantation in winter was a constant watching for spring. May, June, and July were the leafless months, but not wholly songless. On any genial and windless day of sunshine in winter a few swallows would reappear, nobody could guess from where, to spend the bright hours wheeling like house-martins about the house, revisiting their old breeding-holes under the eaves, and uttering their lively little rippling songs, as of water running in a pebbly stream. When the sun declined they would vanish, to be seen no more until we had another perfect spring-like day.

On such days in July and on any mild misty morning, standing on the mound within the moat I would listen to the sounds from the wide open plain, and they were sounds of spring—the constant drumming and rhythmic cries of the spur-wing lapwings engaged in their social meetings and 'dances,' and the song of the pipit soaring high up and pouring out its thick prolonged strains as it slowly floated downwards to the earth.

48   FAR AWAY AND LONG AGO

In August the peach blossomed. The great old trees standing wide apart on their grassy carpet, barely touching each other with the tips of their widest branches, were like great mound-shaped clouds of exquisite rosy-pink blossoms. There was then nothing in the universe which could compare in loveliness to that spectacle. I was a worshipper of trees at this season, and I remember the feelings I experienced when one day a flock of green paroquets came screaming down and alighted on one of the trees near me. This paroquet never bred in our plantation; they were occasional visitors from their home in an old grove about nine miles away, and their visits were always a great pleasure to us. On this occasion I was particularly glad, because the birds had elected to settle on a tree close to where I was standing. But the blossoms thickly covering every twig annoyed the parrots, as they could not find space enough to grasp a twig without grasping its flower as well; so what did the birds do in their impatience but begin stripping the blossoms off the branches on which they were perched with their sharp beaks, so rapidly that the flowers came down in a pink shower, and in this way in half a minute every bird made a twig bare where he could sit perched at ease. There were millions of blossoms; only one here and there would ever be a peach, yet it angered me to see the parrots cut them off in that heedless way: it was a desecration, a crime even in a bird.

Even now when I recall the sight of those old flowering peach trees, with trunks as thick as a man's body, and the huge mounds or clouds of myriads of roseate blossoms seen against the blue ethereal sky, I am not sure that I have seen anything in my life more perfectly beautiful. Yet this great beauty was but half the charm I found in these trees: the other half was in the bird-music that issued from them. It was the music

THE PLANTATION 49

of but one kind of bird, a small greenish-yellow field finch, in size like the linnet though with a longer and slimmer body, and resembling a linnet too in its general habits. Thus, in autumn it unites in immense flocks, which keep together during the winter months and sing in concert and do not break up until the return of the breeding season. In a country where there were no bird-catchers or human persecutors of small birds, the flocks of this finch, called *misto* by the natives, were far larger than any linnet flocks ever seen in England. The flock we used to have about our plantation numbered many thousands, and you would see them like a cloud wheeling about in the air, then suddenly dropping and vanishing from sight in the grass, where they fed on small seeds and tender leaves and buds. On going to the spot they would rise with a loud humming sound on innumerable wings, and begin rushing and whirling about again, chasing each other in play and chirping, and presently all would drop to the ground again.

In August, when the spring begins to infect their blood, they repair to the trees at intervals during the day, where they sit perched and motionless for an hour or longer, all singing together. This singing time was when the peach trees were in blossom, and it was invariably in the peach trees they settled and could be seen, the little yellow birds in thousands amid the millions of pink blossoms, pouring out their wonderful music.

One of the most delightful bird sounds or noises to be heard in England is the concert-singing of a flock of several hundreds, and sometimes of a thousand or more linnets in September and October, and even later in the year, before these great congregations have been broken up or have migrated. The effect produced by the small field finch of the pampas was quite different. The linnet has a little twittering song with breaks in it and small

50   FAR AWAY AND LONG AGO

chirping sounds, and when a great multitude of birds sing together the sound at a distance of fifty or sixty yards is as of a high wind among the trees, but on a nearer approach the mass of sound resolves itself into a tangle of thousands of individual sounds, resembling that of a great concourse of starlings at roosting-time, but more musical in character. It is as if hundreds of fairy minstrels were all playing on stringed and wind instruments of various forms, every one intent on his own performance without regard to the others.

The field finch does not twitter or chirp and has no break or sudden change in his song, which is composed of a series of long-drawn notes, the first somewhat throaty but growing clearer and brighter towards the end, so that when thousands sing together it is as if they sang in perfect unison, the effect on the hearing being like that on the sight of flowing water or of rain when the multitudinous falling drops appear as silvery-grey lines on the vision. It is an exceedingly beautiful effect, and so far as I know unique among birds that have the habit of singing in large companies.

I remember that we had a carpenter in those days, an Englishman named John, a native of Cumberland, who used to make us laugh at his slow heavy way when, after asking him some simple question, we had to wait until he put down his tools and stared at us for about twenty seconds before replying. One of my elder brothers had dubbed him the 'Cumberland boor.' I remember one day on going to listen to the choir of finches in the blossoming orchard, I was surprised to see John standing near the trees doing nothing, and as I came up to him he turned towards me with a look which astonished me on his dull old face—that look which perhaps one of my readers has by chance seen on the face of a religious mystic in a moment of exaltation. 'Those little birds! I never heard anything like

THE PLANTATION

it!' he exclaimed, then trudged off to his work. Like most Englishmen, he had, no doubt, a vein of poetic feeling hidden away somewhere in his soul.

We also had the other kind of concert-singing by another species in the plantation. This was the common purple cow-bird, one of the Troupial family, exclusively American, but supposed to have affinities with the starlings of the Old World. This cow-bird is parasitical (like the European cuckoo) in its breeding habits, and having no domestic affairs of its own to attend to it lives in flocks all the year round, leading an idle vagabond life. The male is of a uniform deep purple-black, the female a drab or mouse-colour. The cow-birds were excessively numerous among the trees in summer, perpetually hunting for nests in which to deposit their eggs: they fed on the ground out on the plain and were often in such big flocks as to look like a huge black carpet spread out on the green sward. On a rainy day they did not feed: they congregated on the trees in thousands and sang by the hour. Their favourite gathering-place at such times was behind the house, where the trees grew pretty thick and were sheltered on two sides by the black acacias and double rows of Lombardy poplars, succeeded by double rows of large mulberry trees, forming walks, and these by pear, apple, and cherry trees. From whichever side the wind blew it was calm here, and during the heaviest rain the birds would sit here in their thousands, pouring out a continuous torrent of song, which resembled the noise produced by thousands of starlings at roosting-time, but was louder and differed somewhat in character owing to the peculiar song of the cow-bird, which begins with hollow guttural sounds, followed by a burst of loud clear ringing notes.

These concert-singers, the little green and yellow field finch and the purple cow-bird, were with us all the year round, with many others which it would take a whole

52 FAR AWAY AND LONG AGO

chapter to tell of. When, in July and August, I watched
for the coming spring, it was the migrants, the birds
that came annually to us from the far north, that
chiefly attracted me. Before their arrival the bloom
was gone from the peach trees, and the choir of countless
little finches broken up and scattered all over the plain.
Then the opening leaves were watched, and after the
willows the first and best-loved were the poplars.
During all the time they were opening, when they were
still a yellowish-green in colour, the air was full of the
fragrance, but not satisfied with that I would crush and
rub the new small leaves in my hands and on my face
to get the delicious balsamic smell in fuller measure.
And of all the trees, after the peach, the poplars appeared
to feel the new season with the greatest intensity, for it
seemed to me that they felt the sunshine even as I did,
and they expressed it in their fragrance just as the peach
and other trees did in their flowers. And it was also
expressed in the new sound they gave out to the wind.
The change was really wonderful when the rows on rows
of immensely tall trees which for months had talked
and cried in that strange sibilant language, rising to
shrieks when a gale was blowing, now gave out a larger
volume of sound, more continuous, softer, deeper, and
like the wash of the sea on a wide shore.

The other trees would follow, and by and by all
would be in full foliage once more, and ready to receive
their strange beautiful guests from the tropical forests
in the distant north.

The most striking of the new-comers was the small
scarlet tyrant-bird, which is about the size of our
spotted flycatcher; all a shining scarlet except the black
wings and tail. This bird had a delicate bell-like voice,
but it was the scarlet colour shining amid the green
foliage which made me delight in it above all other
birds. Yet the humming-bird, which arrived at the

THE PLANTATION 53

same time, was wonderfully beautiful too, especially when he flew close to your face and remained suspended motionless on mist-like wings for a few moments, his feathers looking and glittering like minute emerald scales.

Then came other tyrant-birds and the loved swallows —the house-swallow, which resembles the English house-martin, the large purple martin, the *golondrina doméstica*, and the brown tree-martin. Then, too, came the yellow-billed cuckoo—the *kowe-kowe* as it is called from its cry. Year after year I listened for its deep mysterious call, which sounded like *gow-gow-gow-gow-gow*, in late September, even as the small English boy listens for the call of *his* cuckoo in April; and the human-like character of the sound, together with the startlingly impressive way in which it was enunciated, always produced the idea that it was something more than a mere bird call. Later, in October when the weather was hot, I would hunt for the nest, a frail platform made of a few sticks with four or five oval eggs like those of the turtle-dove in size and of a pale green colour.

There were other summer visitors, but I must not speak of them as this chapter contains too much on that subject. My feathered friends were so much to me that I am constantly tempted to make this sketch of my first years a book about birds and little else. There remains, too, much more to say about the plantation, the trees and their effect on my mind, also some adventures I met with, some with birds and others with snakes, which will occupy two or three or more chapters later on.

CHAPTER V

ASPECTS OF THE PLAIN

Appearance of a green level land—Cardoon and giant thistles—
Villages of the *vizcacha*, a large burrowing rodent—Groves
and plantations seen like islands on the wide level plains—
Trees planted by the early colonists—Decline of the colonists
from an agricultural to a pastoral people—Houses as part of
the landscape—Flesh diet of the gauchos—Summer change in
the aspect of the plain—The water-like mirage—The giant
thistle and a 'thistle year'—Fear of fires—An incident at a
fire—The *pampero*, or south-west wind, and the fall of the
thistles—Thistle-down and thistle-seed as food for animals—
A great *pampero* storm—Big hailstones—Damage caused by
hail—Zango, an old horse, killed—Zango and his master.

As a small boy of six but well able to ride bare-backed
at a fast gallop without falling off, I invite the reader,
mounted too, albeit on nothing but an imaginary animal,
to follow me a league or so from the gate to some spot
where the land rises to a couple or three or four feet
above the surrounding level. There, sitting on our
horses, we shall command a wider horizon than even the
tallest man would have standing on his own legs, and
in this way get a better idea of the district in which
ten of the most impressionable years of my life, from
five to fifteen, were spent.

We see all round us a flat land, its horizon a perfect
ring of misty blue colour where the crystal-blue dome
of the sky rests on the level green world. Green in late
autumn, winter, and spring, or say from April to November, but not all like a green lawn or field: there were smooth
areas where sheep had pastured, but the surface varied
greatly and was mostly more or less rough. In places
the land as far as one could see was covered with a dense
growth of cardoon thistles, or wild artichoke, of a bluish

ASPECTS OF THE PLAIN   55

or grey-green colour, while in other places the giant
thistle flourished, a plant with big variegated green and
white leaves, and standing when in flower six to ten feet
high.

There were other breaks and roughnesses on that flat
green expanse caused by the *vizcachas*, a big rodent the
size of a hare, a mighty burrower in the earth. *Vizcachas*
swarmed in all that district where they have now
practically been exterminated, and lived in villages,
called *vizcacheras*, composed of thirty or forty huge
burrows—about the size of half a dozen badgers' earths
grouped together. The earth thrown out of these
diggings formed a mound, and being bare of vegetation
it appeared in the landscape as a clay-coloured spot on
the green surface. Sitting on a horse one could count
a score to fifty or sixty of these mounds or *vizcacheras*
on the surrounding plain.

On all this visible earth there were no fences, and no
trees excepting those which had been planted at the old
estancia houses, and these being far apart the groves and
plantations looked like small islands of trees, or mounds,
blue in the distance, on the great plain or pampa.
They were mostly shade trees, the commonest being
the Lombardy poplar, which of all trees is the easiest
one to grow in that land. And these trees at the
estancias or cattle-ranches were, at the time I am
writing about, almost invariably aged and in many
instances in an advanced state of decay. It is interesting to know how these old groves and plantations ever
came into existence in a land where at that period there
was practically no tree-planting.

The first colonists who made their homes in this vast
vacant space, called the pampas, came from a land
where the people are accustomed to sit in the shade of
trees, where corn and wine and oil are supposed to be
necessaries, and where there is salad in the garden.

56   FAR AWAY AND LONG AGO

Naturally they made gardens and planted trees, both for shade and fruit, wherever they built themselves a house on the pampas, and no doubt for two or three generations they tried to live as people live in Spain, in the rural districts. But now the main business of their lives was cattle-raising, and as the cattle roamed at will over the vast plains and were more like wild than domestic animals, it was a life on horseback. They could no longer dig or plough the earth or protect their crops from insects and birds and their own animals. They gave up their oil and wine and bread and lived on flesh alone. They sat in the shade and ate the fruit of trees planted by their fathers or their great-grandfathers until the trees died of old age, or were blown down or killed by the cattle, and there was no more shade and fruit.

It thus came about that the Spanish colonists on the pampas declined from the state of an agricultural people to that of an exclusively pastoral and hunting one; and later, when the Spanish yoke, as it was called, was shaken off, the incessant throat-cutting wars of the various factions, which were like the wars of 'crows and pies,' except that knives were used instead of beaks, confirmed and sunk them deeper in their wild and barbarous manner of life.

Thus, too, the tree-clumps on the pampas were mostly remains of a vanished past. To these clumps or planta-tions we shall return later on when I come to describe the home life of some of our nearest neighbours; here the houses only, with or without trees growing about them, need be mentioned as parts of the landscape. The houses were always low and scarcely visible at a distance of a mile and a half: one always had to stoop on entering a door. They were built of burnt or unburnt brick, more often clay and brushwood, and thatched with sedges or bulrushes. At some of the better houses

ASPECTS OF THE PLAIN 57

there would be a small garden, a few yards of soil protected in some way from the poultry and animals, in which a few flowers and herbs were grown, especially parsley, rue, sage, tansy, and horehound. But there was no other cultivation attempted, and no vegetables were eaten except onions and garlic, which were bought at the stores, with bread, rice, maté tea, oil, vinegar, raisins, cinnamon, pepper, cummin seed, and whatever else they could afford to season their meat-pies or give a flavour to the monotonous diet of cow's flesh and mutton and pig. Almost the only game eaten was ostrich, armadillo, and tinamou (the partridge of the country), which the boys could catch by snaring or running them down. Wild duck, plover, and such birds they rarely or never tasted, as they could not shoot; and as to the big rodent, the *vizcacha*, which swarmed everywhere, no gaucho would touch its flesh, although to my taste it was better than rabbit.

The summer change in the aspect of the plain would begin in November: the dead dry grass would take on a yellowish-brown colour, the giant thistle a dark rust-brown, and at this season, from November to February, the grove or plantation at the estancia house, with its deep fresh unchanging verdure and shade, was a veritable refuge on the vast flat yellow earth. It was then, when the water-courses were gradually drying up and the thirsty days coming to flocks and herds, that the mocking illusion of the mirage was constantly about us. Quite early in spring, on any warm cloudless day, this water-mirage was visible, and was like the appearance on a hot summer's day of the atmosphere in England when the air near the surface becomes visible, when one sees it dancing before one's eyes, like thin wavering and ascending tongues of flame—crystal-clear flames mixed with flames of a faint pearly or silver grey. On the level and hotter pampas this appearance is intensified,

58   FAR AWAY AND LONG AGO

and the faintly visible wavering flames change to an appearance of lakelets or sheets of water looking as if ruffled by the wind and shining like molten silver in the sun. The resemblance to water is increased when there are groves and buildings on the horizon, which look like dark blue islands or banks in the distance, while the cattle and horses feeding not far from the spectator appear to be wading knee- or belly-deep in the brilliant water.

The aspect of the plain was different in what was called a 'thistle year,' when the giant thistles, which usually occupied definite areas or grew in isolated patches, suddenly sprang up everywhere, and for a season covered most of the land. In these luxuriant years the plants grew as thick as sedges and bulrushes in their beds, and were taller than usual, attaining a height of about ten feet. The wonder was to see a plant which throws out leaves as large as those of the rhubarb, with its stems so close together as to be almost touching. Standing among the thistles in the growing season one could in a sense *hear* them growing, as the huge leaves freed themselves with a jerk from a cramped position, producing a crackling sound. It was like the crackling sound of the furze seed-vessels which one hears in June in England, only much louder.

To the gaucho who lives half his day on his horse and loves his freedom as much as a wild bird, a thistle year was a hateful period of restraint. His small, low-roofed, mud house was then too like a cage to him, as the tall thistles hemmed it in and shut out the view on all sides. On his horse he was compelled to keep to the narrow cattle track and to draw in or draw up his legs to keep them from the long pricking spines. In those distant primitive days the gaucho if a poor man was usually shod with nothing but a pair of iron spurs.

By the end of November the thistles would be dead,

ASPECTS OF THE PLAIN 59

and their huge hollow stalks as dry and light as the shaft of a bird's feather—a feather-shaft twice as big round as a broomstick and six to eight feet long. The roots were not only dead but turned to dust in the ground, so that one could push a stalk from its place with one finger, but it would not fall since it was held up by scores of other sticks all round it, and these by hundreds more, and the hundreds by thousands and millions. The thistle dead was just as great a nuisance as the thistle living, and in this dead dry condition they would sometimes stand all through December and January when the days were hottest and the danger of fire was ever present to people's minds. At any moment a careless spark from a cigarette might kindle a dangerous blaze. At such times the sight of smoke in the distance would cause every man who saw it to mount his horse and fly to the danger-spot, where an attempt would be made to stop the fire by making a broad path in the thistles some fifty to a hundred yards ahead of it. One way to make the path was to lasso and kill a few sheep from the nearest flock and drag them up and down at a gallop through the dense thistles until a broad space was clear where the flames could be stamped and beaten out with horse-rugs. But sheep to be used in this way were not always to be found on the spot, and even when a broad space could be made, if a hot north wind was blowing it would carry showers of sparks and burning sticks to the other side and the fire would travel on.

I remember going to one of these big fires when I was about twelve years old. It broke out a few miles from home and was travelling in our direction; I saw my father mount and dash off, but it took me half an hour or more to catch a horse for myself, so that I arrived late on the scene. A fresh fire had broken out a quarter of a mile in advance of the main one, where most of the men were fighting the flames; and to this spot I went

60   FAR AWAY AND LONG AGO

first, and found some half a dozen neighbours who had
just arrived on the scene.   Before we started operations
about twenty men from the main fire came galloping up
to us.   They had made their path, but seeing this new
fire so far ahead, had left it in despair after an hour's
hard hot work, and had flown to the new danger-spot.
As they came up I looked in wonder at one who rode
ahead, a tall black man in his shirtsleeves who was a
stranger to me.   'Who is this black fellow, I wonder?'
said I to myself, and just then he shouted to me in
English: 'Hallo, my boy, what are you doing here?'
It was my father; an hour's fighting with the flames in
a cloud of black ashes in that burning sun and wind
had made him look like a pure-blooded negro!

During December and January when this desert world
of thistles dead and dry as tinder continued standing,
a menace and danger, the one desire and hope of every
one was for the *pampero*—the south-west wind, which
in hot weather is apt to come with startling suddenness,
and to blow with extraordinary violence.   And it would
come at last, usually in the afternoon of a close hot day,
after the north wind had been blowing persistently for
days with a breath as from a furnace.   At last the
hateful wind would drop and a strange gloom that was
not from any cloud would cover the sky; and by and
by a cloud would rise, a dull dark cloud as of a mountain
becoming visible on the plain at an enormous distance.
In a little while it would cover half the sky, and there
would be thunder and lightning and a torrent of rain,
and at the same moment the wind would strike and
roar in the bent-down trees and shake the house.   And
in an hour or two it would perhaps be all over, and
next morning the detested thistles would be gone, or at
all events levelled to the ground.

After such a storm the sense of relief to the horseman,
now able to mount and gallop forth in any direction

ASPECTS OF THE PLAIN 61

over the wide plain and see the earth once more spread out for miles before him, was like that of a prisoner released from his cell, or of the sick man when he at length repairs his vigour lost, and breathes and walks again.

To this day it gives me a thrill, or perhaps it would be safer to say the ghost of a vanished thrill, when I remember the relief it was in my case, albeit I was never so tied to a horse, so parasitical, as the gaucho, after one of these great thistle-levelling *pampero* winds. It was a rare pleasure to ride out and gallop my horse over wide brown stretches of level land, to hear his hard hoofs crushing the hollow desiccated stalks covering the earth in millions like the bones of a countless host of perished foes. It was a queer kind of joy, a mixed feeling with a dash of gratified revenge to give it a sharp savour.

After all this abuse of the giant thistle, the *cardo asnal* of the natives and *Carduus mariana* of the botanists, it may sound odd to say that a 'thistle year' was a blessing in some ways. It was an anxious year on account of the fear of fire, and a season of great apprehension too when reports of robberies and other crimes were abroad in the land, especially for the poor women who were left so much alone in their low-roofed hovels, shut in by the dense prickly growth. But a thistle year was called a fat year, since the animals—cattle, horses, sheep, and even pigs—browsed freely on the huge leaves and soft sweetish-tasting stems, and were in excellent condition. The only drawbacks were that the riding-horses lost strength as they gained in fat, and cow's milk didn't taste nice.

The best and fattest time would come when the hardening plant was no longer fit to eat and the flowers began to shed their seed. Each flower, in size like a small coffee-cup, would open out in a white mass and

62 FAR AWAY AND LONG AGO

shed its scores of silvery balls, and these when freed of
heavy seed would float aloft in the wind, and the whole
air as far as one could see would be filled with millions
and myriads of floating balls. The fallen seed was so
abundant as to cover the ground under the dead but
still standing plants. It is a long, slender seed, about
the size of a grain of Carolina rice, of a greenish or
bluish-grey colour, spotted with black. The sheep
feasted on it, using their mobile and extensible upper
lips like a crumb-brush to gather it into their mouths.
Horses gathered it in the same way, but the cattle were
out of it, either because they could not learn the trick,
or because their lips and tongues cannot be used to
gather a crumb-like food. Pigs, however, flourished on
it, and to birds, domestic and wild, it was even more
than to the mammals.

In conclusion of this chapter I will return for a page
or two to the subject of the *pampero*, the south-west
wind of the Argentine pampas, to describe the greatest
of all the great *pampero* storms I have witnessed. This
was when I was in my seventh year.

The wind blowing from this quarter is not like the
south-west wind of the North Atlantic and Britain, a
warm wind laden with moisture from hot tropical seas
—that great wind which Joseph Conrad in his *Mirror
of the Sea* has personified in one of the sublimest passages
in recent literature. It is an excessively violent wind, as
all mariners know who have encountered it on the South
Atlantic off the River Plate, but it is cool and dry,
although it frequently comes with great thunder-clouds
and torrents of rain and hail. The rain may last half
an hour to half a day, but when over the sky is without
a vapour and a spell of fine weather ensues.

It was in sultry summer weather, and towards evening all of us boys and girls went out for a ramble on the

ASPECTS OF THE PLAIN   63

plain, and were about a quarter of a mile from home when a blackness appeared in the south-west, and began to cover the sky in that quarter so rapidly that, taking alarm, we started homeward as fast as we could run. But the stupendous slaty-black darkness, mixed with yellow clouds of dust, gained on us, and before we got to the gate the terrified screams of wild birds reached our ears, and glancing back we saw multitudes of gulls and plover flying madly before the storm, trying to keep ahead of it. Then a swarm of big dragon-flies came like a cloud over us, and was gone in an instant, and just as we reached the gate the first big drops splashed down in the form of liquid mud. We had hardly got indoors before the tempest broke in its full fury, a blackness as of night, a blended uproar of thunder and wind, blinding flashes of lightning, and torrents of rain. Then as the first thick darkness began to pass away, we saw that the air was white with falling hailstones of an extraordinary size and appearance. They were big as fowls' eggs, but not egg-shaped: they were flat, and about half an inch thick, and being white, looked like little blocks or bricklets made of compressed snow. The hail continued falling until the earth was white with them, and in spite of their great size they were driven by the furious wind into drifts two or three feet deep against the walls of the buildings.

It was evening and growing dark when the storm ended, but the light next morning revealed the damage we had suffered. Pumpkins, gourds, and water-melons were cut to pieces, and most of the vegetables, including the Indian corn, were destroyed. The fruit trees, too, had suffered greatly. Forty or fifty sheep had been killed outright, and hundreds more were so much hurt that for days they went limping about or appeared stupefied from blows on the head. Three of our heifers were dead, and one horse—an old loved riding-horse

64   FAR AWAY AND LONG AGO

with a history, poor old Zango—the whole house was in grief at his death! He belonged originally to a cavalry officer who had an extraordinary affection for him—a rare thing in a land where horseflesh was too cheap, and men as a rule careless of their animals and even cruel. The officer had spent years in the Banda Oriental, in guerrilla warfare, and had ridden Zango in every fight in which he had been engaged. Coming back to Buenos Ayres he brought the old horse home with him. Two or three years later he came to my father, whom he had come to know very well, and said he had been ordered to the upper provinces and was in great trouble about his horse. He was twenty years old, he said, and no longer fit to be ridden in a fight; and of all the people he knew there was but one man in whose care he wished to leave his horse. I know, he said, that if you will take him and promise to care for him until his old life ends, he will be safe; and I should be happy about him—as happy as I can be without the horse I have loved more than any other being on earth. My father consented, and had kept the old horse for over nine years when he was killed by the hail. He was a well-shaped dark brown animal, with long mane and tail, but, as I knew him, always lean and old-looking, and the chief use he was put to was for the children to take their first riding-lessons on his back.

My parents had already experienced one great sadness on account of Zango before his strange death. For years they had looked for a letter, a message, from the absent officer, and had often pictured his return and joy at finding alive still and embracing his beloved old friend again. But he never returned, and no message came and no news could be heard of him, and it was at last concluded that he had lost his life in that distant part of the country, where there had been much fighting.

To return to the hailstones. The greatest destruction

ASPECTS OF THE PLAIN 65

had fallen on the wild birds. Before the storm immense numbers of golden plover had appeared and were in large flocks on the plain. One of our native boys rode in and offered to get a sackful of plover for the table, and getting the sack he took me up on his horse behind him. A mile or so from home we came upon scores of dead plover lying together where they had been in close flocks, but my companion would not pick up a dead bird. There were others running about with one wing broken, and these he went after, leaving me to hold his horse, and catching them would wring their necks and drop them in the sack. When he had collected two or three dozen he remounted and we rode back.

Later that morning we heard of one human being, a boy of six, in one of our poor neighbours' houses, who had lost his life in a curious way. He was standing in the middle of the room, gazing out at the falling hail, when a hailstone, cutting through the thatched roof, struck him on the head and killed him instantly.

CHAPTER VI

SOME BIRD ADVENTURES

Visit to a river on the pampas—A first long walk—Water-fowl
—My first sight of flamingoes—A great dove visitation—
Strange tameness of the birds—Vain attempts at putting salt
on their tails—An ethical question: When is a lie not a lie?
—The *carancho*, a vulture-eagle—Our pair of *caranchos*—Their
nest in a peach tree—I am ambitious to take their eggs—
The birds' crimes—I am driven off by the birds—The nest
pulled down.

Just before my riding days began in real earnest, when
I was not yet quite confident enough to gallop off alone
for miles to see the world for myself, I had my first long
walk on the plain. One of my elder brothers invited me
to accompany him to a watercourse, one of the slow-
flowing shallow marshy rivers of the pampas which was
but two miles from home. The thought of the half-
wild cattle we would meet terrified me, but he was
anxious for my company that day and assured me that
he could see no herd in that direction and he would be
careful to give a wide berth to anything with horns we
might come upon. Then I joyfully consented and we
set out, three of us, to survey the wonders of a great
stream of running water, where bulrushes grew and
large wild birds, never seen by us at home, would be
found. I had had a glimpse of the river before, as,
when driving to visit a neighbour, we had crossed it at
one of the fords and I had wished to get down and run
on its moist green low banks, and now that desire would
be gratified. It was for me a tremendously long walk,
as we had to take many a turn to avoid the patches of
cardoon and giant thistles, and by and by we came to
low ground where the grass was almost waist-high and

66

SOME BIRD ADVENTURES   67

full of flowers. It was all like an English meadow in
June, when every grass and every herb is in flower,
beautiful and fragrant, but tiring to a boy six years old
to walk through. At last we came out to a smooth
grass turf, and in a little while were by the stream, which
had overflowed its banks owing to recent heavy rains
and was now about fifty yards wide. An astonishing
number of birds were visible—chiefly wild duck, a few
swans, and many waders—ibises, herons, spoonbills, and
others, but the most wonderful of all were three immensely
tall white-and-rose-coloured birds, wading solemnly in a
row a yard or so apart from one another some twenty
yards out from the bank. I was amazed and enchanted
at the sight, and my delight was intensified when the
leading bird stood still and, raising his head and long
neck aloft, opened and shook his wings. For the wings
when open were of a glorious crimson colour, and the
bird was to me the most angel-like creature on earth.

What were these wonderful birds? I asked of my
brothers, but they could not tell me. They said they
had never seen birds like them before, and later I found
that the flamingo was not known in our neighbourhood
as the watercourses were not large enough for it, but
that it could be seen in flocks at a lake less than a day's
journey from our home.

It was not for several years that I had an opportunity of seeing the bird again; later I have seen it
scores and hundreds of times, at rest or flying, at all
times of the day and in all states of the atmosphere, in
all its most beautiful aspects, as when at sunset or in
the early morning it stands motionless in the still water
with its clear image reflected below; or when seen flying
in flocks—seen from some high bank beneath one—
moving low over the blue water in a long crimson line
or half-moon, the birds at equal distances apart, their
wing-tips all but touching; but the delight in these

68 FAR AWAY AND LONG AGO

spectacles has never equalled in degree that which I experienced on this occasion when I was six years old.

The next little bird adventure to be told exhibits me more in the character of an innocent and exceedingly credulous baby of three than of a field naturalist of six with a considerable experience of wild birds.

One spring day an immense number of doves appeared and settled in the plantation. It was a species common in the country and bred in our trees, and in fact in every grove or orchard in the land—a pretty dove-coloured bird with a pretty sorrowful song, about a third less in size than the domestic pigeon, and belonging to the American genus *Zenaida*. This dove was a resident with us all the year round, but occasionally in spring and autumn they were to be seen travelling in immense flocks, and these were evidently strangers in the land and came from some sub-tropical country in the north where they had no fear of the human form. At all events, on going out into the plantation I found them all about on the ground, diligently searching for seeds, and so tame and heedless of my presence that I actually attempted to capture them with my hands. But they wouldn't be caught: the bird when I stooped and put out my hands slipped away, and flying a yard or two would settle down in front of me and go on looking for and picking up invisible seeds.

My attempts failing I rushed back to the house, wildly excited, to look for an old gentleman who lived with us and took an interest in me and my passion for birds, and finding him I told him the whole place was swarming with doves and they were perfectly tame but wouldn't let me catch them—could he tell me how to catch them? He laughed and said I must be a little fool not to know how to catch a bird. The only way was to put salt on their tails. There would be no difficulty in doing that, I thought, and how delighted I was to know that birds

SOME BIRD ADVENTURES 69

could be caught so easily! Off I ran to the salt-barrel
and filled my pockets and hands with coarse salt used
to make brine in which to dip the hides; for I wanted
to catch a great many doves—armfuls of doves.

In a few minutes I was out again in the plantation,
with doves in hundreds moving over the ground all
about me and taking no notice of me. It was a joyful
and exciting moment when I started operations, but
I soon found that when I tossed a handful of salt at the
bird's tail it never fell on its tail—it fell on the ground
two or three or four inches short of the tail. If, I
thought, the bird would only keep still a moment
longer! But then it wouldn't, and I think I spent
quite two hours in these vain attempts to make the
salt fall on the right place. At last I went back to my
mentor to confess that I had failed and to ask for fresh
instructions, but all he would say was that I was on
the right track, that the plan I had adopted was the
proper one, and all that was wanted was a little more
practice to enable me to drop the salt on the right spot.
Thus encouraged I filled my pockets again and started
afresh, and then finding that by following the proper
plan I made no progress I adopted a new one, which
was to take a handful of salt and hurl it at the bird's
tail. Still I couldn't touch the tail; my violent action
only frightened the bird and caused it to fly away, a
dozen yards or so, before dropping down again to
resume its seed-searching business.

By and by I was told by somebody that birds could
not be caught by putting salt on their tails, that I was
being made a fool of, and this was a great shock to me,
since I had been taught to believe that it was wicked
to tell a lie. Now for the first time I discovered that
there were lies and lies, or untruths that were not lies,
which one could tell innocently although they were
invented and deliberately told to deceive. This angered

70   FAR AWAY AND LONG AGO

me at first, and I wanted to know how I was to distinguish between real lies and lies that were not lies, and the only answer I got was that I could distinguish them by not being a fool!

In the next adventure to be told we pass from the love (or tameness) of the turtle to the rage of the vulture. It may be remarked in passing that the vernacular name of the dove I have described is *torcasa*, which I take it is a corruption of *tortola*, the name first given to it by the early colonists on account of its slight resemblance to the turtle-dove of Europe.

Then, as to the vulture, it was not a true vulture nor a strictly true eagle, but a carrion-hawk, a bird the size of a small eagle, blackish-brown in colour with a white neck and breast suffused with brown and spotted with black; also it had a very big eagle-shaped beak, and claws not so strong as an eagle's nor so weak as a vulture's. In its habits it was both eagle and vulture, as it fed on dead flesh, and was also a hunter and killer of animals and birds, especially of the weakly and young. A somewhat destructive creature to poultry and young sucking lambs and pigs. Its feeding habits were, in fact, very like those of the raven, and its voice, too, was raven-like, or rather like that of the carrion-crow at his loudest and harshest. Considering the character of this big rapacious bird, the *Polyborus tharus* of naturalists and the *carancho* of the natives, it may seem strange that a pair were allowed to nest and live for years in our plantation, but in those days people were singularly tolerant not only of injurious birds and beasts but even of beings of their own species of predaceous habits.

On the outskirts of our old peach orchard, described in a former chapter, there was a solitary tree of a somewhat singular shape, standing about forty yards from the others on the edge of a piece of waste weedy land. It was a big old tree like the others, and had a smooth

SOME BIRD ADVENTURES 71

round trunk standing about fourteen feet high and
throwing out branches all round, so that its upper part
had the shape of an open inverted umbrella. And in
the convenient hollow formed by the circle of branches
the *caranchos* had built their huge nest, composed of
sticks, lumps of turf, dry bones of sheep and other
animals, pieces of rope and raw hide, and any other
object they could carry. The nest was their home; they
roosted in it by night and visited it at odd times during
the day, usually bringing a bleached bone or thistle-
stalk or some such object to add to the pile.

Our birds never attacked the fowls, and were not
offensive or obtrusive, but kept to their own end of the
plantation furthest away from the buildings. They only
came when an animal was killed for meat, and would
then hang about, keeping a sharp eye on the proceedings
and watching their chance. This would come when the
carcass was dressed and lights and other portions thrown
to the dogs; then the *carancho* would swoop down like
a kite, and snatching up the meat with his beak would
rise to a height of twenty or thirty yards in the air, and
dropping his prize would deftly catch it again in his
claws and soar away to feed on it at leisure. I was
never tired of admiring this feat of the *carancho*, which
is, I believe, unique in birds of prey.

The big nest in the old inverted-umbrella-shaped peach
tree had a great attraction for me; I used often to visit
it and wonder if I would ever have the power of getting
up to it. Oh, what a delight it would be to get up
there, above the nest, and look down into the great
basin-like hollow lined with sheep's wool and see the
eggs, bigger than turkey's eggs, all marbled with deep
red, or creamy white splashed with blood-red! For I
had seen *carancho* eggs brought in by a gaucho, and I
was ambitious to take a clutch from a nest with my own
hands. It was true I had been told by my mother that

72 FAR AWAY AND LONG AGO

if I wanted wild birds' eggs I was never to take more
than one from a nest, unless it was of some injurious
species. And injurious the *carancho* certainly was, in
spite of his good behaviour when at home. On one of
my early rides on my pony I had seen a pair of them,
and I think they were our own birds, furiously attacking
a weak and sickly ewe; she had refused to lie down to
be killed, and they were on her neck, beating and
tearing at her face and trying to pull her down. Also I
had seen a litter of little pigs a sow had brought
forth on the plain attacked by six or seven *caranchos*,
and found on approaching the spot that they had
killed half of them (about six, I think), and were de-
vouring them at some distance from the old pig and the
survivors of the litter. But how could I climb the tree
and get over the rim of the huge nest? And I was
afraid of the birds, they looked so unspeakably savage
and formidable whenever I went near them. But my
desire to get the eggs was overmastering, and when it
was spring and I·had reason to think that eggs were
being laid, I went oftener than ever to watch and wait
for an opportunity. And one evening just after sunset
I could not see the birds anywhere about and thought
my chance had now come. I managed to swarm up
the smooth trunk to the branches, and then with wildly
beating heart began the task of trying to get through
the close branches and to work my way over the huge
rim of the nest. Just then I heard the harsh grating
cry of the bird, and peering through the leaves in the
direction it came from I caught sight of the two birds
flying furiously towards me, screaming again as they
came nearer. Then terror seized me, and down I went
through the branches, and catching hold of the lowest
one managed to swing myself clear, and dropped to the
ground. It was a good long drop, but I fell on a soft
turf, and springing to my feet fled to the shelter of the

SOME BIRD ADVENTURES 73

orchard and then on towards the house, without ever looking back to see if they were following.

That was my only attempt to raid the nest, and from that time the birds continued in peaceful possession of it until it came into some person's mind that this huge nest was detrimental to the tree, and was the cause of its producing so little fruit compared with any other tree, and the nest was accordingly pulled down, and the birds forsook the place.

In the description in a former chapter of our old peach trees in their blossoming time I mentioned the paroquets which occasionally visited us but had their breeding-place some distance away. This bird was one of the two common parrots of the district, the other larger species being the Patagonian parrot, *Conarus patagonus*, the *loro barranquero* or cliff parrot of the natives. In my early years this bird was common on the treeless pampas extending for hundreds of miles south of Buenos Ayres as well as in Patagonia, and bred in holes it excavated in cliffs and steep banks at the side of lakes and rivers. These breeding-sites were far south of my home, and I did not visit them until my boyhood's days were over.

In winter these birds had a partial migration to the north: at that season we were visited by flocks, and as a child it was a joy to me when the resounding screams of the travelling parrots, heard in the silence long before the birds became visible in the sky, announced their approach. Then, when they appeared flying at a moderate height, how strange and beautiful they looked, with long pointed wings and long graduated tails, in their sombre green plumage touched with yellow, blue, and crimson colour! How I longed for a nearer acquaintance with these winter visitors and hoped they would settle on our trees! Sometimes they did settle to rest, perhaps to spend half a day or longer in the plantation; and sometimes, to my great happiness, a flock would

74 FAR AWAY AND LONG AGO

elect to remain with us for whole days and weeks, feeding on the surrounding plain, coming at intervals to the trees during the day, and at night to roost. I used to go out on my pony to follow and watch the flock at feed, and wondered at their partiality for the bitter-tasting seeds of the wild pumpkin. This plant, which was abundant with us, produced an egg-shaped fruit about half the size of an ostrich's egg, with a hard shell-like rind, but the birds with their sharp iron-hard beaks would quickly break up the dry shell and feast on the pips, scattering the seed-shells about till the ground was whitened with them. When I approached the feeding flock on my pony the birds would rise up and, flying to and at me, hover in a compact crowd just above my head, almost deafening me with their angry screams.

The smaller bird, the paroquet, which was about the size of a turtle-dove, had a uniform rich green colour above and ashy-grey beneath, and, like most parrots, it nested in trees. It is one of the most social birds I know; it lives all the year round in communities and builds huge nests of sticks near together as in a rookery, each nest having accommodation for two or three to half a dozen pairs. Each pair has an entrance and nest cavity of its own in the big structure.

The only breeding-place in our neighbourhood was in a grove or remains òf an ancient ruined plantation at an estancia house, about nine miles from us, owned by an Englishman named Ramsdale. Here there was a colony of about a couple of hundred birds, and the dozen or more trees they had built on were laden with their great nests, each one containing as much material as would have filled a cart.

Mr Ramsdale was not our nearest English neighbour —the one to be described in another chapter; nor was he a man we cared much about, and his meagre establishment was not attractive, as his old slatternly native

SOME BIRD ADVENTURES   75

housekeeper and the other servants were allowed to do just what they liked. But he was English and a neighbour, and my parents made it a point of paying him an occasional visit, and I always managed to go with them —certainly not to see Mr Ramsdale, who had nothing to say to a shy little boy and whose hard red face looked the face of a hard drinker. *My* visits were to the paroquets exclusively. Oh, why, thought I many and many a time, did not these dear green people come over to us and have their happy village in our trees! Yet when I visited them they didn't like it; no sooner would I run out to the grove where the nests were than the place would be in an uproar. Out and up they would rush, to unite in a flock and hover shrieking over my head, and the commotion would last until I left them.

On our return late one afternoon in early spring from one of our rare visits to Mr Ramsdale, we witnessed a strange thing. The plain at that place was covered with a dense growth of cardoon thistle or wild artichoke, and leaving the estancia house in our trap, we followed the cattle tracks as there was no road on that side. About half-way home we saw a troop of seven or eight deer in an open green space among the big grey thistle bushes, but instead of uttering their whistling alarm-cry and making off at our approach they remained at the same spot, although we passed within forty yards of them. The troop was composed of two bucks engaged in a furious fight, and five or six does walking round and round the two fighters. The bucks kept their heads so low down that their noses were almost touching the ground, while with their horns locked together they pushed violently, and from time to time one would succeed in forcing the other ten or twenty feet back. Then a pause, then another violent push, then with horns still together they would move sideways, round

76   FAR·AWAY AND LONG AGO

and round, and so on until we left them behind and lost sight of them.

This spectacle greatly excited us at the time and was vividly recalled several months afterwards when one of our gaucho neighbours told us of a curious thing he had just seen. He had been out on that cardoon-covered spot where we had seen the fighting deer, and at that very spot in the little green space he had come upon the skeletons of two deer with their horns interlocked!

Tragedies of this kind in the wild animal world have often been recorded, but they are exceedingly rare on the pampas, as the smooth few-pronged antlers of the native deer, *Cervus campestris*, are not so liable to get hopelessly interlocked together as in many other species.

Deer were common in our district in those days, and were partial to land overgrown with cardoon thistle, which in the absence of trees and thickets afforded them some sort of cover. I seldom rode to that side without getting a sight of a group of deer, often looking exceedingly conspicuous in their bright fawn colour as they stood gazing at the intruder amidst the wide waste of grey cardoon bushes.

These rough plains were also the haunt of the rhea, our ostrich, and it was here that I first had a close sight of this greatest and most unbird-like bird of our continent. I was eight years old then, when one afternoon in late summer I was just setting off for a ride on my pony, when I was told to go out on the east side till I came to the cardoon-covered land about a mile beyond the shepherd's ranch. The shepherd was wanted in the plantation and could not go to the flock just yet, and I was told to look for the flock and turn it towards home.

I found the flock just where I had been told to look for it, the sheep very widely scattered, and some groups of a dozen or two to a hundred were just visible at a distance among the rough bushes. Just where these

SOME BIRD ADVENTURES

furthest sheep were grazing there was a scattered troop of seventy or eighty horses grazing too, and when I rode to that spot I all at once found myself among a lot of rheas, feeding too among the sheep and horses. Their grey plumage being so much like the cardoon bushes in colour had prevented me from seeing them before I was right among them.

The strange thing was that they paid not the slightest attention to me, and pulling up my pony I sat staring in astonishment at them, particularly at one, a very big one and nearest to me, engaged in leisurely pecking at the clover plants growing among the big prickly thistle leaves, and as it seemed carefully selecting the best sprays.

What a great noble-looking bird it was, and how beautiful in its loose grey-and-white plumage, hanging like a picturesquely worn mantle about its body! Why were they so tame? I wondered. The sight of a mounted gaucho, even at a great distance, will invariably set them off at their topmost speed; yet here I was within a dozen yards of one of them, with several others about me, all occupied in examining the herbage and selecting the nicest-looking leaves to pluck, just as if I was not there at all! I suppose it was because I was only a small boy on a small horse and was not associated in the ostrich brain with the wild-looking gaucho on his big animal charging upon him with a deadly purpose. Presently I went straight at the one near me, and he then raised his head and neck and moved carelessly away before to a distance of a few yards, then began cropping the clover once more. I rode at him again, putting my pony to a trot, and when within two yards of him he all at once swung his body round in a quaint way towards me, and breaking into a sort of dancing trot brushed past me.

Pulling up again and looking back I found he was ten

D. 956

78   FAR AWAY AND LONG AGO

or twelve yards behind me, once more quietly engaged in cropping clover leaves!

Again and again this bird, and one of the others I rode at, practised the same pretty trick, first appearing perfectly unconcerned at my presence and then, when I made a charge at them, with just one little careless movement placing themselves a dozen yards behind me.

But this same trick of the rhea is wonderful to see when the hunted bird is spent with running and is finally overtaken by one of the hunters who has perhaps lost the *bolas* with which he captures his quarry, and who endeavours to pláce himself side by side with it so as to reach it with his knife.   It seems an easy thing to do: the bird is plainly exhausted, panting, his wings hanging, as he lopes on, yet no sooner is the man within striking distance than the sudden motion comes into play, and the bird as by a miracle is now behind instead of at the side of the horse.   And before the horse going at top speed can be reined in and turned round, the rhea has had time to recover his wind and get a hundred yards away or more.   It is on account of this tricky instinct of the rhea that the gauchos say, 'El avestruz es el mas *gaucho* de los animales,' which means that the ostrich, in its resourcefulness and the tricks it practises to save itself when hard pressed, is as clever as the gaucho knows himself to be.

CHAPTER VII

MY FIRST VISIT TO BUENOS AYRES

Happiest time—First visit to the capital—Old and New Buenos
Ayres—Vivid impressions—Solitary walk—How I learnt to
go alone—Lost—The house we stayed at and the sea-like
river—Rough and narrow streets—Rows of posts—Carts and
noise—A great church festival—Young men in black and
scarlet—River scenes—Washerwomen and their language—
Their word-fights with young fashionables—Night watchmen—
A young gentleman's pastime—A fishing dog—A fine gentleman seen stoning little birds—A glimpse of Don Eusebio, the
Dictator's fool.

THE happiest time of my boyhood was at that early
period, a little past the age of six, when I had my own
pony to ride on, and was allowed to stay on his back
just as long and go as far from home as I liked. I was
like the young bird when on first quitting the nest it
suddenly becomes conscious of its power to fly. My
early flying days were, however, soon interrupted, when
my mother took me on my first visit to Buenos Ayres;
that is to say, the first I remember, as I must have been
taken there once before as an infant in arms, since we
lived too far from town for any missionary-clergyman
to travel all that distance just to baptize a little baby.
Buenos Ayres is now the wealthiest, most populous,
Europeanized city in South America: what it was like
at that time these glimpses into a far past will serve to
show. Coming as a small boy of an exceptionally impressionable mind from that green plain where people
lived the simple pastoral life, everything I saw in the city
impressed me deeply, and the sights which impressed
me the most are as vivid in my mind to-day as they
ever were. I was a solitary little boy in my rambles
about the streets, for though I had a younger brother

79

80   FAR AWAY AND LONG AGO

who was my only playmate, he was not yet five, and
too small to keep me company in my walks. Nor did
I mind having no one with me. Very, very early in
my boyhood I had acquired the habit of going about
alone to amuse myself in my own way, and it was only
after years, when my age was about twelve, that my
mother told me how anxious this singularity in me used
to make her. She would miss me when looking out to
see what the children were doing, and I would be called
and searched for, to be found hidden away somewhere
in the plantation. Then she began to keep an eye on
me, and when I was observed stealing off she would
secretly follow and watch me, standing motionless among
the tall weeds or under the trees by the half-hour,
staring at vacancy. This distressed her very much;
then to her great relief and joy she discovered that I
was there with a motive which she could understand
and appreciate: that I was watching some living thing,
an insect perhaps, but oftener a bird—a pair of little
scarlet flycatchers building a nest of lichen on a peach
tree, or some such beautiful thing. And as she loved
all living things herself she was quite satisfied that I was
not going queer in my head, for that was what she had
been fearing.

The strangeness of the streets was a little too much
for me at the start, and I remember that on first ven-
turing out by myself a little distance from home I got
lost. In despair of ever finding my way back I began to
cry, hiding my face against a post at a street corner,
and was there soon surrounded by quite a number of
passers-by; then a policeman came up, with brass
buttons on his blue coat and a sword at his side, and
taking me by the arm he asked me in a commanding
voice where I lived—the name of the street and the
number of the house. I couldn't tell him; then I began
to get frightened on account of his sword and big black

FIRST VISIT TO BUENOS AYRES 81

moustache and loud rasping voice, and suddenly ran away, and after running for about six or eight minutes found myself back at home, to my surprise and joy.

The house where we stayed with English friends was near the front, or what was then the front, that part of the city which faced the Plata river, a river which was like the sea, with no visible shore beyond; and like the sea it was tidal, and differed only in its colour, which was a muddy red instead of blue or green. The house was roomy, and like most of the houses at that date had a large courtyard paved with red tiles and planted with small lemon trees and flowering shrubs of various kinds. The streets were straight and narrow, paved with round boulder stones the size of a football, the pavements with brick or flagstones, and so narrow they would hardly admit of more than two persons walking abreast. Along the pavements on each side of the street were rows of posts placed at a distance of ten yards apart. These strange-looking rows of posts, which foreigners laughed to see, were no doubt the remains of yet ruder times, when ropes of hide were stretched along the side of the pavements to protect the foot-passengers from runaway horses, wild cattle driven by wild men from the plains, and other dangers of the narrow streets. As they were then paved the streets must have been the noisiest in the world, on account of the immense numbers of big springless carts in them. Imagine the thunderous racket made by a long procession of these carts, when they were returning empty, and the drivers, as was often the case, urged their horses to a gallop, and they bumped and thundered over the big round stones!

Just opposite the house we stayed at there was a large church, one of the largest of the numerous churches of the city, and one of my most vivid memories relates to a great annual festival at the church—that of the patron

82   FAR AWAY AND LONG AGO

saint's day. It had been open to worshippers all day, but the chief service was held about three o'clock in the afternoon; at all events it was at that hour when a great attendance of fashionable people took place. I watched them as they came in couples, families, and small groups, in every case the ladies, beautifully dressed, attended by their cavaliers. At the door of the church the gentleman would make his bow and withdraw to the street before the building, where a sort of outdoor gathering was formed of all those who had come as escorts to the ladies, and where they would remain until the service was over. The crowd in the street grew and grew until there were about four or five hundred gentlemen, mostly young, conversing in an animated way, so that the street was filled with the loud humming sound of their blended voices. These men were all natives, all of the good or upper class of the native society, and all dressed exactly alike in the fashion of that time. It was their dress and the uniform appearance of so large a number of persons, most of them with young, handsome, animated faces, that fascinated me and kept me on the spot gazing at them until the big bells began to thunder at the conclusion of the service and the immense concourse of gaily dressed ladies swarmed out, and immediately the meeting broke up, the gentlemen hurrying back to meet them.

They all wore silk hats and the glossiest black broadcloth, not even a pair of trousers of any other shade was seen; and all wore the scarlet silk or fine cloth waistcoat which, at that period, was considered the right thing for every citizen of the republic to wear; also, in lieu of buttonhole, a scarlet ribbon pinned to the lapel of the coat. It was a pretty sight, and the concourse reminded me of a flock of military starlings, a black- or dark-plumaged bird with a scarlet breast, one of my feathered favourites.

FIRST VISIT TO BUENOS AYRES 83

My rambles were almost always on the front, since I could walk there a mile or two from home, north or south, without getting lost, always with the vast expanse of water on one hand, with many big ships looking dim in the distance, and numerous lighters or berlanders coming from them with cargoes of merchandise which they unloaded into carts, these going out a quarter of a mile in the shallow water to meet them. Then there were the water-carts going and coming in scores and hundreds, for at that period there was no water supply to the houses, and every householder had to buy muddy water by the bucket at his own door from the watermen.

One of the most attractive spots to me was the congregating place of the *lavanderas*, south of my street. Here on the broad beach under the cliff one saw a whiteness like a white cloud, covering the ground for a space of about a third of a mile; and the cloud, as one drew near, resolved itself into innumerable garments, sheets and quilts, and other linen pieces, fluttering from long lines, and covering the low rocks washed clean by the tide and the stretches of green turf between. It was the spot where the washerwomen were allowed to wash all the dirty linen of Buenos Ayres in public. All over the ground the women, mostly negresses, were seen on their knees, beside the pools among the rocks, furiously scrubbing and pounding away at their work, and like all negresses they were exceedingly vociferous, and their loud gabble, mingled with yells and shrieks of laughter, reminded me of the hubbub made by a great concourse of gulls, ibises, godwits, geese, and other noisy waterfowl on some marshy lake. It was a wonderfully animated scene, and drew me to it again and again: I found, however, that it was necessary to go warily among these women, as they looked with suspicion at idling boys, and sometimes, when I picked my way among the spread garments, I was sharply ordered off.

84 FAR AWAY AND LONG AGO

Then, too, they often quarrelled over their right to certain places and spaces among themselves; then very suddenly their hilarious gabble would change to wild cries of anger and torrents of abuse. By and by I discovered that their greatest rages and worst language were when certain young gentlemen of the upper classes visited the spot to amuse themselves by baiting the *lavanderas*. The young gentleman would saunter about in an absent-minded manner and presently walk right on to a beautifully embroidered and belaced nightdress or other dainty garment spread out to dry on the sward or rock, and, standing on it, calmly proceed to take out and light a cigarette. Instantly the black virago would be on her feet confronting him and pouring out a torrent of her foulest expressions and deadliest curses. He, in a pretended rage, would reply in even worse language. That would put her on her mettle; for now all her friends and foes scattered about the ground would suspend their work to listen with all their ears; and the contest of words growing louder and fiercer would last until the combatants were both exhausted and unable to invent any more new and horrible expressions of opprobrium to hurl at each other. Then the insulted young gentleman would kick the garment away in a fury and hurling the unfinished cigarette in his adversary's face would walk off with his nose in the air.

I laugh to recall these unseemly word-battles on the beach, but they were shocking to me when I first heard them as a small, innocent-minded boy, and it only made the case worse when I was assured that the young gentleman was only acting a part, that the extreme anger he exhibited, which might have served as an excuse for using such language, was all pretence.

Another favourite pastime of these same idle, rich young gentlemen offended me as much as the one I have related. The night-watchmen, called *serenos*, of that

FIRST VISIT TO BUENOS AYRES 85

time interested me in an extraordinary way. When
night came it appeared that the fierce policemen, with
their swords and brass buttons, were no longer needed
to safeguard the people, and their place in the streets
was taken by a quaint, frowsy-looking body of men,
mostly old, some almost decrepit, wearing big cloaks
and carrying staffs and heavy iron lanterns with a tallow
candle alight inside. But what a pleasure it was to lie
awake at night and listen to their voices calling the
hours! The calls began at the stroke of eleven, and
then from beneath the window would come the wonderful long drawling call of *Las ón—ce han dá—do y se—
ré—no*, which means eleven of the clock and all serene,
but if clouded the concluding word would be *nu—blá—
do*, and so on, according to the weather. From all the
streets, from all over the town, the long-drawn calls
would float to my listening ears, with infinite variety
in the voices—the high and shrill, the falsetto, the harsh,
raucous note like the caw of the carrion-crow, the
solemn, booming bass, and then some fine, rich, pure
voice that soared heavenwards above all the others and
was like the pealing notes of an organ.

I loved the poor night-watchmen and their cries, and
it grieved my little soft heart to hear that it was considered fine sport by the rich young gentlemen to sally
forth at night and do battle with them, and to deprive
them of their staffs and lanterns, which they took home
and kept as trophies.

Another human phenomenon which annoyed and
shocked my tender mind, like that of the contests on
the beach between young gentlemen and washerwomen,
was the multitude of beggars which infested the town.
These were not like our dignified beggar on horseback,
with his red poncho, spurs, and tall straw hat, who rode
to your gate, and having received his tribute, blessed
you and rode away to the next estancia. These city

*D 95⁶

86   FAR AWAY AND LONG AGO

beggars on the pavement were the most brutal, even
fiendish, looking men I had ever seen. Most of them
were old soldiers, who, having served their ten, fifteen,
or twenty years, according to the nature of the crime
for which they had been condemned to the army, had
been discharged or thrown out to live like carrion-hawks
on what they could pick up. Twenty times a day at
least you would hear the iron gate opening from the
courtyard into the street swung open, followed by the
call or shout of the beggar demanding charity in the
name of God. Outside you could not walk far without
being confronted by one of these men, who would boldly
square himself in front of you on the narrow pavement
and beg for alms. If you had no change and said,
'Perdón, por Dios,' he would scowl and let you pass;
but if you looked annoyed or disgusted, or ordered him
out of the way, or pushed by without a word, he would
glare at you with a concentrated rage which seemed to
say, 'Oh, to have you down at my mercy, bound hand
and foot, a sharp knife in my hand!' And this would
be followed by a blast of the most horrible language.

One day I witnessed a very strange thing, the action
of a dog, by the waterside. It was evening and the
beach was forsaken; cartmen, fishermen, boatmen all
gone, and I was the only idler left on the rocks; but the
tide was coming in, rolling quite big waves on to the
rocks, and the novel sight of the waves, the freshness,
the joy of it, kept me at that spot, standing on one of
the outermost rocks not yet washed over by the water.
By and by a gentleman, followed by a big dog, came
down on to the beach and stood at a distance of forty
or fifty yards from me, while the dog bounded forward
over the flat, slippery rocks and through pools of water
until he came to my side, and sitting on the edge of the
rock began gazing intently down at the water. He was
a big, shaggy, round-headed animal, with a greyish coat

FIRST VISIT TO BUENOS AYRES 87

with some patches of light reddish colour on it; what his breed was I cannot say, but he looked somewhat like a sheep-dog or an otter-hound. Suddenly he plunged in, quite disappearing from sight, but quickly reappeared with a big shad of about three and a half or four pounds weight in his jaws. Climbing on to the rock he dropped the fish, which he did not appear to have injured much, as it began floundering about in an exceedingly lively manner. I was astonished and looked back at the dog's master; but there he stood in the same place, smoking and paying no attention to what his animal was doing. Again the dog plunged in and brought out a second big fish and dropped it on the flat rock, and again and again he dived, until there were five big shads all floundering about on the wet rock and likely soon to be washed back into the water.

The shad is a common fish in the Plata and the best to eat of all its fishes, resembling the salmon in its rich flavour, and is eagerly watched for when it comes up from the sea by the Buenos Ayres fishermen, just as our fishermen watch for mackerel on our coasts. But on this evening the beach was deserted by every one, watchers included, and the fish came and swarmed along the rocks, and there was no one to catch them—not even some poor hungry idler to pounce upon and carry off the five fishes the dog had captured. One by one I saw them washed back into the water, and presently the dog, hearing his master whistling to him, bounded away.

For many years after this incident I failed to find any one who had even seen or heard of a dog catching fish. Eventually, in reading I met with an account of fishing-dogs in Newfoundland and other countries.

One other strange adventure met with on the front remains to be told. It was about eleven o'clock in the morning and I was on the Parade, walking north,

88   FAR AWAY AND LONG AGO

pausing from time to time to look over the sea-wall
to watch the flocks of small birds that came to feed on
the beach below. Presently my attention was drawn
to a young man walking on before me, pausing and
peering too from time to time over the wall, and when
he did so throwing something at the small birds. I ran
on and overtook him, and was rather taken aback at
his wonderfully fine appearance. He was like one of the
gentlemen of the gathering before the church, described
a few pages back, and wore a silk hat and fashionable
black coat and trousers and scarlet silk waistcoat; he
was also a remarkably handsome young gentleman, with
a golden-brown curly beard and moustache and dark
liquid eyes that studied my face with a half-amused
curiosity when I looked up at him. In one hand he
carried a wash-leather bag by its handle, and holding a
pebble in his right hand he watched the birds, the small
parties of crested song-sparrows, yellow house-sparrows,
siskins, field finches, and other kinds, and from time to
time he would hurl a pebble at the bird he had singled
out forty yards down below us on the rocks. I did not
see him actually hit a bird, but his precision was
amazing, for almost invariably the missile, thrown from
such a distance at so minute an object, appeared to
graze the feathers and to miss killing by but a fraction
of an inch.

I followed him for some distance, my wonder and
curiosity growing every minute to see such a superior-
looking person engaged in such a pastime. For it is a
fact that the natives do not persecute small birds. On
the contrary, they despise the aliens in the land who
shoot and trap them. Besides, if he wanted small birds
for any purpose, why did he try to get them by throwing
pebbles at them? As he did not order me off, but looked
in a kindly way at me every little while, with a slight
smile on his face, I at length ventured to tell him that

FIRST VISIT TO BUENOS AYRES 89

he would never get a bird that way—that it would be impossible at that distance to hit one with a small pebble. 'Oh, no, not impossible,' he returned, smiling and walking on, still with an eye on the rocks. 'Well, you haven't hit one yet,' I was bold enough to say, and at that he stopped, and putting his finger and thumb in his waistcoat pocket he pulled out a dead male siskin and put it in my hands.

This was the bird called 'goldfinch' by the English resident in La Plata, and to the Spanish it is also goldfinch; it is, however, a siskin, *Chrysomitris magellanica*, and has a velvet-black head, the rest of its plumage being black, green, and shining yellow. It was one of my best-loved birds, but I had never had one in my hand, dead or alive, before, and now its wonderful unimagined loveliness, its graceful form, and the exquisitely pure flower-like yellow hue affected me with a delight so keen that I could hardly keep from tears.

After gloating a few moments over it, touching it with my finger-tips and opening the little black and gold wings, I looked up pleadingly and begged him to let me keep it. He smiled and shook his head: he would not waste his breath talking; all his energy was to be spent in hurling pebbles at other lovely little birds.

'Oh, señor, will you not give it to me?' I pleaded still; and then, with sudden hope: 'Are you going to sell it?'

He laughed, and taking it from my hand put it back in his waistcoat pocket; then, with a pleasant smile and a nod to say that the interview was now over, he went on his way.

Standing on the spot where he left me, and still bitterly regretting that I had failed to get the bird, I watched him until he disappeared from sight in the distance, walking towards the suburb of Palermo; and a mystery he remains to this day, the one and only

90 FAR AWAY AND LONG AGO

Argentine gentleman, a citizen of the Athens of South
America, amusing himself by killing little birds with
pebbles. But I do not know that it was an amusement.
He had perhaps in some wild moment made a vow to
kill so many siskins in that way, or a bet to prove his
skill in throwing a pebble; or he might have been
practising a cure for some mysterious deadly malady,
prescribed by some wandering physician, from Bagdad
or Ispahan; or, more probably still, some heartless,
soulless woman he was in love with had imposed this
fantastical task on him.

Perhaps the most wonderful thing I saw during that
first eventful visit to the capital was the famed Don
Eusebio, the court jester or fool of the President or
Dictator Rosas, the 'Nero of South America,' who lived
in his palace at Palermo, just outside the city. I had
been sent with my sisters and little brother to spend
the day at the house of an Anglo-Argentine family in
another part of the town, and we were in the large
courtyard playing with the children of the house when
someone opened a window above us and called out,
'Don Eusebio!' That conveyed nothing to me, but the
little boys of the house knew what it meant; it meant
that if we went quickly out to the street we might catch
a glimpse of the great man in all his glory. At all
events, they jumped up, flinging their toys away, and
rushed to the street door, and we after them. Coming
out we found quite a crowd of lookers-on, and then
down the street, in his general's dress—for it was one
of the Dictator's little jokes to make his fool a general—
all scarlet, with a big scarlet three-cornered hat surmounted by an immense aigrette of scarlet plumes,
came Don Eusebio. He marched along with tremendous dignity, his sword at his side, and twelve soldiers,
also in scarlet, his bodyguard, walking six on each side
of him with drawn swords in their hands.

FIRST VISIT TO BUENOS AYRES 91

We gazed with joyful excitement at this splendid spectacle, and it made it all the more thrilling when one of the boys whispered in my ear that if any person in the crowd laughed or made any insulting or rude remark, he would be instantly cut to pieces by the guard. And they looked truculent enough for anything.

The great Rosas himself I did not see, but it was something to have had this momentary sight of General Eusebio, his fool, on the eve of his fall after a reign of over twenty years, during which he proved himself one of the bloodiest as well as the most original-minded of the Caudillos and Dictators, and altogether, perhaps, the greatest of those who have climbed into power in this continent of republics and revolutions.

CHAPTER VIII

THE TYRANT'S FALL AND WHAT FOLLOWED

The portraits in our drawing-room—The Dictator Rosas who was
like an Englishman—The strange face of his wife, Encarnacion—The traitor Urquiza—The Minister of War, his peacocks and his son—Home again from the city—The war
deprives us of our playmate—Natalia, our shepherd's wife—
Her son, Medardo—The Alcalde, our grand old man—Battle
of Monte Caseros—The defeated army—Demands for fresh
horses—In peril—My father's shining defects—His pleasure
in a thunderstorm—A childlike trust in his fellow-men—
Soldiers turn upon their officer—A refugee given up and
murdered—Our Alcalde again—On cutting throats—Ferocity
and cynicism—Native blood-lust and its effect on a boy's
mind—Feeling about Rosas—A bird poem or tale—Vain search
for lost poem and story of its authorship—The Dictator's
daughter—Time, the old god.

AT the end of the last chapter, when describing my one
sight of the famous jester, Don Eusebio, in his glory,
attended by a bodyguard with drawn swords who were
ready to cut down any one of the spectators who failed
to remove his hat or laughed at the show, I said it was
on the eve of the fall of the President of the Republic,
or Dictator, 'the Tyrant,' as he was called by his
adversaries when they didn't call him the 'Nero of
South America' or the 'Tiger of Palermo'—this being
the name of a park on the north side of Buenos Ayres
where Rosas lived in a white stuccoed house called
his palace.

At that time the portrait, in colours, of the great man
occupied the post of honour above the mantelpiece in
our *sala*, or drawing-room—the picture of a man with
fine clear-cut regular features, light reddish-brown hair
and side-whiskers, and blue eyes; he was sometimes

92

THE TYRANT'S FALL 93

called 'Englishman' on account of his regular features
and blond complexion. That picture of a stern handsome face, with flags and cannon and olive-branch—
the arms of the republic—in its heavy gold frame, was
one of the principal ornaments of the room, and my
father was proud of it, since he was, for reasons to be
stated by and by, a great admirer of Rosas, an out-and-
out Rosista, as the loyal ones were called. This portrait
was flanked by two others; one of Doña Encarnacion,
the wife, long dead, of Rosas; a handsome, proud-looking
young woman with a vast amount of black hair piled up
on her head in a fantastic fashion, surmounted by a large
tortoiseshell comb. I remember that as small children
we used to look with a queer, almost uncanny sort of
feeling at this face under its pile of black hair, because
it was handsome but not sweet nor gentle, and because
she was dead and had died long ago; yet it was like the
picture of one alive when we looked at it, and those
black unloving eyes gazed straight back into ours. Why
did those eyes, unless they moved, which they didn't,
always look back into ours no matter in what part of
the room we stood?—a perpetual puzzle to our childish
uninformed brains.

On the other side was the repellent, truculent countenance of the Captain-General Urquiza, who was the
Dictator's right-hand man, a ferocious cut-throat if
ever there was one, who had upheld his authority for
many years in the rebellious upper provinces, but who
had just now raised the standard of revolt against him
and in a little while, with the aid of a Brazilian army,
would succeed in overthrowing him.

The central portrait inspired us with a kind of awe
and reverential feeling, since even as small children we
were made to know that he was the greatest man in
the republic, that he had unlimited power over all men's
lives and fortunes and was terrible in his anger against

94   FAR AWAY AND LONG AGO

evil-doers, especially those who rebelled against his authority.

Two more portraits of the famous men of the republic of that date adorned the same wall. Next to Urquiza was General Oribe, commander of the army sent by Rosas against Montevideo, which maintained the siege of that city for the space of ten years. On the other side, next to Doña Encarnacion, was the portrait of the Minister of War, a face which had no attraction for us children, as it was not coloured like that of the Dictator, nor had any romance or mystery in it like that of his dead wife; yet it served to bring all these pictured people into our actual world—to make us realize that they were the counterfeit presentments of real men and women. For it happened that this same Minister of War was in a way a neighbour of ours, as he owned an estancia, which he sometimes visited, about three leagues from us, on that part of the plain to the east of our place which I have described in a former chapter as being covered with a dense growth of the bluish-grey wild artichoke, the *cardo de Castilla*, as it is called in the vernacular. Like most of the estancia houses of that day it was a long low building of brick with thatched roof, surrounded by an enclosed *quinta*, or plantation, with rows of century-old Lombardy poplars conspicuous at a great distance, and many old acacia, peach, quince, and cherry trees. It was a cattle- and horse-breeding establishment, but the beasts were of less account to the owner than his peacocks, a fowl for which he had so great a predilection that he could not have too many of them; he was always buying more peacocks to send out to the estate, and they multiplied until the whole place swarmed with them. And he wanted them all for himself, so that it was forbidden to sell or give even an egg away. The place was in the charge of a major-domo, a good-natured fellow, and when he discovered

THE TYRANT'S FALL 95

that we liked peacocks' feathers for decorative purposes
in the house, he made it a custom to send us each year
at the moulting-time large bundles, whole armfuls, of
feathers.

Another curious thing in the estancia was a large room
set apart for the display of trophies sent from Buenos
Ayres by the Minister's eldest son. I have already
given an account of a favourite pastime of the young
gentlemen of the capital—that of giving battle to the
night-watchmen and wresting their staffs and lanterns
from them. Our Minister's heir was a leader in this
sport, and from time to time sent consignments of his
trophies to the country place, where the walls of
the room were covered with staffs and festoons of
lanterns.

Once or twice as a small boy I had the privilege of
meeting this young gentleman and looked at him with
an intense curiosity which has served to keep his image
in my mind till now. His figure was slender and
graceful, his features good, and he had a rather long
Spanish face; his eyes were grey-blue, and his hair and
moustache a reddish golden-brown. It was a handsome
face, but with a curiously repelling, impatient, reckless,
almost devilish expression.

I was at home again, back in the plantation among
my beloved birds, glad to escape from the noisy dusty
city into the sweet green silences, with the great green
plain glittering with the false water of the mirage spreading around our shady oasis, and the fact that war, which
for the short period of my own little life and for many
long years before I was born had not visited our province,
thanks to Rosas the Tyrant, the man of blood and iron,
had now come to us did not make the sunshine less
sweet and pleasant to behold. Our elders, it is true,
showed anxious faces, but they were often anxious about
matters which did not affect us children, and therefore

96 FAR AWAY AND LONG AGO

didn't matter. But by and by even we little ones were made to realize that there was a trouble in the land which touched us too, since it deprived us of the companionship of the native boy who was our particular friend and guardian during our early horseback rambles on the plain. This boy, Medardo, or Dardo, was the fifteen-years-old son — illegitimate of course — of the native woman our English shepherd had made his wife. Why he had done so was a perpetual mystery and marvel to every one on account of her person and temper. The very thought of this poor Natalia, or Doña Nata as she was called, long dead and turned to dust in that far pampa, troubles my spirit even now and gives me the uncomfortable feeling that in putting her portrait on this paper I am doing a mean thing.

She was an excessively lean creature, careless, and even dirty in her person, with slippers but no stockings on her feet, and a large coloured cotton handkerchief or piece of calico wound turban-wise about her head. She was of a yellowish parchment colour, the skin tight-drawn over the small bony aquiline features, and it would have seemed like the face of a corpse or mummy but for the deeply sunken jet-black eyes burning with a troubled fire in their sockets. There was a tremor and strangely pathetic note in her thin high-pitched voice, as of a woman speaking with effort between half-suppressed sobs, or like the mournful cry of some wild bird of the marshes. Voice and face were true indications of her anxious mind. She was in a perpetual state of worry over some trifling matter, and when a real trouble came, as when our flock 'got mixed' with a neighbour's flock and four or five thousand sheep had to be parted, sheep by sheep, according to their ear-marks, or when her husband came home drunk and tumbled off his horse at the door instead of dismounting in the usual manner, she would be almost out of her mind and wring her

THE TYRANT'S FALL   97

hands and shriek and cry out that such conduct would
not be endured by his long-suffering master, and they
would no longer have a roof over their heads!

Poor anxious-minded Nata, who moved us both to
pity and repulsion, it was impossible not to admire her
efforts to keep her stolid inarticulate husband in the
right path and her intense wild animal-like love of her
children—the three dirty-faced English-looking offspring
of her strange marriage, and Dardo, her firstborn, the
son of the wind. He, too, was an interesting person;
small or short for his years, he was thick and had a
curiously solid mature appearance, with a round head,
wide-open, startlingly bright eyes, and aquiline features
which gave him a resemblance to a sparrow-hawk. He
was mature in mind, too, and had all the horse lore of
the seasoned gaucho, and at the same time he was like
a child in his love of fun and play, and wanted nothing
better than to serve us as a perpetual playmate. But he
had his work, which was to look after the flock when
the shepherd's services were required elsewhere; an easy
task for him on his horse, especially in summer when
for long hours the sheep would stand motionless on the
plain. Dardo, who was teaching us to swim, would
then invite us to go to the river—to one of two streams
within half an hour's ride from home, where there were
good bathing-pools; but always before starting he would
have to go and ask his mother's consent. Mounting my
pony I would follow him to the *puesto* or shepherd's
ranch, only to be denied permission: 'No, you are not
to go to-day: you must not think of such a thing. I
forbid you to take the boys to the river this day!'

Then Dardo, turning his horse's head, would exclaim:
'Oh, caram-bam-bam-ba!' And she, seeing him going,
would rush out after us, shrieking: 'Don't caram-bam-
bam-ba me! You are not to go to the river this day—
I forbid it! I know if you go to the river this day there

98   FAR AWAY AND LONG AGO

will be a terrible calamity! Listen to me, Dardo, rebel-
devil that you are, you shall not go bathing to-day!'
And the cries would continue until, breaking into a
gallop, we would quickly be out of earshot. Then Dardo
would say: 'Now we 'll go back to the house for the
others and go to the river. You see, she made me kneel
before the crucifix and promise never to take you to
bathe without asking her consent. And that 's all I 've
got to do; I never promised to obey her commands, so
it 's all right.'

These pleasant adventures with Dardo on the plain
were suddenly put a stop to by the war. One morning
a number of persons on foot and on horseback were seen
coming to us over the green plain from the shepherd's
ranch, and as they drew nearer we recognized our old
Alcalde on his horse as the leader of the procession, and
behind him walked Doña Nata, holding her son by the
hand; then followed others on foot, and behind them all
rode four old gauchos, the Alcalde's henchmen, wearing
their swords.

What matter of tremendous importance had brought
this crowd to our house? The Alcalde, Don Amáro
Avalos, was not only the representative of the 'authorities' in our parts—police officer, petty magistrate of
sorts, and several other things besides—but a grand
old man in himself, and he looms large in memory among
the old gaucho patriarchs in our neighbourhood. He
was a big man, about six feet high, exceedingly dignified
in manner, his long hair and beard of a silvery whiteness;
he wore the gaucho costume with a great profusion of
silver ornaments, including ponderous silver spurs weigh-
ing about four pounds, and heavy silver whip-handle.
As a rule he rode on a big black horse which admirably
suited his figure and the scarlet colour and silver of
his costume.

On arrival Don Amáro was conducted to the drawing-

THE TYRANT'S FALL 99

room, followed by all the others; and when all were seated, including the four old gauchos wearing swords, the Alcalde addressed my parents and informed them of the object of the visit. He had received an imperative order from his superiors, he said, to take at once and send to headquarters twelve more young men as recruits for the army from his small section of the district. Now most of the young men had already been taken, or had disappeared from the neighbourhood in order to avoid service, and to make up this last twelve he had even to take boys of the age of this one, and Medardo would have to go. But this woman would not have her boy taken, and after spending many words in trying to convince her that she must submit he had at last, to satisfy her, consented to accompany her to her master's house to discuss the matter again in her master and mistress's presence.

It was a long speech, pronounced with great dignity; then, almost before it finished, the distracted mother jumped up and threw herself on her knees before my parents, and in her wild tremulous voice began crying to them, imploring them to have compassion on her and help her to save her boy from such a dreadful destiny. What would he be, she cried, a boy of his tender years dragged from his home, from his mother's care, and thrown among a crowd of old hardened soldiers, and of evil-minded men—murderers, robbers, and criminals of all descriptions drawn from all the prisons of the land to serve in the army!

It was dreadful to see her on her knees wringing her hands, and to listen to her wild lamentable cries; and again and again while the matter was being discussed between the old Alcalde and my parents, she would break out and plead with such passion and despair in her voice and words, that all the people in the room were affected to tears. She was like some wild animal

100 FAR AWAY AND LONG AGO

trying to save her offspring from the hunters. Never, exclaimed my mother, when the struggle was over, had she passed so painful, so terrible, an hour! And the struggle had all been in vain, and Dardo was taken from us.

One morning, some weeks later, the dull roar from distant big guns came to our ears, and we were told that a great battle was being fought, that Rosas himself was at the head of his army—a poor little force of twenty-five thousand men got together in hot haste to oppose a mixed Argentine and Brazilian force of about forty thousand men commanded by the traitor Urquiza. During several hours of that anxious day the dull, heavy sound of firing continued and was like distant thunder: then in the evening came the tidings of the overthrow of the defending army, and of the march of the enemy on Buenos Ayres city! On the following day, from dawn to dark, we were in the midst of an incessant stream of the defeated men, flying to the south, in small parties of two or three to half a dozen men, with some larger bands, all in their scarlet uniforms and armed with lances and carbines and broadswords, many of the bands driving large numbers of horses before them.

My father was warned by the neighbours that we were in great danger, since these men were now lawless and would not hesitate to plunder and kill in their retreat, and that all riding-horses would certainly be seized by them. As a precaution he had the horses driven in and concealed in the plantation, and that was all he would do. 'Oh no,' he said, with a laugh, 'they won't hurt us,' and so we were all out and about all day with the front gate and all doors and windows standing open. From time to time a band on tired horses rode to the gate and, without dismounting, shouted a demand for

THE TYRANT'S FALL

fresh horses. In every case he went out and talked to them, always with a smiling, pleasant face, and after assuring them that he had no horses for them they slowly and reluctantly took their departure.

About three o'clock in the afternoon, the hottest hour of the day, a troop of ten men rode up at a gallop, raising a great cloud of dust, and coming in at the gate drew rein before the veranda. My father as usual went out to meet them, whereupon they demanded fresh horses in loud menacing voices.

Indoors we were all gathered in the large sitting-room, waiting the upshot in a state of intense anxiety, for no preparations had been made and no means of defence existed in the event of a sudden attack on the house. We watched the proceedings from the interior, which was too much in shadow for our dangerous visitors to see that they were only women and children there and one man, a visitor, who had withdrawn to the further end of the room and sat leaning back in an easy-chair, trembling and white as a corpse, with a naked sword in his hand. He explained to us afterwards, when the danger was all over, that fortunately he was an excellent swordsman, and that having found the weapon in the room, he had resolved to give a good account of the ten ruffians if they had made a rush to get in.

My father replied to these men as he had done to the others, assuring them that he had no horses to give them. Meanwhile we who were indoors all noticed that one of the ten men was an officer, a beardless young man of about twenty-one or two, with a singularly engaging face. He took no part in the proceedings, but sat silent on his horse, watching the others with a peculiar expression, half contemptuous and half anxious, on his countenance. And he alone was unarmed, a circumstance which struck us as very strange. The others were all old veterans, middle-aged and oldish men with

102   FAR AWAY AND LONG AGO

grizzled beards, all in scarlet jacket and scarlet *chiripá*
and a scarlet cap of the quaint form then worn, shaped
like a boat turned upside down, with a horn-like peak
in front, and beneath the peak a brass plate on which
was the number of the regiment.

The men appeared surprised at the refusal of horses,
and stated plainly that they would not accept it; at
which my father shook his head and smiled. One of
the men then asked for water to quench his thirst.
Someone in the house then took out a large jug of cold
water, and my father taking it handed it up to the man;
he drank, then passed the jug on to the other thirsty
ones, and after going its rounds the jug was handed
back and the demand for fresh horses renewed in
menacing tones. There was some water left in the jug,
and my father began pouring it out in a thin stream,
making little circles and figures on the dry dusty ground,
then once more shook his head and smiled very pleasantly
on them. Then one of the men, fixing his eyes on my
father's face, bent forward and suddenly struck his hand
violently on the hilt of his broadsword and, rattling the
weapon, half drew it from its sheath. This nerve-
trying experiment was a complete failure, its only effect
being to make my father smile up at the man even more
pleasantly than before, as if the little practical joke had
greatly amused him.

The strange thing was that my father was not playing
a part—that it was his nature to act in just that way.
It is a curious thing to say of any person that his highest
or most shining qualities were nothing but defects, since,
apart from these same singular qualities, he was just an
ordinary person with nothing to distinguish him from
his neighbours, excepting perhaps that he was not
anxious to get rich and was more neighbourly or more
brotherly towards his fellows than most men. The
sense of danger, the instinct of self-preservation supposed

THE TYRANT'S FALL   103

to be universal, was not in him, and there were occasions when this extraordinary defect produced the keenest distress in my mother. In hot summers we were subject to thunderstorms of an amazing violence, and at such times, when thunder and lightning were nearest together and most terrifying to everybody else, he would stand out of doors gazing calmly up at the sky as if the blinding flashes and world-shaking thunder-crashes had some soothing effect, like music, on his mind. One day, just before noon, it was reported by one of the men that the saddle-horses could not be found, and my father, with his spy-glass in his hand, went out and ran up the wooden stairs to the *mirador* or look-out constructed at the top of the big barn-like building used for storing wool. The *mirador* was so high that standing on it one was able to see even over the tops of the tall plantation trees, and to protect the looker-out there was a high wooden railing round it, and against this the tall flagstaff was fastened. When my father went up to the look-out a terribly violent thunderstorm was just bursting on us. The dazzling, almost continuous lightning appeared to be not only in the black cloud over the house but all round us, and crash quickly followed crash, making the doors and windows rattle in their frames, while there high above us in the very midst of the awful tumult stood my father calm as ever. Not satisfied that he was high enough on the floor of the look-out he had got up on the topmost rail, and standing on it, with his back against the tall pole, he surveyed the open plain all round through his spy-glass in search of the lost horses. I remember that indoors my mother with white terror-stricken face stood gazing out at him, and that the whole house was in a state of terror, expecting every moment to see him struck by lightning and hurled down to the earth below.

A second and in its results a more disastrous shining

104   FAR AWAY AND LONG AGO

quality was a childlike trust in the absolute good faith of every person with whom he came into business relations. Things being what they are this inevitably led to his ruin.

To return to our unwelcome visitors. ˙ On this occasion my father's perfectly cool smiling demeanour, resulting from his foolhardiness, served him and the house well: it deceived them, for they could not believe that he would have acted in that way if they had not been watched by men with rifles in their hands from the interior who would open fire on the least hostile movement on their part.

Suddenly the scowling spokesman of the troop, with a shouted 'Vamos!' turned his horse's head and, followed by all the others, rode out and broke into a gallop. We too then hurried out, and from the screen of poplar and black acacia trees growing at the side of the moat, watched their movements, and saw, when they had got away a few hundred yards from the gate, the young unarmed officer break away from them and start off at the greatest speed he could get out of his horse. The others quickly gave chase and at length disappeared from sight in the direction of the Alcalde's or local petty magistrate's house, about a mile and a half away. It was a long low thatched ranch without trees, and could not be seen from our house as it stood behind a marshy lake overgrown with tall bulrushes.

While we were straining our eyes to see the result of the chase, and after the hunted man and his pursuers had vanished from sight among the herds of cattle and horses grazing on the plain, the tragedy was being carried out in exceedingly painful circumstances. The young officer, whose home was more than a day's journey from our district, had visited the neighbourhood on a former occasion and remembered that he had relations in it; and when he broke away from the men, divining

THE TYRANT'S FALL 105

that it was their intention to murder him, he made for the old Alcalde's house. He succeeded in keeping ahead of his pursuers until he arrived at the gate, and throwing himself from his horse and rushing into the house, and finding the old Alcalde surrounded by the women of the house, addressed him as uncle and claimed his protection. The Alcalde was not, strictly speaking, his uncle but was his mother's first cousin. It was an awful moment: the nine armed ruffians were already standing outside, shouting to the owner of the place to give them up their prisoner, and threatening to burn down the house and kill all the inmates if he refused. The old Alcalde stood in the middle of the room, surrounded by a crowd of women and children, his own two handsome daughters, aged about twenty and twenty-two respectively, among them, fainting with terror and crying for him to save them, while the young officer on his knees implored him for the sake of his mother's memory, and of the Mother of God and of all he held sacred, to refuse to give him up to be slaughtered.

The old man was not equal to the situation: he trembled and sobbed with anguish, and at last faltered out that he could not protect him—that he must save his own daughters and the wives and children of his neighbours who had sought refuge in his house. The men outside, hearing how the argument was going, came to the door, and finally seizing the young man by the arm led him out and made him mount his horse again and ride with them. They rode back the way they had gone for half a mile towards our house, then pulled him off his horse and cut his throat.

On the following day a mulatto boy who looked after the flock and went on errands for the Alcalde, came to me and said that if I would mount my pony and go with him he would show me something. It was not seldom this same little fellow came to me to offer to

106   FAR AWAY AND LONG AGO

show me something, and it usually turned out to be a
bird's nest, an object which keenly interested us both.
I gladly mounted my pony and followed. The broken
army had ceased passing our way by now, and it was
peaceful and safe once more on the great plain. We
rode about a mile, and he then pulled up his horse and
pointed to the turf at our feet, where I saw a great stain
of blood on the short dry grass. Here, he told me, was
where they had cut the young officer's throat: the body
had been taken by the Alcalde to his house, where it
had been lying since the evening before, and it would
be taken for burial next day to our nearest village,
about eight miles distant.

The murder was the talk of the place for some days,
chiefly on account of the painful facts of the case—that
the old Alcalde, who was respected and even loved by
every one, should have failed in so pitiful a way to make
any attempt at saving his young relation. But the
mere fact that the soldiers had cut the throat of their
officer surprised no one; it was a common thing in the
case of a defeat in those days for the men to turn upon
and murder their officers. Nor was throat-cutting a
mere custom or convention: to the old soldier it was the
only satisfactory way of finishing off your adversary,
or prisoner of war, or your officer who had been your
tyrant, on the day of defeat. Their feeling was similar
to that of the man who is inspired by the hunting
instinct in its primitive form, as described by Richard
Jefferies.   To kill the creatures with bullets at a distance
was no satisfaction to him: he must with his own hands
drive the shaft into the quivering flesh—he must feel
its quivering and see the blood gush up beneath his hand.
One smiles at a vision of the gentle Richard Jefferies
slaughtering wild cattle in the palaeolithic way, but
that feeling and desire which he describes with such

THE TYRANT'S FALL 107

passion in his *Story of My Heart*, that survival of the
past, is not uncommon in the hearts of hunters, and if
we were ever to drop out of our civilization I fancy we
should return rather joyfully to the primitive method.
And so in those dark times in the Argentine Republic
when, during half a century of civil strife which followed on casting off the Spanish 'yoke,' as it was called,
the people of the plains had developed an amazing
ferocity, they loved to kill a man not with a bullet
but in a manner to make them know and feel that they
were really and truly killing.

As a child those dreadful deeds did not impress me,
since I did not witness them myself, and after looking
at that stain of blood on the grass the subject faded
out of my mind. But as time went on and I heard
more about this painful subject I began to realize what
it meant. The full horror of it came only a few years
later, when I was big enough to go about to the native
houses and among the gauchos in their gatherings, at
cattle-partings and brandings, races, and on other
occasions. I listened to the conversation of groups of
men whose lives had been mostly spent in the army,
as a rule in guerrilla warfare, and the talk turned with
surprising frequency to the subject of cutting throats.
Not to waste powder on prisoners was an unwritten law
of the Argentine army at that period, and the veteran
gaucho clever with the knife took delight in obeying it.
It always came as a relief, I heard them say, to have as
victim a young man with a good neck after an experience
of tough, scraggy old throats: with a person of that sort
they were in no hurry to finish the business; it was
performed in a leisurely, loving way. Darwin, writing
in praise of the gaucho in his *Voyage of a Naturalist*, says
that if a gaucho cuts your throat he does it like a gentleman: even as a small boy I knew better—that he did
his business rather like a hellish creature revelling in his

108   FAR AWAY AND LONG AGO

cruelty. He would listen to all his captive could say
to soften his heart—all his heartrending prayers and
pleadings; and would reply: 'Ah, friend,'—or little
friend, or brother—'your words pierce me to the heart
and I would gladly spare you for the sake of that poor
mother of yours who fed you with her milk, and for
your own sake too, since in this short time I have con-
ceived a great friendship towards you; but your beautiful
neck is your undoing, for how could I possibly deny
myself the pleasure of cutting such a throat—so shapely,
so smooth and soft and so white! Think of the sight
of warm red blood gushing from that white column!'
And so on, with wavings of the steel blade before the
captive's eyes, until the end.

When I heard them relate such things—and I am
quoting their very words, remembered all these years
only too well—laughingly, gloating over such memories,
such a loathing and hatred possessed me that ever afterwards the very sight of these men was enough to produce a sensation of nausea, just as when in the dog days
one inadvertently rides too near the putrid carcass of
some large beast on the plain.

As I have said, all this feeling about throat-cutting
and the power to realize and visualize it, came to me
by degrees long after the sight of a blood-stain on the
turf near our home; and in like manner the significance
of the tyrant's fall and the mighty change it brought
about in the land only came to me long after the event.
People were in perpetual conflict about the character
of the great man. He was abhorred by many, perhaps
by most; others were on his side even for years after
he had vanished from their ken, and among these were
most of the English residents of the country, my father
among them. Quite naturally I followed my father and
came to believe that all the bloodshed during a quarter
of a century, all the crimes and cruelties practised by

THE TYRANT'S FALL 109

Rosas, were not like the crimes committed by a private person, but were all for the good of the country, with the result that in Buenos Ayres and throughout our province there had been a long period of peace and prosperity, and that all this ended with his fall and was succeeded by years of fresh revolutionary outbreaks and bloodshed and anarchy. Another thing about Rosas which made me ready to fall in with my father's high opinion of him was the number of stories about him which appealed to my childish imagination. Many of these related to his adventures when he would disguise himself as a person of humble status and prowl about the city by night, especially in the squalid quarters, where he would make the acquaintance of the very poor in their hovels. Most of these stories were probably inventions and need not be told here; but there was one which I must say something about because it is a bird story and greatly excited my boyish interest.

I was often asked by our gaucho neighbours when I talked with them about birds—and they all knew that that subject interested me above all others—if I had ever heard *el canto*, or *el cuento del Bien-te-veo*. That is to say, the ballad or tale of the *Bien-te-veo*—a species of tyrant-bird quite common in the country, with a brown back and sulphur-yellow under-parts, a crest on its head, and face barred with black and white. It is a little larger than our butcher bird and, like it, is partly rapacious in its habits. The barred face and long kingfisher-like beak give it a peculiarly knowing or cunning look, and the effect is heightened by the long trisyllabic call constantly uttered by the bird, from which it derives its name of Bien-te-veo, which means I-can-see-you. He is always letting you know that he is there, that he has got his eye on you, so that you had better be careful about your actions.

The Bien-te-veo, I need hardly say, was one of my
E 956

110   FAR AWAY AND LONG AGO

feathered favourites, and I begged my gaucho friends
to tell me this *cuento*, but although I met scores of men
who had heard it, not one remembered it: they could
only say that it was very long—very few persons could
remember such a long story; and I further gathered
that it was a sort of history of the bird's life and his
adventures among the other birds; that the Bien-te-veo
was always doing clever naughty things and getting into
trouble, but invariably escaping the penalty. From all
I could hear it was a tale of the Reynard the Fox order,
or like the tales told by the gauchos of the armadillo
and how that quaint little beast always managed to fool
his fellow-animals, especially the fox, who regarded himself as the cleverest of all the beasts and who looked
on his honest, dull-witted neighbour the armadillo as a
born fool. Old gauchos used to tell me that twenty or
more years ago one often met with a reciter of ballads
who could relate the whole story of the Bien-te-veo.
Good reciters were common enough in my time: at
dances it was always possible to find one or two to
amuse the company with long poems and ballads in the
intervals of dancing, and first and last I questioned
many who had this talent, but failed to find one who
knew the famous bird-ballad, and in the end I gave up
the quest.

The story invariably told was that a man convicted
of some serious crime and condemned to suffer the last
penalty, and left, as the custom then was, for long
months in the jail in Buenos Ayres, amused himself by
composing the story of the Bien-te-veo, and thinking
well of it he made a present of the manuscript to the
jailer in acknowledgment of some kindness he had
received from that person. The condemned man had
no money and no friends to interest themselves on his
behalf; but it was not the custom at that time to execute
a criminal as soon as he was condemned. The prison

THE TYRANT'S FALL

authorities preferred to wait until there were a dozen
or so to execute; these would then be taken out, ranged
against a wall of the prison, opposite a file of soldiers
with muskets in their hands, and shot, the soldiers after
the first discharge reloading their weapons and going up
to the fallen men to finish off those who were still
kicking. This was the prospect our prisoner had to
look forward to. Meanwhile his ballad was being circu-
lated and read with immense delight by various persons
in authority, and one of these who was privileged to
approach the Dictator, thinking it would afford him a
little amusement, took the ballad and read it to him.
Rosas was so pleased with it that he pardoned the
condemned man and ordered his liberation.

All this, I conjectured, must have happened at least
twenty years before I was born. I also concluded that
the ballad had never been printed, otherwise I would
most probably have found it; but some copies in writing
had evidently been made and it had become a favourite
composition with the reciters at festive gatherings, but
had now gone out and was hopelessly lost.

These, as I have already intimated, were but the little
things that touched a child's fancy; there was another
romantic circumstance in the life of Rosas which
appealed to everybody, adult as well as child. He was
the father of Doña Manuela, known by the affectionate
diminutive, Manuelita, throughout the land, and loved
and admired by all, even by her father's enemies, for
her compassionate disposition. Perhaps she was the
one being in the world for whom he, a widower and
lonely man, cherished a great tenderness. It is certain
that her power over him was very great and that many
lives that would have been taken for State reasons were
saved by her interposition. It was a beautiful and
fearful part that she, a girl, was called on to play on that
dreadful stage; and very naturally it was said that she,

112 FAR AWAY AND LONG AGO

who was the very spirit of mercy incarnate, could not
have acted as the loving, devoted daughter to one
who was the monster of cruelty his enemies proclaimed
him to be.

Here, in conclusion to this chapter, I had intended
to introduce a few sober reflections on the character of
Rosas—certainly the greatest and most interesting of
all the South American Caudillos, or leaders, who rose
to absolute power during the long stormy period that
followed on the war of independence—reflections which
came to me later, in my teens, when I began to think
for myself and form my own judgments. This I now
perceive would be a mistake, if not an impertinence,
since I have not the temper of mind for such exercises
and should give too much importance to certain singular
acts on the Dictator's part which others would perhaps
regard as political errors, or due to sudden fits of passion
or petulance rather than as crimes. And some of his
acts are inexplicable, as for instance the public
execution in the interests of religion and morality of a
charming young lady of good family and her lover, the
handsome young priest who had captivated the town
with his eloquence. Why he did it will remain a puzzle
for ever. There were many other acts which to foreigners
and to those born in later times might seem the result of
insanity, but which were really the outcome of a peculiar,
sardonic, and somewhat primitive sense of humour on
his part which appeals powerfully to the men of the
plains, the gauchos, among whom Rosas lived from boyhood, when he ran away from his father's house, and by
whose aid he eventually rose to supreme power.

All these things do not much affect the question of
Rosas as a ruler and his place in history. Time, the
old god, says the poet, invests all things with honour,
and makes them white. The poet-prophet is not to be
taken literally, but his words do undoubtedly contain a

THE TYRANT'S FALL

tremendous truth. And here, then, one may let the question rest. If after half a century, and more, the old god is still sitting, chin on hand, revolving this question, it would be as well to give him, say, another fifty years to make up his mind and pronounce a final judgment.

CHAPTER IX

OUR NEIGHBOURS AT THE POPLARS

Homes on the great green plain—Making the acquaintance of our neighbours—The attraction of birds—Los Alamos and the old lady of the house—Her treatment of St Anthony—The strange Barboza family—The man of blood—Great fighters—Barboza as a singer—A great quarrel but no fight—A cattle-marking—Doña Lucía del Ombú—A feast—Barboza sings and is insulted by El Rengo—Refuses to fight—The two kinds of fighters—A poor little angel on horseback—My feeling for Anjelita—Boys unable to express sympathy—A quarrel with a friend—Enduring image of a little girl.

In a former chapter on the aspects of the plain I described the groves and plantations, which marked the sites of the estancia houses, as appearing like banks or islands of trees, blue in the distance, on the vast flat sea-like plain. Some of these were many miles away and were but faintly visible on the horizon, others nearer, and the nearest of all was but two miles from us, on the hither side of that shallow river to which my first long walk was taken, where I was amazed and enchanted with my first sight of flamingoes. This place was called Los Alamos, or The Poplars, a name which would have suited a large majority of the estancia houses with trees growing about them, seeing that the tall Lombardy poplar was almost always there in long rows towering high above all other trees and a landmark in the district. It is about the people dwelling at Los Alamos I have now to write.

When I first started on my riding rambles about the plain I began to make the acquaintance of some of our nearest neighbours, but at first it was a slow process. As a child I was excessively shy of strangers, and I also greatly feared the big savage house-dogs that would

114

NEIGHBOURS AT THE POPLARS 115

rush out to attack any one approaching the gate. But a house with a grove or plantation fascinated me, for where there were trees birds were abundant, and I had soon made the discovery that you could sometimes meet with birds of a new kind in a plantation quite near to your own. Little by little I found out that the people were invariably friendly towards a small boy, even the child of an alien and heretic race; also that the dogs in spite of all their noise and fury never really tried to pull me off my horse and tear me to pieces. In this way, thinking of and looking only for the birds, I became acquainted with some of the people individually, and as I grew to know them better from year to year I sometimes became interested in them too, and in this and three or four succeeding chapters I will describe those I knew best or that interested me the most. Not only as I first knew or began to know them in my seventh year, but in several instances I shall be able to trace their lives and fortunes for some years further on.

When out riding I went oftenest in the direction of Los Alamos, which was west of us, or as the gauchos would say, 'on the side where the sun sets.' For just behind the plantation, enclosed in its rows of tall old poplars, was that bird-haunted stream which was an irresistible attraction. The sight of running water, too, was a never-failing joy, also the odours which greeted me in that moist green place—odours earthy, herby, fishy, flowery, and even birdy, particularly that peculiar musky odour given out on hot days by large flocks of the glossy ibis.

The person—owner or tenant, I forget which—who lived in the house was an old woman named Doña Pascuala, whom I never saw without a cigar in her mouth. Her hair was white, and her thousand-wrinkled face was as brown as the cigar, and she had fun-loving eyes, a loud authoritative voice and a masterful manner,

116   FAR AWAY AND LONG AGO

and she was esteemed by her neighbours as a wise and good woman. I was shy of her and avoided the house while anxious to get peeps into the plantation to watch the birds and look for nests, as whenever she caught sight of me she would not let me off without a sharp cross-examination as to my motives and doings. She would also have a hundred questions besides about the family, how they were, what they were all doing, and whether it was really true that we drank coffee every morning for breakfast; also if it was true that all of us children, even the girls, when big enough were going to be taught to read the almanac.

I remember once when we had been having a long spell of wet weather, and the low-lying plain about Los Alamos was getting flooded, she came to visit my mother and told her reassuringly that the rain would not last much longer. St Anthony was the saint she was devoted to, and she had taken his image from its place in her bedroom and tied a string round its legs and let it down the well and left it there with its head in the water. He was her own saint, she said, and after all her devotion to him, and all the candles and flowers, this was how he treated her! It was all very well, she told her saint, to amuse himself by causing the rain to fall for days and weeks just to find out whether men would be drowned or turn themselves into frogs to save themselves: now she, Doña Pascuala, was going to find out how _he_ liked it. There, with his head in the water, he would have to hang in the well until the weather changed.

Four years later, in my tenth year, Doña Pascuala moved away and was succeeded at Los Alamos by a family named Barboza: strange people! Half a dozen brothers and sisters, one or two married, and one, the head and leader of the tribe, or family, a big man aged about forty with fierce eagle-like eyes under bushy black

NEIGHBOURS AT THE POPLARS 117

eyebrows that looked like tufts of feathers. But his chief glory was an immense crow-black beard, of which he appeared to be excessively proud and was usually seen stroking it in a slow deliberate manner, now with one hand, then with both, pulling it out, dividing it, then spreading it over his chest to display its full magnificence. He wore at his waist, in front, a knife or *facon*, with a sword-shaped hilt and a long curved blade about two-thirds the length of a sword.

He was a great fighter: at all events he came to our neighbourhood with that reputation, and I at that time, at the age of nine, like my elder brothers had come to take a keen interest in the fighting gaucho. A duel between two men with knives, their ponchos wrapped round their left arms and used as shields, was a thrilling spectacle to us; I had already witnessed several encounters of this kind; but these were fights of ordinary or small men and were very small affairs compared with the encounters of the famous fighters, about which we had news from time to time. Now that we had one of the genuine big ones among us it would perhaps be our great good fortune to witness a real big fight; for sooner or later some champion duellist from a distance would appear to challenge our man, or else someone of our own neighbours would rise up one day to dispute his claim to be cock of the walk. But nothing of the kind happened, although on two occasions I thought the wished moment had come.

The first occasion was at a big gathering of gauchos when Barboza was asked and graciously consented to sing a *décima*—a song or ballad consisting of four ten-line stanzas. Now Barboza was a singer but not a player on the guitar, so that an accompanist had to be called for. A stranger at the meeting quickly responded to the call. Yes, he could play to any man's singing —any tune he liked to call. He was a big, loud-voiced,

*E 95⁶

118   FAR AWAY AND LONG AGO

talkative man, not known to any person present; he
was a passer-by, and seeing a crowd at a rancho had
ridden up and joined them, ready to take a hand in
whatever work or games might be going on. Taking
the guitar he settled down by Barboza's side and began
tuning the instrument and discussing the question of
the air to be played. And this was soon settled.

Here I must pause to remark that Barboza, although
almost as famous for his *décimas* as for his sanguinary
duels, was not what one would call a musical person.
His singing voice was inexpressibly harsh, like that, for
example, of the carrion-crow when that bird is most
vocal in its love season and makes the woods resound
with its prolonged grating metallic calls. The interesting
point was that his songs were his own composition and
were recitals of his strange adventures, mixed with his
thoughts and feelings about things in general—his
philosophy of life. Probably if I had these composi-
tions before me now in manuscript they would strike
me as dreadfully crude stuff; nevertheless I am sorry
I did not write some of them down and that I can
only recall a few lines.

The *décima* he now started to sing related to his early
experiences, and swaying his body from side to side
and bending forward until his beard was all over his
knees he began in his raucous voice:

> En el año mil ochocientos y quarenta,
> Quando citaron todos los enrolados,

which, roughly translated, means:

> Eighteen hundred and forty was the year
> When all the enrolled were cited to appear.

Thus far he had got when the guitarist, smiting angrily
on the strings with his palm, leaped to his feet, shouting:
'No, no—no more of that! What! do you sing to me
of 1840—that cursed year! I refuse to play to you!

NEIGHBOURS AT THE POPLARS 119

Nor will I listen to you, nor will I allow any person to sing of that year and that event in my presence.'

Naturally every one was astonished, and the first thought was, What will happen now? Blood would assuredly flow, and I was there to see—and how my elder brothers would envy me!

Barboza rose scowling from his seat, and dropping his hand on the hilt of his *facon* said: 'Who is this who forbids me, Basilio Barboza, to sing of 1840?'

'I forbid you!' shouted the stranger in a rage and smiting his breast. 'Do you know what it is to me to hear that date—that fatal year? It is like the stab of a knife. I, a boy, was of that year; and when the fifteen years of my slavery and misery were over there was no longer a roof to shelter me, nor father nor mother nor land nor cattle!'

Every one instantly understood the case of this poor man, half crazed at the sudden recollection of his wasted and ruined life, and it did not seem right that he should bleed and perhaps die for such a cause, and all at once there was a rush and the crowd thrust itself between him and his antagonist and hustled him a dozen yards away. Then one in the crowd, an old man, shouted: 'Do you think, friend, that you are the only one in this gathering who lost his liberty and all he possessed on earth in that fatal year? I, too, suffered as you have suffered——'

'And I!' 'And I!' shouted others, and while this noisy demonstration was going on some of those who were pressing close to the stranger began to ask him if he knew who the man was he had forbidden to sing of 1840? Had he never heard of Barboza, the celebrated fighter who had killed so many men in fights?

Perhaps he had heard and did not wish to die just yet: at all events a change came over his spirit; he became more rational and even apologetic, and Barboza

120   FAR AWAY AND LONG AGO

graciously accepted the assurance that he had no desire
to provoke a quarrel.

And so there was no fight after all!

The second occasion was about two years later—a
long period, during which there had been a good many
duels with knives in our neighbourhood; but Barboza
was not in any of them, no person had come forward
to challenge his supremacy. It is commonly said among
the gauchos that when a man has proved his prowess
by killing a few of his opponents, he is thereafter
permitted to live in peace.

One day I attended a cattle-marking at a small native
estancia a few miles from home, owned by an old woman
whom I used to think the oldest person in the world as
she hobbled about supporting herself with two sticks,
bent nearly double, with her half-blind, colourless eyes
always fixed on the ground. But she had grand-
daughters living with her who were not bad-looking:
the eldest, Antonia, a big, loud-voiced young woman,
known as the 'white mare' on account of the whiteness
of her skin and large size, and three others. It was not
strange that cattle-branding at this estancia brought all
the men and youths for leagues around to do a service
to the venerable Doña Lucía del Ombú. That was
what she was called, because there was a solitary grand
old ombú tree growing about a hundred yards from the
house—a well-known landmark in the district. There
were also half a dozen weeping willows close to the
house, but no plantation, no garden, and no ditch or
enclosure of any kind. The old mud-built rancho,
thatched with rushes, stood on the level naked plain;
it was one of the old decayed establishments, and the
cattle were not many, so that by midday the work was
done and the men, numbering about forty or fifty,
trooped to the house to be entertained at dinner.

As the day was hot and the indoor accommodation

NEIGHBOURS AT THE POPLARS   121

insufficient, the tables were in the shade of the willows, and there we had our feast of roast and boiled meat, with bread and wine and big dishes of *aros con leche*—rice boiled in milk with sugar and cinnamon. Next to cummin-seed cinnamon is the spice best loved of the gaucho: he will ride long leagues to get it.

The dinner over and tables cleared, the men and youths disposed themselves on the benches and chairs and on their spread ponchos on the ground, and started smoking and conversing. A guitar was produced, and Barboza being present, surrounded as usual by a crowd of his particular friends or parasites, all eagerly listening to his talk and applauding his sallies with bursts of laughter, he was naturally first asked to sing. The accompanist in this case was Goyo Montes, a little thick-set gaucho with round staring blue eyes set in a round pinky-brown face, and the tune agreed on was one known as *La Lechera*—The Milkmaid.

Then, while the instrument was being tuned and Barboza began to sway his body about, and talking ceased, a gaucho named Marcos, but usually called *El Rengo* on account of his lameness, pushed himself into the crowd surrounding the great man and seated himself on a table and put the foot of his lame leg on the bench below.

El Rengo was a strange being, a man with remark-ably fine aquiline features, piercing black eyes, and long black hair. As a youth he had distinguished him-self among his fellow-gauchos by his daring feats of horsemanship, mad adventures, and fights; then he met with the accident which lamed him for life and at the same time saved him from the army: when, at a cattle-parting, he was thrown from his horse and gored by a furious bull, the animal's horn having been driven deep into his thigh. From that time Marcos was a man of peace and was liked and respected by every one as a

122 FAR AWAY AND LONG AGO

good neighbour and a good fellow. He was also admired for the peculiarly amusing way of talking he had, when in the proper mood, which was usually when he was a little exhilarated by drink. His eyes would sparkle and his face light up, and he would set his listeners laughing at the queer way in which he would play with his subject; but there was always some mockery and bitterness in it which served to show that something of the dangerous spirit of his youth still survived in him.

On this occasion he was in one of his most wilful, mocking, reckless moods, and was no sooner seated than he began smilingly, in his quiet conversational tone, to discuss the question of the singer and the tune. Yes, he said, 'The Milkmaid' was a good tune, but another name to it would have suited the subject better. Oh, the subject! · Any one might guess what that would be. The words mattered more than the air. For here we had before us not a small sweet singer, a goldfinch in a cage, but a cock—a fighting cock with well-trimmed comb and tail and a pair of sharp spurs to its feet. Listen, friends, he is now about to flap his wings and crow.

I was leaning against the table on which he sat and began to think it was a dangerous place for me, since I was certain that every word was distinctly heard by Barboza; yet he made no sign, but went on swaying from side to side as if no mocking word had reached him, then launched out in one of his most atrocious *décimas*, autobiographical and philosophical. In the first stanza he mentions that he had slain eleven men, but using a poet's licence he states the fact in a roundabout way, saying that he slew six men, and then five more, making eleven in all:

Seis muertes hé hecho y cinco son once;

which may be paraphrased thus:

NEIGHBOURS AT THE POPLARS   123

Six men had I sent to hades or heaven,
Then added five more to make them eleven.

The stanza ended, Marcos resumed his comments.
What I desire to know, said he, is, why eleven? It
is not the proper number in this case. One more is
wanted to make the full dozen. He who rests at eleven
has not completed his task and should not boast of
what he has done. Here am I at his service: here is
a life worth nothing to any one waiting to be taken if
he is willing and has the power to take it.

This was a challenge direct enough, yet strange to
say no sudden furious action followed, no flashing of
steel and blood splashed on table and benches; nor was
there the faintest sign of emotion in the singer's face,
or any tremor or change in his voice when he resumed
his singing. And so it went on to the end—boastful
stanza and insulting remarks from Marcos; and by the
time the *décima* ended a dozen or twenty men had
forced themselves in between the two so that there
could be no fight on this occasion.

Among those present was an old gaucho who took a
peculiar interest in me on account of my bird lore and
who used to talk and expound gaucho philosophy to
me in a fatherly way. Meeting him a day or two later
I remarked I did not think Barboza deserving of his
fame as a fighter. I thought him a coward. No, he
said, he was not a coward. He could have killed Marcos,
but he considered that it would be a mistake, since it
would add nothing to his reputation and would probably make him disliked in the district. That was all
very well, I replied, but how could any one who was not
a poltroon endure to be publicly insulted and challenged
without flying into a rage and going for his enemy?

He smiled and answered that I was an ignorant boy
and would understand these things better some day,
after knowing a good many fighters. There were some,

124 FAR AWAY AND LONG AGO

he said, who were men of fiery temper, who would fly
at and kill any one for the slightest cause—an idle or
imprudent word perhaps. There were others of a cool
temper whose ambition it was to be great fighters, who
fought and killed people not because they hated or were
in a rage with them, but for the sake of the fame it would
give them. Barboza was one of this cool kind, who
when he fought killed, and he was not to be drawn
into a fight by any ordinary person or any fool who
thought proper to challenge him.

Thus spoke my mentor and did not wholly remove
my doubts. But I must now go back to the earlier
date, when this strange family were newly come to our
neighbourhood.

All of the family appeared proud of their strangeness
and of the reputation of their fighting brother, their
protector and chief. No doubt he was an unspeakable
ruffian, and although I was accustomed to ruffians even
as a child and did not find that they differed much
from other men, this one with his fierce piercing eyes
and cloud of black beard and hair somehow made me
uncomfortable, and I accordingly avoided Los Alamos.
I disliked the whole tribe, except a little girl of about
eight, a child, it was said, of one of the unmarried
sisters. I never discovered which of her aunts, as she
called all these tall, white-faced, heavy-browed women,
was her mother. I used to see her almost every day,
for though a child she was out on horseback early and
late, riding bare-backed and boy fashion, flying about
the plain, now to drive in the horses, now to turn back
the flock when it was getting too far afield, then the
cattle, and finally to ride on errands to neighbours'
houses or to buy groceries at the store. I can see her
now at full gallop on the plain, bare-footed and bare-
legged, in her thin old cotton frock, her raven-black
hair flying loose behind. The strangest thing in her was

NEIGHBOURS AT THE POPLARS   125

her whiteness: her beautifully chiselled face was like alabaster, without a freckle or trace of colour in spite of the burning hot sun and wind she was constantly exposed to.   She was also extremely lean, and strangely serious for a little girl: she never laughed and rarely smiled.   Her name was Angela, and she was called Anjelita, the affectionate diminutive, but I doubt that much affection was ever bestowed on her.

To my small-boy's eyes she was a beautiful being with a cloud on her, and I wished it had been in my power to say something to make her laugh and forget, though but for a minute, the many cares and anxieties which made her so unnaturally grave for a little girl. Nothing proper to say ever came to me, and if it had come it would no doubt have remained unspoken.   Boys are always inarticulate where their deepest feelings are concerned; however much they may desire it they cannot express kind and sympathetic feelings.   In a halting way they may sometimes say a word of that nature to another boy, or pal, but before a girl, however much she may move their compassion, they remain dumb. I remember, when my age was about nine, the case of a quarrel about some trivial matter I once had with my closest friend, a boy of my own age who, with his people, used to come yearly on a month's visit to us from Buenos Ayres.   For three whole days we spoke not a word and took no notice of each other, whereas before we had been inseparable.   Then he all at once came up to me and holding out his hands said: 'Let's be friends.'   I seized the proffered hand, and was more grateful to him than I have ever felt towards any one since, just because by approaching me first I was spared the agony of having to say those three words to him. Now that boy—that is to say, the material part of him —is but a handful of grey ashes, long, long ago at rest; but I can believe that if the other still living part should

126   FAR AWAY AND LONG AGO

by chance be in this room now, peeping over my shoulder to see what I am writing, he would burst into as hearty a laugh as a ghost is capable of at this ancient memory, and say to himself that it took him all his courage to speak those three simple words.

And so it came about that I said no gentle word to white-faced Anjelita, and in due time she vanished out of my life with all that queer tribe of hers, the bloody uncle included, to leave an enduring image in my mind which has never quite lost a certain disturbing effect.

CHAPTER X

OUR NEAREST ENGLISH NEIGHBOUR

Casa Antigua, our nearest English neighbour's house—Old Lombardy poplars—Cardoon thistle or wild artichoke—Mr Royd, an English sheep-farmer—Making sheep's-milk cheeses under difficulties—Mr Royd's native wife—The negro servants—The two daughters: a striking contrast—The white blue-eyed child and her dusky playmate—A happy family—Our visits to Casa Antigua—Gorgeous dinners—Estanislao and his love of wild life—The Royds' return visits—A home-made carriage—The gaucho's primitive conveyance—The happy home broken up.

ONE of the most important estancias in our neighbourhood, at all events to us, was called Casa Antigua, and that it was an ancient dwelling-place in that district appeared likely enough, since the trees were the largest and had an appearance of extreme age. It must, however, be remembered that in speaking of ancient things on the pampas we mean things a century or two old, not many hundreds or thousands of years as in Europe. Three centuries in that part of South America takes us back to prehistoric times. These Lombardy poplars, planted in long rows, were the largest I had seen: they were very tall; many of them appeared to be dying of old age, and all had enormous rough-barked buttressed trunks. The other shade trees were also old and gnarled, some of them dying. The house itself did not look ancient, and was built of unburnt bricks and thatched, and had a broad corridor supported by wooden posts or pillars.

The Casa Antigua was situated about six miles from our house, but looked no more than three on account of the great height of the trees, which made it appear large and conspicuous on that wide level plain. The

128   FAR AWAY AND LONG AGO

land for miles round it was covered with a dense growth
of cardoon thistles. Now the cardoon is the European
artichoke run wild and its character somewhat altered
in a different soil and climate. The large deep-cut
leaves are of a palish grey-green colour, the stalks
covered with a whitish-grey down, and the leaves and
stems thickly set with long yellow spines. It grows in
thick bushes, and the bushes grow close together to the
exclusion of grasses and most other plant-life, and produces purple blossoms big as a small boy's head, on
stems four or five feet high. The stalks, which are
about as thick as a man's wrist, were used when dead
and dry as firewood; and this indeed was the only fuel
obtainable at that time in the country, except 'cow
chips' from the grazing lands and 'peat' from the
sheepfold. At the end of summer, in February, the
firewood-gathers would set to work gathering the
cardoon-stalks, their hands and arms protected with
sheepskin gloves, and at that season our carters would
bring in huge loads, to be stacked up in piles high as a
house for the year's use.

 The land where the cardoon grows so abundantly is
not good for sheep, and at Casa Antigua all the land
was of this character. The tenant was an Englishman,
a Mr George Royd, and it was thought by his neighbours
that he had made a serious mistake which would perhaps lead to disastrous consequences, when investing
his capital in the expensive fine-wool breeds to put them
on such land. All this I heard years afterwards. At
that time I only knew that he was our nearest English
neighbour, and more to us on that account than any
other. We certainly had other English neighbours—
those who lived half a day's journey on horseback from
us were our neighbours there—English, Welsh, Irish,
Scotch, but they were not like Mr Royd. These others,
however prosperous (and some were the owners of large

NEAREST ENGLISH NEIGHBOUR 129

estates), came mostly from the working or lower middle class in their own country and were interested solely in their own affairs. Mr Royd was of a different order. He was about forty-five when my years were seven, a handsome clean-shaved man with bright blue humorous eyes and brown hair. He was an educated man, and loved to meet with others of like mind with himself, with whom he could converse in his own language. There was no English in his house. He had a bright genial disposition, a love of fun, and a hearty ringing laugh it was a pleasure to hear. He was an enthusiast about his sheep-farming, always full of fine projects, always dreaming of the things he intended doing and of the great results which would follow. One of his pet notions was that cheeses made with sheep's milk would be worth any price he liked to put on them, and he accordingly began to make them under very great difficulties, since the sheep had to be broken to it and they yielded but a small quantity compared with the sheep of certain districts in France and other countries where they have been milked for many generations and have enlarged their udders. Worst of all, his native servants considered it a degradation to have to stoop to milk such creatures as sheep. 'Why not milk the cats?' they scornfully demanded. However, he succeeded in making cheeses, and very nice they were, far nicer in fact than any native cheeses made from cows' milk we had ever tasted. But the difficulties were too great for him to produce them in sufficient quantity for the market, and eventually the sheep-milking came to an end.

Unfortunately Mr Royd had no one to help him in his schemes, or to advise and infuse a little more practicality into him. His family could never have been anything but a burden and drag on him in his struggle, and his disaster probably resulted from his romantic

130   FAR AWAY AND LONG AGO

and over-sanguine temper, which made him the husband
of his wife and caused him to dream of a fortune built
on cheeses made from sheep's milk.

His wife was a native; in other words, a lady of
Spanish blood, of a good family, city born and bred.
They had met in Buenos Ayres when in their bloom,
at the most emotional period of life, and in spite of
opposition from her people and of the tremendous
difficulties in the way of a union between one of the
Faith and a heretic in those religious days, they were
eventually made man and wife. As a girl she had been
beautiful; now, aged about forty, she was only fat—a
large fat woman, with an extremely white skin, raven-
black hair and eyebrows, and velvet-black eyes. That
was Doña Mercedes as I knew her. She did no work
in the house, and never went for a walk or a ride on horseback: she spent her time in an easy chair, always well
dressed, and in warm weather always with a fan in her
hand. I can hear the rattle of that fan now as she
played with it, producing a succession of graceful
waving motions and rhythmic sounds as an accompaniment to the endless torrent of small talk which she
poured out; for she was an exceedingly voluble person,
and to assist in making the conversation more lively
there were always two or three screaming parrots on their
perches near her. She also liked to be surrounded by
all the other females in the house, her two daughters
and the indoor servants, four or five in number, all
full-blooded negresses, black but comely, fat, pleasant-
looking, laughing young and middle-aged women, all
as a rule dressed in white. They were unmarried, but
two or three of them were the mothers of certain small
darkies to be seen playing about and rolling in the dust
near the servants' quarters at the far end of the long
low house.

The eldest daughter, Eulodia, was about fifteen as I

NEAREST ENGLISH NEIGHBOUR   131

first remember her, a tall, slim handsome girl with blue-black hair, black eyes, coral-red lips, and a remarkably white skin without a trace of red colour in it. She was no doubt just like what her mother had been when the dashing, impressionable young George Royd had first met her and lost his heart—and soul. The younger sister, about eight at that time, was a perfect contrast to Eulodia: she had taken after her father, and in colour and appearance generally was a perfect little English girl of the usual angel type, with long shining golden hair, worn in curls, eyes of the purest turquoise blue, and a complexion like the petals of a wild rose. Adelina was her pretty name, and to us Adelina was the most beautiful human being in the world, especially when seen with her dusky little playmate Liberata, who was of the same age and height and was the child of one of the black servants. These two had grown fond of each other from the cradle, and so Liberata had been promoted to be Adelina's constant companion in the house and to wear pretty dresses. Being a *mulatita* she was dark or dusky skinned, with a reddish tinge in the duskiness, purple-red lips, and liquid black eyes with orange-brown reflections in them—the eyes called tortoiseshell in America. Her crisp cast-iron-coloured hair was worn like a fleece round her small head, and her features were so refined one could only suppose that her father had been a singularly handsome as well as a white man. Adelina and Liberata were inseparable, except at meal-times, when the dusky little girl had to go back among her own tribe on the mother's side; and they formed an exquisite picture as one often saw them, standing by the Señora's chair with their arms round each other's necks—the pretty dark-skinned child and the beautiful white child with shining hair and blue forget-me-not eyes.

Adelina was her father's favourite, but he was fond

132 FAR AWAY AND LONG AGO

of all his people, the black servants included, and they of him, and the life at Casa Antigua appeared to be an exceedingly happy and harmonious one.

Looking back at this distance of time it strikes me when I come to think of it, that it was a most extraordinary *ménage*, a collection of the most incongruous beings it would be possible to bring together—a sort of Happy Family in the zoological sense. It did not seem so at the time, when in any house on the wide pampas one would meet with people whose lives and characters would be regarded in civilized countries as exceedingly odd and almost incredible.

It was a red-letter day to us children when, almost once a month, we were packed into a trap and driven with our parents to spend a day at Casa Antigua. The dinner at noon was the most gorgeous affair of the kind we knew. One of Mr Royd's enthusiasms was cookery —the making of rare and delicate dishes—and the servants had been taught so well that we used to be amazed at the richness and profusion of the repast. These dinners were to us like the 'collations' and feasts so minutely and lovingly described in the *Arabian Nights*, especially that dinner of many courses given by the Barmecide to his hungry guest which followed the first tantalizing imaginary one. The wonder was that any man in the position of a sheep-farmer in a semi-barbarous land, far from any town, could provide such dinners for his visitors.

After dinner my best time would come, when I would steal off to look for Estanislao, the young native horseman, who was only too enthusiastic about wild life and spent more time hunting rheas than in attending to his duties. 'When I see an ostrich,' he would say, 'I leave the flock and drop my work no matter what it is. I would rather lose my place on the estancia than not chase it.' But he never lost his place, since it appeared

NEAREST ENGLISH NEIGHBOUR   133

that no one could do anything wrong on the estancia and not be forgiven by its master. Then Estanislao, a big fellow in gaucho dress, wearing a red handkerchief tied round his head in place of hat, and a mass or cloud of blackish crinkled hair on his neck and shoulders, would take me round the plantation to show me any nests he had found and any rare birds that happened to be about.

Towards evening we would be bundled back into the trap and driven home. Then, when the day came round for the return visit, Mr Royd would bundle his family into their 'carriage,' which he, without being a carriage-builder or even a carpenter, had made with his own hands. It had four solid wooden wheels about a yard in diameter, and upright wooden sides about four or five feet high. It was springless and without seats, and had a long pole to which two horses were fastened, and Estanislao, mounted on one, would thrash them into a gallop and carry the thing bounding over the roadless plain. The fat lady and other passengers were saved from being bumped to death by several mattresses, pillows, and cushions heaped inside. It was the strangest, most primitive conveyance I ever saw, except the one commonly used by a gaucho to take his wife on a visit to a neighbour's house when she was in a delicate condition or too timid to ride on a horse or not well enough off to own a side-saddle. This was a well-stretched, dried horse-hide, with a lasso attached at one end to the head or fore-part of the hide and the other end to the gaucho's horse, as a rule, to the surcingle. A stool or cushion was placed in the centre of the big hide for the lady to sit on, and when she had established herself on it the man would whip up his horse and away he would gallop, dragging the strange conveyance after him—a sight which filled the foreigner with amazement.

Our intimate happy relations with the Royd family

134 FAR AWAY AND LONG AGO

continued till about my twelfth year, then came rather suddenly to an end. Mr Royd, who had always seemed one of the brightest, happiest men we knew, all at once fell into a state of profound melancholy. No one could guess the cause, as he was quite well and appeared to be prosperous. He was at length persuaded by his friends to go to Buenos Ayres to consult a doctor, and went alone and stayed in the house of an Anglo-Argentine family who were also friends of ours. By and by the dreadful news came that he had committed suicide by cutting his throat with a razor. His wife and daughters then left the Casa Antigua, and not long afterwards Doña Mercedes wrote to my mother that they were left penniless; that their flocks and other possessions at the estancia were to be sold for the benefit of their creditors, and that she and her daughters were living on the charity of some of her relations who were not well off. Her only hope was that her two daughters, being good-looking girls, would find husbands and be in a position to keep her from want. Her one word about her dead husband, the lovable, easy-going George Royd, the bright, handsome English boy who had wooed and won her so many years before, was that she looked upon her meeting with him in girlhood as the great calamity of her life, that in killing himself and leaving his wife and daughters to poverty and suffering he had committed an unpardonable crime.

So ends the story of our nearest English neighbour.

CHAPTER XI

A BREEDER OF PÏEBALDS

La Tapera, a native estancia—Don Gregorio Gandara—His
grotesque appearance and strange laugh—Gandara's wife and
her habits and pets—My dislike of hairless dogs—Gandara's
daughters—A pet ostrich—In the peach orchard—Gandara's
herds of piebald brood mares—His masterful temper—His
own saddle-horses—Creating a sensation at gaucho gatherings
—The younger daughter's lovers—Her marriage at our house
—The priest and the wedding breakfast—Demetria forsaken
by her husband.

WHEN, standing by the front gate of our home, we
looked out to the north over the level plain and let our
eyes rove west from the tall Lombardy poplars of Casa
Antigua, they presently rested on another pile or island
of trees, blue in the distance, marking the site of another
estancia house. This was the estancia called La Tapera,
with whose owner we also had friendly relations during
all the years we lived in that district. The owner was
Don Gregorio Gandara, a native, and like our nearest
English neighbour, Mr Royd, an enthusiast, and was
also like him in being the husband of a fat indolent
wife who kept parrots and other pet animals, and the
father of two daughters. In this case, too, there were
no sons. There, however, all resemblance ceased, since
two men more unlike in their appearance, character,
and fortune it would not be easy to find. Don Gregorio
was an extraordinary person to look at; he had a round
or barrel-shaped body, short bow legs, and a big round
head, which resembled a ball fashioned out of a block
of dark-coloured wood with a coarse human face and
huge ears rudely carved on it. He had a curly head,
the crisp dark hair growing as knobs, which gave his
round skull the appearance of being embossed like the

136   FAR AWAY AND LONG AGO

head of a curly retriever. The large brown eyes were extremely prominent, with a tremendous staring power in them, and the whole expression was one of toad-like gravity. But he could laugh on occasion, and his laugh to us children was the most grotesque and consequently the most delightful thing about him. Whenever we saw him ride up and dismount, and after fastening his magnificently caparisoned horse to the outer gate come in to make a call on our parents, we children would abandon our sports or whatever we were doing and joyfully run to the house; then distributing ourselves about the room on chairs and stools, sit, silent and meek, listening and watching for Don Gregorio's laugh. He talked in a startlingly emphatic way, almost making one jump when he assented to what was being said with his loud, sudden *si-si-si-si-si*, and when he spoke bringing out his sentences two or three words at a time, sounding like angry barks. And by and by something would be said to touch his risible faculties, which would send him off in a sort of fit, and throwing himself back in his chair, closing his eyes and opening wide his big mouth he would draw his breath in with a prolonged wailing or sibilant sound until his lungs were too full to hold any more, and it would then be discharged with a rush, accompanied by a sort of wild animal scream, something like the scream of a fox. Then instantly, almost before the scream was over, his countenance would recover its preternatural gravity and intense staring attention.

Our keen delight in this performance made it actually painful since the feeling could not be expressed—since we knew that our father knew that we were only too liable to explode in the presence of an honoured guest, and nothing vexed him more. While in the room we dared not exchange glances or even smile; but after seeing and hearing the wonderful laugh a few times

A BREEDER OF PIEBALDS 137

we would steal off and going to some quiet spot sit in a circle and start imitating it, finding it a very delightful pastime.

After I had learnt to ride I used sometimes to go with my mother and sisters for an afternoon's visit to La Tapera. The wife was the biggest and fattest woman in our neighbourhood and stood a head and shoulders taller than her barrel-shaped husband. She was not, like Doña Mercedes, a lady by birth, nor an educated person, but resembled her in her habits and tastes. She sat always in a large cane easy chair, outdoors or in, invariably with four hairless dogs in her company, one on her broad lap, another on a lambskin rug at her feet, and one on rugs at each side. The three on the floor were ever patiently waiting for their respective turns to occupy the broad warm lap when the time came to remove the last-favoured one from that position. I had an invincible dislike to these dogs with their shiny blue-black naked skins, like the bald head of an old negro, and their long white scattered whiskers. These white stiff hairs on their faces and their dim blinking eyes gave them a certain resemblance to very old ugly men with black blood in them, and made them all the more repulsive.

The two daughters, both grown to womanhood, were named Marcelina and Demetria; the first big, brown, jolly, and fat like her mother, the other with better features, a pale olive skin, dark melancholy eyes, and a gentle pensive voice and air which made her seem like one of a different family and race. The daughters would serve maté to us, a beverage which as a small boy I did not like, but there was no chocolate or tea in that house for visitors, and in fruit-time I was always glad to get away to the orchard. As at our own home the old peach trees grew in the middle part of the plantation, the other parts being planted with rows of

138 FAR AWAY AND LONG AGO

Lombardy poplars and other large shade trees. A tame ostrich, or rhea, was kept at the house, and as long as we remained indoors or seated in the veranda he would hang about close by, but would follow us as soon as we started off to the orchard. He was like a pet dog and could not endure to be left alone or in the uncongenial company of other domestic creatures—dogs, cats, fowls, turkeys, and geese. He regarded men and women as the only suitable associates for an ostrich, but was not allowed in the rooms on account of his inconvenient habit of swallowing metal objects such as scissors, spoons, thimbles, bodkins, copper coins, and anything of the kind he could snatch up when no one was looking. In the orchard when he saw us eating peaches he would do the same, and if he couldn't reach high enough to pluck them for himself he would beg of us. It was great fun to give him half a dozen or more at a time, then, when they had been quickly gobbled up, watch their progress as the long row of big round lumps slowly travelled down his neck and disappeared one by one as the peaches passed into his crop.

Gandara's great business was horse-breeding, and as a rule he kept about a thousand brood mares, so that the herds usually numbered about three thousand head. Strange to say, they were nearly all piebalds. The gaucho, from the poorest worker on horseback to the largest owner of lands and cattle, has, or had in those days, a fancy for having all his riding-horses of one colour. Every man as a rule had his *tropilla*—his own half a dozen or a dozen or more saddle-horses, and he would have them all as nearly alike as possible, so that one man had chestnuts, another browns, bays, silver- or iron-greys, duns, fawns, cream-noses, or blacks, or whites, or piebalds. On some estancias the cattle, too, were all of one colour, and I remember one estate where the cattle, numbering about six thousand, were all black.

A BREEDER OF PIEBALDS 139

Our neighbour's fancy was for piebald horses, and so
strong was it that he wished not to have any one-
coloured animals in his herd, despite the fact that he
bred horses for sale and that piebalds were not so
popular as horses of a more normal colouring. He
would have done better if, sticking to one colour, he
had bred iron-greys, cream-noses, chestnuts, or fawns
or duns—all favourite colours; or better still if he had
not confined himself to any one colour. The stallions
were all piebalds, but many of the brood mares were
white, as he had discovered that he could get as good
if not better results from keeping white as well as piebald mares. Nobody quarrelled with Gandara on account
of his taste in horses; on the contrary, he and his vast
parti-coloured herds were greatly admired, but his ambition to have a monopoly in piebalds was sometimes a
cause of offence. He sold two-year-old geldings only,
but never a mare unless for slaughter, for in those days
the half-wild horses of the pampas were annually
slaughtered in vast numbers just for the hides and
grease. If he found a white or piebald mare in a neighbour's herd he would not rest until he got possession
of it, and by giving double its value in money or horses
he seldom found any difficulty in getting what he
wanted. But occasionally some poor gaucho with only
a few animals would refuse to part with a piebald mare,
either out of pride, or 'cussedness' as an American
would say, or because he was attached to it, and this
would stir Gandara's soul to its deepest depth and bring
up all the blackness in him to the surface. 'What do
you want, then?' he would shout, sitting on his horse
and making violent gestures with his right hand and
arm, barking out his words. 'Have I not offered you
enough? Listen! What is a white mare to you—to
you, a poor man—more than a mare of any other
colour? If your riding-horses must be of one colour,

140 FAR AWAY AND LONG AGO

tell me the colour you want. Black or brown or bay
or chestnut, or what? Look! you shall have two young
unbroken geldings of two years in exchange for the
mare. Could you make a better exchange? Were you
ever treated more generously? If you refuse it will be
out of spite, and I shall know how to treat you. When
you lose your animals and are broken, when your
children are sick with fever, when your wife is starving,
you shall not come to me for a horse to ride on, nor for
money, nor meat, nor medicine, since you will have me
for an enemy instead of a friend.'

That, they say, was how he raged and bullied when
he met with a repulse from a poor neighbour. So fond
was Don Gregorio of his piebalds that he spent the
greater part of every day on horseback with his different
herds of mares, each led by its own proud piebald
stallion. He was perpetually waiting and watching with
anxious interest for the appearance of a new foal. If it
turned out not a piebald he cared nothing more about
it, no matter how beautiful in colour it might be or
what good points it had: it was to go as soon as he
could get rid of it; but if a piebald, he would rejoice,
and if there was anything remarkable in its colouring
he would keep a sharp eye on it, to find out later perhaps
that he liked it too well to part with it. Eventually,
when broken, it would go into his private *tropilla*, and
in this way he would always possess three or four times
as many saddle-horses as he needed. If you met
Gandara every day for a week or two you would see
him each time on a different horse, and every one of
them would be more or less a surprise to you on account
of its colouring.

There was something fantastic in this passion. It
reminds one of the famous eighteenth-century miller of
Newhaven, described by Mark Anthony Lower in his
book about the strange customs and quaint characters

A BREEDER OF PIEBALDS   141

in the Sussex of the old days. The miller used to pay
weekly visits on horseback to his customers in the neigh-
bouring towns and villages, his horse, originally a white
one, having first been painted some brilliant colour—
blue, green, yellow, orange, purple, or scarlet. The
whole village would turn out to look at the miller's
wonderful horse and speculate as to the colour he would
exhibit on his next appearance. Gandara's horses were
strangely coloured by nature aided by artificial selection,
and I remember that as a boy I thought them very
beautiful. Sometimes it was a black- or brown- or
bay-and-white, or a chestnut- or silver-grey- or strawberry - red - and - white, but the main point was the
pleasing arrangement and shading of the dark colour.
Some of his best selected specimens were iron- or blue-
grey-and-white; others, finer still, fawn-and-white and
dun-and-white, and the best of all, perhaps, white and
a metallic tawny yellow, the colour the natives call
bronze or brassy, which I never see in England. Horses
of this colour have the ears edged and tipped with black,
the muzzle, fetlocks, mane, and tail also black. I do not
know if he ever succeeded in breeding a tortoiseshell.

Gandara's pride in the horses he rode himself—the
rare blooms selected from his equine garden—showed
itself in the way in which he decorated them with silver
headstalls and bit and the whole gear sparkling with
silver, while he was careless of his own dress, going
about in an old rusty hat, unpolished boots, and a
frayed old Indian poncho or cloak over his gaucho
garments. Probably the most glorious moment of his
life was when he rode to a race-meeting or cattle-marking
or other gathering of the gaucho population of the
district, when all eyes would be turned to him on his
arrival. Dismounting, he would hobble his horse, tie
the glittering reins to the back of the saddle, and leave
him proudly champing his big native bit and tossing

F 956

142   FAR AWAY AND LONG AGO

his decorated head, while the people gathered round to admire the strangely coloured animal as if it had been a Pegasus just alighted from the skies to stand for a while exhibiting itself among the horses of the earth.

My latest recollections of La Tapera are concerned more with Demetria than the piebalds. She was not an elegant figure, as was natural in a daughter of the grotesque Don Gregorio, but her countenance, as I have said, was attractive on account of its colour and gentle wistful expression, and being the daughter of a man rich in horses she did not want for lovers. In those far-off days the idle, gay, well-dressed young gambler was always a girl's first and often most successful wooer, but at La Tapera the young lovers had to reckon with one who, incredible as it seemed in a gaucho, hated gambling and kept a hostile and rather terrifying eye on their approaches. Eventually Demetria became engaged to a young stranger from a distance who had succeeded in persuading the father that he was an eligible person and able to provide for a wife.

Now it happened that the nearest priest in our part of the country lived a long distance away, and to get to him and his little thatched chapel one had to cross a swamp two miles wide in which one's horse would sink belly-deep in miry holes at least a dozen times before one could get through. In these circumstances the Gandara family could not go to the priest, but managed to persuade him to come to them, and as La Tapera was not considered a good enough place in which to hold so important a ceremony, my parents invited them to have the marriage in our house. The priest arrived on horseback about noon on a sultry day, hot and tired and well splashed with dried mud, and in a rather bad temper. It must also have gone against him to unite these young people in the house of heretics who were doomed to a dreadful future after their

A BREEDER OF PIEBALDS 143

rebellious lives had ended. However, he got through with the business, and presently recovered his good temper and grew quite genial and talkative when he was led into the dining-room and found a grand wedding-breakfast with wine in plenty on the table. During the breakfast I looked often and long at the faces of the newly-married pair, and pitied our nice gentle Demetria, and wished she had not given herself to that man. He was not a bad-looking young man and was well dressed in the gaucho costume, but he was strangely silent and ill at ease the whole time and did not win our regard. I never saw him again. It soon came out that he was a gambler and had nothing but his skill with a pack of cards to live by, and Don Gregorio in a rage told him to go back to his native place. And go he did very soon, leaving poor Demetria on her parents' hands.

Shortly after this unhappy experience Don Gregorio bought a house in Buenos Ayres for his wife and daughters, so that they could go and spend a month or two when they wanted a change, and I saw them on one or two occasions when in town. He himself would have been out of his element in such a place, shut up in a close room or painfully waddling over the rough boulder-stones of the narrow streets on his bow legs. Life for him was to be on the back of a piebald horse on the wide green plain, looking after his beloved animals.

CHAPTER XII

THE HEAD OF A DECAYED HOUSE

The Estancia Cañada Seca—Low lands and floods—Don Anastacio, a gaucho exquisite—A greatly respected man—Poor
relations—Don Anastacio a pig-fancier—Narrow escape from
a pig—Charm of the low green lands—The flower called
mácachina—A sweet-tasting bulb—Beauty of the green
flower-sprinkled turf—A haunt of the golden plover—The
bolas—My plover-hunting experience—Rebuked by a gaucho
—A green spot, our playground in summer and lake in winter
—The venomous toad-like *Ceratophrys*—Vocal performance
of the toad-like creature—We make war on them—The great
lake battle and its results.

In this chapter I wish to introduce the reader to the
last but one of the half-dozen of our nearest neighbours,
selected as typical of the small estancieros—a class of
landowners and cattle-breeders then in their decay and
probably now fast vanishing. This was Don Anastacio
Buenavida, who was an original person too in his little
way. He was one of our very nearest neighbours, his
estancia house being no more than two short miles
from us on the south side. Like most of these old
establishments, it was a long, low building with a thatched
roof, enclosures for cattle and sheep close by, and an
old grove or plantation of shade trees bordered with
rows of tall Lombardy poplars. The whole place had a
decayed and neglected appearance, the grounds being
weedy and littered with bleached bones and other
rubbish: fences and ditches had also been destroyed
and obliterated, so that the cattle were free to rub
their hides on the tree trunks and gnaw at the bark.
The estancia was called Cañada Seca, from a sluggish
muddy stream near the house which almost invariably
dried up in summer; in winter after heavy rains it

144

HEAD OF A DECAYED HOUSE 145

overflowed its low banks, and in very wet seasons lake-like ponds of water were formed all over the low-lying plain between Cañada Seca and our house. A rainy season was welcome to us children: the sight of wide sheets of clear shallow water with a vivid green turf beneath excited us joyfully, and also afforded us some adventurous days, one of which will be related by and by.

Don Anastacio Buenavida was a middle-aged man, a bachelor, deeply respected by his neighbours, and even looked on as a person of considerable importance. So much did I hear in his praise that as a child I had a kind of reverential feeling for him, which lasted for years and did not, I think, wholly evaporate until I was in my teens and began to form my own judgments. He was quite a little man, not more than an inch or two over five feet high, slim, with a narrow waist and small ladylike hands and feet. His small oval face was the colour of old parchment; he had large dark pathetic eyes, a beautifully shaped black moustache, and long black hair, worn in symmetrical ringlets to his shoulders. In his dress too he was something of an exquisite. He wore the picturesque gaucho costume; a *camiseta*, or blouse, of the finest black cloth, profusely decorated with silver buttons, puffs and pleats, and scarlet and green embroidery; a *chiripá*, the shawl-like garment worn in place of trousers, of the finest yellow or vicuña-coloured wool; the white *carsoncillos*, or wide drawers, showing below, of the finest linen, with more fringe and lace-work than was usual in that garment. His boots were well polished, and his poncho, or cloak, of the finest blue cloth, lined with scarlet.

It must have taken Don Anastacio a couple of hours each morning to get himself up in this fashion, ringlets and all, and once up he did nothing but sit in the living-room, sipping bitter maté and taking part from time to

146   FAR AWAY AND LONG AGO

time in the general conversation, speaking always in
low but impressive tones. He would say something
about the weather, the lack or superabundance of water,
according to the season, the condition of his animals
and the condition of the pasture—in fact, just what
everybody else was saying but of more importance as
coming from him. All listened to his words with the
profoundest attention and respect, and no wonder, since
most of those who sat in his living-room, sucking maté,
were his poor relations who fed on his bounty.

Don Anastacio was the last of a long line of estancieros
once rich in land and cattle, but for generations the
Cañada Seca estate had been dwindling as land was
sold, and now there was little left, and the cattle and
horses were few, and only a small flock of sheep kept
just to provide the house with mutton. His poor relations living scattered about the district knew that he
was not only an improvident but an exceedingly weak
and soft-hearted man, in spite of his grand manner,
and many of the poorest among them had been allowed
to build their ranchos on his land and to keep a few
animals for their sustenance: most of these had built
their hovels quite close to the estancia house, behind
the plantation, so that it was almost like a hamlet at
this point. These poor neighbours had the freedom of
the kitchen or living-room; it was usually full of them,
especially of the women, gossiping, sipping endless maté,
and listening with admiring attention to the wise words
which fell at intervals from the lips of the head of the
family or tribe.

Altogether, Don Anastacio in his ringlets was an
ineffectual, colourless, effeminate person, a perfect contrast to his ugly, barrel-shaped, badly dressed but
robust-minded neighbour, Gandara. Yet he too had
a taste in animals which distinguished him among his
fellow-landowners, and even reminded one of Gandara

HEAD OF A DECAYED HOUSE   147

in a ridiculous way. For just as Gandara was devoted
to piebald horses, so Don Anastacio was devoted to
pigs. It would not have been like him if these had
been pigs for profit: they were not animals fit to be
fattened for the market, and no person would have
thought of buying such beasts. They were of the wild-
pig breed, descended originally from the European
animal introduced by the early Spanish colonists, but
after two or three centuries of feral life a good deal
changed in appearance from their progenitors. This
feral pig was called *barráco* in the vernacular, and was
about a third less in size than the domestic animal,
with longer legs and more pointed face, and of a uniform
deep rust-red in colour. Among hundreds I never saw
one with any black or white on it.

I believe that before Don Anastacio's time a few of
these wild pigs had been kept as a curiosity at the
estancia, and that when he came into possession he
allowed them to increase and roam in herds all over the
place, doing much harm by rooting up many acres of
the best grazing land in their search after grubs, earth-
worms, mole-crickets, and blind snakes, along with
certain roots and bulbs which they liked. This was
their only provender when there happened to be no
carcasses of cows, horses, or sheep for them to feed on
in company with the dogs and carrion-hawks. He
would not allow his pigs to be killed, but probably his
poor relations and pensioners were out occasionally by
night to stick a pig when beef and mutton were wanting.
I never tasted or wanted to taste their flesh. The gaucho
is inordinately fond of the two gamiest-flavoured animals
in the pampas—the ostrich or rhea and the hairy armadillo. These I could eat and enjoy eating, although I
was often told by English friends that they were too
strong for their stomachs; but the very thought of this
wild-pig flesh produced a sensation of disgust.

148 FAR AWAY AND LONG AGO

One day when I was about eight years old I was
riding home at a lonely spot three or four miles out,
going at a fast gallop by a narrow path through a dense
growth of giant thistles seven or eight feet high, when
all at once I saw a few yards before me a big round
heap of thistle plants, which had been plucked up entire
and built into a shelter from the hot sun about four
feet high. As I came close to it a loud savage grunt
and the squealing of many little piglets issued from the
mound, and out from it rushed a furious red sow and
charged me. The pony suddenly swerved aside in
terror, throwing me completely over on one side, but
luckily I had instinctively gripped the mane with both
hands, and with a violent effort succeeded in getting
a leg back over the horse, and we swiftly left the
dangerous enemy behind. Then, remembering all I had
been told about the ferocity of these pigs, it struck me
that I had had an extremely narrow escape, since if
I had been thrown off the savage beast would have had
me at her mercy and would have certainly killed me in
a couple of minutes; and as she was probably mad with
hunger and thirst in that lonely hot spot, with a lot of
young to feed, it would not have taken her long to
devour me, bones and boots included.

This set me thinking on the probable effect of my
disappearance, of my mother's terrible anxiety, and
what they would think and do about it. They would
know from the return of the pony that I had fallen
somewhere: they would have searched for me all over
the surrounding plain, especially in all the wilder,
lonelier places where birds breed; on lands where the
cardoon thistle flourished most, and in the vast beds
of bulrushes in the marshes, but would not have found
me. And at length when the searching was all over,
some gaucho riding by that cattle-path through the
thistles would catch sight of a piece of cloth, a portion

HEAD OF A DECAYED HOUSE 149

of a boy's garment, and the secret of my end would be discovered.

I had never liked the red pigs, on account of the way they ploughed up and disfigured the beautiful green sward with their iron-hard snouts, also because of the powerful and disgusting smell they emitted, but after this adventure with the sow the feeling was much stronger, and I wondered more and more why that beautiful soul, Don Anastacio, cherished an affection for such detestable beasts.

In spring and early summer the low-lying areas about Cañada Seca were pleasant places to see and ride on where the pigs had not defaced them: they kept their bright verdure when the higher grounds were parched and brown; then too, after rain, they were made beautiful with the bright little yellow flower called *mácachina*.

As the *mácachina* was the first wild flower to blossom in the land, it had as great an attraction to us children as the wild strawberry, ground-ivy, celandine, and other first blooms for the child in England. Our liking for our earliest flower was all the greater because we could eat it and liked its acid taste, also because it had a bulb very nice to eat—a small round bulb the size of a hazel nut, of a pearly white, which tasted like sugar and water. That little sweetness was enough to set us all digging the bulbs up with table-knives, but even little children can value things for their beauty as well as taste. The *mácachina* was like the wood-sorrel in shape, both flower and leaf, but the leaves were much smaller and grew close to the ground, as the plant flourished most where the grass was close-cropped by the sheep, forming a smooth turf like that of our chalk downs. The flowers were never crowded together, like the buttercup, forming sheets of shining yellow, but grew two or three inches apart, each slender stem producing a single flower, which stood a couple of inches

*F 956

150 FAR AWAY AND LONG AGO

above the turf. So fine were the stems that the slightest breath of wind would set the blossoms swaying, and it was then a pretty sight, and often held me motionless in the midst of some green place, when all around me for hundreds of yards the green carpet of grass was abundantly sprinkled with thousands of the little yellow blossoms all swaying to the light wind.

These green level lands were also a favourite haunt of the golden plover on their first arrival in September from their breeding-places many thousands of miles away in the arctic regions. Later in the season, as the water dried up, they would go elsewhere. They came in flocks and were then greatly esteemed as a table-bird, especially by my father, but we could only have them when one of my elder brothers, who was the sportsman of the family, went out to shoot them. As a very small boy I was not allowed to use a gun, but as I had been taught to throw the *bolas* by the little native boys I sometimes associated with, I thought I might be able to procure a few of the birds with it. The *bolas*, used for such an object, is a string a couple of yards long, made from fine threads cut from a colt's hide, twisted or braided, and a leaden ball at each end, one being the size of a hen's egg, the other less than half the size. The small ball is held in the hand, the other swung round three or four times and the *bolas* then launched at the animal or bird one wishes to capture.

I spent many hours on several consecutive days following the flocks about on my pony, hurling the *bolas* at them without bringing down more than one bird. My proceedings were no doubt watched with amusement by the people of the estancia house, who were often sitting out of doors at the everlasting maté-drinking; and perhaps Don Anastacio did not like it, as he was, I imagine, something of a St Francis with regard to the lower animals. He certainly loved his

HEAD OF A DECAYED HOUSE 151

abominable pigs. At all events on the last day of my vain efforts to procure golden plover, a big, bearded gaucho, with hat stuck on the back of his head, rode forth from the house on a large horse, and was passing at a distance of about fifty yards when he all at once stopped, and turning came at a gallop to within a few feet of me and shouted in a loud voice: 'Why do you come here, English boy, frightening and chasing away God's little birds? Don't you know that they do no harm to any one, and it is wrong to hurt them?' And with that he galloped off.

I was angry at being rebuked by an ignorant ruffianly gaucho, who like most of his kind would tell lies, gamble, cheat, fight, steal, and do other naughty things without a qualm. Besides, it struck me as funny to hear the golden plover, which I wanted for the table, called 'God's little birds,' just as if they were wrens or swallows or humming-birds, or the darling little many-coloured kinglet of the bulrush beds. But I was ashamed, too, and gave up the chase.

The nearest of the moist green low-lying spots I have described as lying south of us, between our house and Cañada Seca, was not more than twenty minutes' walk from the gate. It was a flat, oval-shaped area of about fifty acres, and kept its vivid green colour and freshness when in January the surrounding land was all of a rusty-brown colour. It was to us a delightful spot to run about and play on, and though the golden plover did not come there it was haunted during the summer by small flocks of the pretty buff-coloured sandpiper, a sandpiper with the habits of a plover, one, too, which breeds in the arctic regions and spends half the year in southern South America. This green area would become flooded after heavy rains. It was then like a vast lake to us, although the water was not more than about three feet deep, and at such times it was infested with the big venomous toad-like creature called *escuerzo* in the vernacular, which simply means toad, but naturalists have placed it in quite a different family of the batrachians and call it *Ceratophrys ornata*. It is toad-like in form but more lumpish, with a bigger head; it is as big as a man's fist, of a vivid green with black symmetrical markings on its back, and primrose-yellow beneath. A dreadful-looking creature, a toad that preys on the real or common toads, swallowing them alive just as the hamadryad swallows other serpents, venomous or not, and as the cribo of Martinique, a big non-venomous serpent, kills and swallows the deadly fer-de-lance.

In summer we had no fear of this creature, as it buries itself in the soil and aestivates during the hot, dry season, and comes forth in wet weather. I never knew any spot where these creatures were more abundant than in that winter lake of ours, and at night in the flooded time we used to lie awake listening to their concerts. The *Ceratophrys* croaks when angry, and as it is the most truculent of all batrachians it works itself into a rage if you go near it. Its first efforts at chanting or singing sounds like the deep, harsh, anger-croak prolonged, but as the time goes on they gradually acquire, night by night, a less raucous and a louder, more sustained and far-reaching sound. There was always very great variety in the tones; and while some continued deep and harsh—the harshest sound in nature—others were clearer and not unmusical; and in a large number there were always a few in the scattered choir that out-soared all the others in high, long-drawn notes, almost organ-like in quality.

Listening to their varied performance one night as we lay in bed, my sporting brother proposed that on the following morning we should drag one of the cattle-troughs to the lake to launch it and go on a voyage in quest of these dangerous, hateful creatures and slay

HEAD OF A DECAYED HOUSE   153

them with our javelins. It was not an impossible
scheme, since the creatures were to be seen at this
season swimming or floating on the surface, and in
our boat or canoe we should also detect them as they
moved about over the green sward at the bottom.

Accordingly, next morning after breakfast we set out,
without imparting our plans to any one, and with great
labour dragged the trough to the water. It was a
box-shaped thing, about twenty feet long and two feet
wide at the bottom and three at the top. We were
also provided with three javelins, one for each of us,
from my brother's extensive armoury.

He had about that time been reading ancient history,
and fired with the story of old wars when men fought
hand to hand, he had dropped guns and pistols for the
moment and set himself with furious zeal to manu-
facture the ancient weapons—bows and arrows, pikes,
shield, battle-axes, and javelins. These last were sticks
about six feet long, nicely made of pine-wood—he had
no doubt bribed the carpenter to make them for him—
and pointed with old knife-blades six or seven inches
long, ground to a fearful sharpness. Such formidable
weapons were not required for our purpose: they would
have served well enough if we had been going out against
Don Anastacio's fierce and powerful swine; but it was
his order, and to his wild and warlike imagination the
toad-like creatures were the warriors of some hostile
tribe opposing us, I forget if in Asia or Africa, which
had to be conquered and extirpated.

No sooner had we got into our long, awkwardly
shaped boat than it capsized and threw us all into the
water; that was but the first of some dozens of upsets
and fresh drenchings we experienced during the day.
However, we succeeded in circumnavigating the lake and
crossing it two or three times from side to side, and in
slaying seventy or eighty of the enemy with our javelins.

154   FAR AWAY AND LONG AGO

At length, when the short, midwinter day was in its decline, and we were all feeling stiff and cold and half-famished, our commander thought proper to bring the great lake battle, with awful slaughter of our barbarian foes, to an end, and we wearily trudged home in our soaking clothes and squeaking shoes. We were too tired to pay much heed to the little sermon we had expected, and glad to get into dry clothes and sit down to food and tea. Then to sit by the fire as close as we could get to it, until we all began to sneeze and to feel our throats getting sore and our faces burning hot. And, finally, when we went burning and shivering with cold to bed we could not sleep; and hark! the grand nightly chorus was going on just as usual. No, in spite of the great slaughter we had not exterminated the enemy; on the contrary, they appeared to be rejoicing over a great victory, especially when high above the deep harsh notes the long-drawn, organ-like sounds of the leaders were heard.

How I then wished, when tossing and burning feverishly in bed, that I had rebelled and refused to take part in that day's adventure! I was too young for it, and again and again, when thrusting one of the creatures through with my javelin, I had experienced a horrible disgust and shrinking at the spectacle. Now in my wakeful hours, with that tremendous chanting in my ears, it all came back to me and was like a nightmare.

CHAPTER XIII

A PATRIARCH OF THE PAMPAS

The grand old man of the plains—Don Evaristo Peñalva, the Patriarch—My first sight of his estancia house—Don Evaristo described—A husband of six wives—How he was esteemed and loved by every one—On leaving home I lose sight of Don Evaristo—I meet him again after seven years—His failing health—His old first wife and her daughter, Cipriana—The tragedy of Cipriana—Don Evaristo dies and I lose sight of the family.

PATRIARCHS were fairly common in the land of my nativity: grave, dignified old men with imposing beards, owners of land and cattle and many horses, though many of them could not spell their own names; handsome too, some of them with regular features, descendants of good old Spanish families who colonized the wide pampas in the seventeenth and early eighteenth centuries. I do not think I have got one of this sort in the preceding chapters which treat of our neighbours, unless it be Don Anastacio Buenavida of the corkscrew curls and quaint taste in pigs. Certainly he was of the old land-owning class, and in his refined features and delicate little hands and feet gave evidence of good blood, but the marks of degeneration were equally plain; he was an effeminate, futile person, and not properly to be ranked with the patriarchs. His ugly grotesque neighbour of the piebald horses was more like one. I described the people that lived nearest to us, our next-door neighbours so to speak, because I knew them from childhood and followed their fortunes when I grew up, and was thus able to give their complete history. The patriarchs, the grand old gaucho estancieros, I came to know, were scattered all over the land, but, with one exception,

155

156   FAR AWAY AND LONG AGO

I did not know them intimately from childhood, and though I could fill this chapter with their portraits I prefer to give it all to the one I knew best, Don Evaristo Peñalva, a very fine patriarch indeed.

I cannot now remember when I first made his acquaintance, but I was not quite six, though very near it, when I had my first view of his house. In the chapter on 'Some Bird Adventures' I have described my first long walk on the plains, when two of my brothers took me to a river some distance from home, where I was enchanted with my first sight of that glorious water-fowl, the flamingo. Now, as we stood on the brink of the flowing water, which had a width of about two hundred yards at that spot when the river had overflowed its banks, one of my elder brothers pointed to a long, low house, thatched with rushes, about three-quarters of a mile distant on the other side of the stream, and informed me that it was the estancia house of Don Evaristo Peñalva, who was one of the principal land-owners in that part.

That was one of the images my mind received on that adventurous day which have not faded—the long, low, mud-built house, standing on the wide, empty, treeless plain, with three ancient, half-dead, crooked acacia trees growing close to it, and a little further away a corral or cattle-enclosure and a sheep-fold. It was a poor, naked, dreary-looking house without garden or shade, and I dare say a little English boy six years old would have smiled, a little incredulous, to be told that it was the residence of one of the principal landowners in that part.

Then, as we have seen, I got my horse, and being delivered from the fear of evil-minded cows with long, sharp horns, I spent a good deal of my time on the plain, where I made the acquaintance of other small boys on horseback, who took me to their homes and introduced

A PATRIARCH OF THE PAMPAS 157

me to their people. In this way I came to be a visitor
to that lonely-looking house on the other side of the
river, and to know all the interesting people in it, including Don Evaristo himself, its lord and master. He
was a middle-aged man at that date, of medium height,
very white-skinned, with long black hair and full beard,
straight nose, fine broad forehead, with large dark eyes.
He was slow and deliberate in all his movements, grave,
dignified, and ceremonious in his manner and speech;
but in spite of this lofty air he was known to have a
sweet and gentle disposition and was friendly towards
every one, even to small boys who are naturally naughty
and a nuisance to their elders. And so it came about
that even as a very small shy boy, a stranger in the
house, I came to know that Don Evaristo was not one
to be afraid of.

I hope that the reader, forgetting all he has learnt
about the domestic life of the patriarchs of an older
time, will not begin to feel disgusted at Don Evaristo
when I proceed to say that he was the husband of six
wives, all living with him at that same house. The
first, the only one he had been permitted to marry in
a church, was as old as or rather older than himself;
she was very dark and was getting wrinkles, and was
the mother of several grown-up sons and daughters,
some married. The others were of various ages, the
youngest two about thirty; and these were twin sisters,
both named Ascension, for they were both born on
Ascension Day. So much alike were these Ascensions
in face and figure that one day, when I was a big boy,
I went into the house, and finding one of the sisters
there began relating something, when she was called
out. Presently she came back, as I thought, and I went
on with my story just where I had left off, and only when
I saw the look of surprise and inquiry on her face did I
discover that I was now talking to the other sister.

158 FAR AWAY AND LONG AGO

How was this man with six wives regarded by his neighbours? He was esteemed and beloved above most men in his position. If any person was in trouble or distress, or suffering from a wound or some secret malady, he would go to Don Evaristo for advice and assistance and for such remedies as he knew; and if he was sick unto death he would send for Don Evaristo to come to him to write down his last will and testament. For Don Evaristo knew his letters and had the reputation of a learned man among the gauchos. They considered him better than any one calling himself a doctor. I remember that his cure for shingles, a common and dangerous ailment in that region, was regarded as infallible. The malady took the form of an eruption, like erysipelas, on the middle of the body and extending round the waist till it formed a perfect zone. 'If the zone is not complete I can cure the disease,' Don Evaristo would say. He would send someone down to the river to procure a good-sized toad, then causing the patient to strip, he would take pen and ink and write on the skin in the space between the two ends of the inflamed region, in stout letters, the words, *In the name of the Father*, etc. This done, he would take the toad in his hand and gently rub it on the inflamed part, and the toad, enraged at such treatment, would swell himself up almost to bursting and exude a poisonous milky secretion from his warty skin. That was all, and the man got well!

If it pleased such a man as that to have six wives instead of one it was right and proper for him to have them; no person would presume to say that he was not a good and wise and religious man on that account. It may be added that Don Evaristo, like Henry VIII, who also had six wives, was a strictly virtuous man. The only difference was that when he desired a fresh wife he did not barbarously execute or put away the one, or the others, he already possessed.

A PATRIARCH OF THE PAMPAS 159

I lost sight of Don Evaristo when I was sixteen, having gone to live in another district about thirty miles from my old home. He was then just at the end of the middle period of life, with a few grey hairs beginning to show in his black beard, but he was still a strong man and more children were being added to his numerous family. Some time later I heard that he had acquired a second estate a long day's journey on horseback from the first, and that some of his wives and children had emigrated to the new estancia, and that he divided his time between the two establishments. But his people were not wholly separated from each other; from time to time some of them would take the long journey to visit the absent ones and there would be an exchange of homes between them. For, incredible as it may seem, they were in spirit, or appeared to be, a united family.

Seven years had passed since I lost sight of them, when it chanced that I was travelling home from the southern frontier with only two horses to carry me. One gave out, and I was compelled to leave him on the road. I put up that evening at a little wayside *pulperia,* or public-house, and was hospitably entertained by the landlord, who turned out to be an Englishman. But he had lived so long among the gauchos, having left his country when very young, that he had almost forgotten his own language. Again and again during the evening he started talking in English as if glad of the opportunity to speak his native tongue once more; but after a sentence or two a word wanted would not come, and it would have to be spoken in Spanish, and gradually he would relapse into unadulterated Spanish again, then, becoming conscious of the relapse, he would make a fresh start in English.

As we sat talking after supper I expressed my intention of leaving early in the morning so as to get over

160   FAR AWAY AND LONG AGO

a few leagues while it was fresh, as the weather was
very hot and I had to consider my one horse. He was
sorry not to be able to provide me with another, but
at one of the large estancias I would come to next
morning I would no doubt be able to get one. He then
mentioned that in about an hour and a half or two hours
I should arrive at an estancia named La Paja Brava,
where many riding-horses were kept.

This was good news indeed! La Paja Brava was the
name of the estate my ancient friend and neighbour,
Don Evaristo, had bought so many years before: no
doubt I should find some of the family, and they would
give me a horse and anything I wanted.

The house, when I approached it next morning,
strongly reminded me of the old home of the family
many leagues away, only it was if possible more lonely
and dreary in appearance, without even an old half-
dead acacia tree to make it less desolate. The plain
all round as far as one could see was absolutely flat and
treeless, the short grass burnt by the January sun to a
yellowish-brown colour; while at the large watering-
well, half a mile distant, the cattle were gathering in
vast numbers, bellowing with thirst and raising clouds of
dust in their struggles to get to the trough.

I found Don Evaristo himself in the house, and with
him his first and oldest wife, with several of the grown-
up children. I was grieved to see the change in my
old friend; he had aged greatly in seven years; his face
was now white as alabaster, and his full beard and long
hair quite grey. He was suffering from some internal
malady, and spent most of the day in the large kitchen
and living-room, resting in an easy chair. The fire
burnt all day in the hearth in the middle of the clay
floor, and the women served maté and did their work
in a quiet way, talking the while; and all day long the
young men and big boys came and went, coming in,

A PATRIARCH OF THE PAMPAS   161

one or two at a time, to sip maté, smoke, and tell the news—the state of the well, the time the water would last, the condition of the cattle, of horses strayed, and so on.

The old first wife had also aged—her whole dark, anxious face had been covered with little interlacing wrinkles; but the greatest change was in the eldest child, her daughter Cipriana, who was living permanently at La Paja Brava. The old mother had a dash of dark or negrine blood in her veins, and this strain came out strongly in the daughter, a tall woman with lustreless crinkled hair of a wrought-iron colour, large voluptuous mouth, pale dark skin, and large dark sad eyes.

I remembered that they had not always been sad, for I had known her in her full bloom—an imposing woman, her eyes sparkling with intense fire and passion, who, despite her coarse features and dark skin, had a kind of strange wild beauty which attracted men. Unhappily she placed her affections on the wrong person, a dashing young gaucho who, albeit landless and poor in cattle, made a brave appearance, especially when mounted and when man and horse glittered with silver ornaments. I recalled how one of my last sights of her had been on a Sunday morning in summer when I had ridden to a spot on the plain where it was overgrown with giant thistles, standing about ten feet high, in full flower and filling the hot air with their perfume. There, in a small open grassy space, I had dismounted to watch a hawk, in hopes of finding its nest concealed somewhere among the thistles close by. And presently two persons came at a swift gallop by the narrow path through the thistles, and bursting out into that small open spot I saw that it was Cipriana, in a white dress, on a big bay horse, and her lover, who was leading the way. Catching sight of me they threw me a 'Good morning,' and galloped on, laughing gaily

162   FAR AWAY AND LONG AGO

at the unexpected encounter. I thought that in her white dress, with the hot sun shining on her, her face flushed with excitement, on her big spirited horse, she looked splendid that morning.

But she gave herself too freely to her lover, and by and by there was a difference, and he rode away to return no more. It was hard for her then to face her neighbours, and eventually she went away with her mother to live at the new estancia; but even now at this distance of time it is a pain to remember her when her image comes back to my mind as I saw her on that chance visit to La Paja Brava.

Every evening during my stay, after maté had been served and there was a long vacant interval before night, she would go out from the gate to a distance of fifty or sixty yards, where an old log was lying on a piece of waste ground overgrown with nettles, burdock, and redweed, now dead and brown, and sitting on the log, her chin resting on her hand, she would fix her eyes on the dusty road half a mile away, and motionless in that dejected attitude she would remain for about an hour. When you looked closely at her you could see her lips moving, and if you came quite near her you could hear her talking in a very low voice, but she would not lift her gaze from the road nor seem to be aware of your presence. The fit or dream over, she would get up and return to the house, where she would quietly set to work with the other women in preparing the great meal of the day — the late supper of roast and boiled meat, when all the men would be back from their work with the cattle.

That was my last sight of Cipriana; what her end was I never heard, nor what was done with the Paja Brava after the death of Don Evaristo, who was gathered to his fathers a year or so after my visit. I only know that the old place where as a child I first knew him,

A PATRIARCH OF THE PAMPAS 163

where his cattle and horses grazed, and the stream where they were watered was alive with herons and spoonbills, black-necked swans, glossy ibises in clouds, and great blue ibises with resounding voices, is now possessed by aliens, who destroy all wild-bird life and grown corn on the land for the markets of Europe.

CHAPTER XIV

THE DOVECOTE

A favourite climbing tree—The desire to fly—Soaring birds—
A peregrine falcon — The dovecote and pigeon-pies — The
falcon's depredations—A splendid aerial feat—A secret enemy
of the dovecote—A short-eared owl in a loft—My father and
birds—A strange flower—The owls' nesting-place—Great owl
visitations.

BY the side of the moat at the far end of the enclosed
ground there grew a big red willow, the tree already
mentioned in a former chapter as the second largest
in the plantation. It had a thick round trunk, wide-
spreading horizontal branches, and rough bark. In
its shape, when the thin foliage was gone, it was more
like an old oak than a red willow. This was my
favourite tree when I had once mastered the difficult
and dangerous art of climbing. It was furthest from the
house of all the trees, on a waste weedy spot which no
one else visited, and this made it an ideal place for me,
and whenever I was in the wild arboreal mood I would
climb the willow to find a good stout branch high up
on which to spend an hour, with a good view of the
wide green plain before me and the sight of grazing
flocks and herds, and of houses and poplar groves
looking blue in the distance. Here, too, in this tree I
first felt the desire for wings, to dream of the delight
it would be to circle upwards to a great height and float
on the air without effort, like the gull and buzzard and
harrier and other great soaring land and water birds.
But from the time this notion and desire began to
affect me I envied most the great crested screamer, an
inhabitant then of all the marshes in our vicinity. For
here was a bird as big or bigger than a goose, as heavy

164

THE DOVECOTE

almost as I was myself, who, when he wished to fly,
rose off the ground with tremendous labour, and then
as he got higher and higher and flew more and more
easily, until he rose so high that he looked no bigger
than a lark or pipit, and at that height he would continue floating round and round in vast circles for hours,
pouring out those jubilant cries at intervals which
sounded to us so far below like clarion notes in the
sky. If I could only get off the ground like that heavy
bird and rise as high, then the blue air would make
me as buoyant and let me float all day without pain
or effort like the bird! This desire has continued with
me through my life, yet I have never wished to fly
in a balloon or airship, since I should then be tied to
a machine and have no will or soul of my own. The
desire has only been gratified a very few times in that
kind of dream called levitation, when one rises and floats
above the earth without effort and is like a ball of
thistledown carried by the wind.

My favourite red willow was also the chosen haunt
of another being, a peregrine falcon, a large handsome
female that used to spend some months each year with
us, and would sit for hours every day in the tree. It
was an ideal tree for the falcon, too, not only because
it was a quiet spot where it could doze the hot hours
away in safety, but also on account of the numbers of
pigeons we used to keep. The pigeon-house, a round,
tower-shaped building, whitewashed outside, with a
small door always kept locked, was usually tenanted
by four or five hundred birds. These cost us nothing
to keep, and were never fed, as they picked up their
own living on the plain, and being strong fliers and
well used to the dangers of the open country abounding in hawks, they ranged far from home, going out
in small parties of a dozen or more to their various
distant feeding-grounds. When out riding we used

166 FAR AWAY AND LONG AGO

to come on these flocks several miles from home, and knew they were our birds since no one else in that neighbourhood kept pigeons. They were highly valued, especially by my father, who preferred a broiled pigeon to mutton cutlets for breakfast, and was also fond of pigeon-pies. Once or twice every week, according to the season, eighteen or twenty young birds, just ready to leave the nest, were taken from the dovecote to be put into a pie of gigantic size, and this was usually the grandest dish on the table when we had a lot of people to dinner or supper.

Every day the falcon, during the months she spent with us, took toll of the pigeons, and though these depredations annoyed my father he did nothing to stop them. He appeared to think that one or two birds a day didn't matter much as the birds were so many. The falcon's custom was, after dozing a few hours in the willow, to fly up and circle high in the air above the buildings, whereupon the pigeons, losing their heads in their terror, would rush up in a cloud to escape their deadly enemy. This was exactly what their enemy wanted them to do, and no sooner would they rise to a proper height than she would make her swoop, and singling out her victim strike it down with a blow of her lacerating claws; down like a stone it would fall, and the hawk, after a moment's pause in mid-air, would drop down after it and catch it in her talons before it touched the tree-tops, then carry it away to feed on at leisure out on the plain. It was a magnificent spectacle, and although witnessed so often it always greatly excited me.

One day my father went to the *galpon*, the big barn-like building used for storing wood, hides, and horse-hair, and seeing him go up the ladder I climbed up after him. It was an immense vacant place containing nothing but a number of empty cases on one side of the floor and empty flour-barrels, standing upright, on

THE DOVECOTE 167

the other. My father began walking about among the cases, and by and by called me to look at a young pigeon, apparently just killed, which he had found in one of the empty boxes. Now, how came it to be there? he asked. Rats, no doubt, but how strange and almost incredible it seemed that a rat, however big, had been able to scale the pigeon-house, kill a pigeon and drag it back a distance of twenty-five yards, then mount with it to the loft, and after all that labour to leave it uneaten! The wonder grew when he began to find more young pigeons, all young birds almost of an age to have left the nest, and only one or two out of half a dozen with any flesh eaten.

Here was an enemy to the dovecote who went about at night and did his killing quietly, unseen by any one, and was ten times more destructive than the falcon, who killed her one adult pigeon daily in sight of all the world and in a magnificent way!

I left him pondering over the mystery, gradually working himself up into a rage against rats, and went off to explore among the empty barrels standing upright on the other side of the loft.

'Another pigeon!' I shouted presently, filled with pride at the discovery and fishing the bird up from the bottom. He came over to me and began to examine the dead bird, his wrath still increasing; then I shouted gleefully again: 'Another pigeon!' and altogether I shouted 'Another pigeon!' about five times, and by that time he was in a quite furious temper. 'Rats—rats!' he exclaimed, 'killing all these pigeons and dragging them up here just to put them away in empty barrels— who ever heard of such a thing!' No stronger language did he use. Like the vicar's wonderfully sober-minded daughter, as described by Marjory Fleming, 'he never said a single dam,' for that was the sort of man he was, but he went back fuming to his boxes.

168   FAR AWAY AND LONG AGO

Meanwhile I continued my investigations, and by and by, peering into an empty barrel, received one of the greatest shocks I had ever experienced. Down at the bottom of the barrel was a big brown-and-yellow mottled owl, one of a kind I had never seen, standing with its claws grasping a dead pigeon and its face turned up in alarm at mine. What a face it was!—a round grey disc, with black lines like spokes radiating from the centre, where the beak was, and the two wide-open staring orange-coloured eyes, the wheel-like head surmounted by a pair of ear- or horn-like black feathers! For a few moments we stared at one another, then recovering myself I shouted: 'Father—an owl!' For although I had never seen its like before I knew it was an owl. Not until that moment had I known any owl except the common burrowing-owl of the plain, a small grey-and-white bird, half diurnal in its habits, with a pretty dove-like voice when it hooted round the house of an evening.

In a few moments my father came running over to my side, an iron bar in his hand, and looking into the barrel began a furious assault on the bird. 'This then is the culprit!' he cried. 'This is the rat that has been destroying my birds by the score! Now he's going to pay for it'; and so on, striking down with the bar while the bird struggled frantically to rise and make its escape; but in the end it was killed and thrown out on the floor.

That was the first and only time I saw my father kill a bird, and nothing but his extreme anger against the robber of his precious pigeons would have made him do a thing so contrary to his nature. He was quite willing to have birds killed—young pigeons, wild ducks, plover, snipe, whimbrel, tinamou, or partridge, and various others which he liked to eat—but the killing always had to be done by others. He hated to see any

THE DOVECOTE 169

bird killed that was not for the table, and that was why he tolerated the falcon, and even allowed a pair of *caranchos*, or carrion-eagles—birds destructive to poultry, and killers when they got the chance of newly born lambs and sucking-pigs—to have their huge nest in one of the old peach trees for several years. I never saw him angrier than once when a visitor staying in the house, going out with his gun one day suddenly threw it up to his shoulder and brought down a passing swallow.

That was my first encounter with the short-eared owl, a world-wandering species, known familiarly to the sportsman in England as the October or woodcock owl; an inhabitant of the whole of Europe, also of Asia, Africa, America, Australasia, and many Atlantic and Pacific islands. No other bird has so vast a range; yet nobody in the house could tell me anything about it, excepting that it was an owl, which I knew, and no such bird was found in our neighbourhood. Several months later I found out more about it, and this was when I began to ramble about the plain on my pony.

One of the most attractive spots to me at that time, when my expeditions were not yet very extended, was a low-lying moist stretch of ground about a mile and a half from home, where on account of the moisture it was always a vivid green. In spring it was like a moist meadow in England, a perfect garden of wild flowers, and as it was liable to become flooded in wet winters it was avoided by the *vizcachas*, the big rodents that make their warrens or villages of huge burrows all over the plain. Here I used to go in quest of the most charming flowers which were not found in other places; one, a special favourite on account of its delicious fragrance, being the small lily called by the natives *Lagrimas de la Virgen*—Tears of the Virgin. Here at one spot the ground to the extent of an acre or so was occupied by one plant of a peculiar appearance, to the

170   FAR AWAY AND LONG AGO

complete exclusion of the tall grasses and herbage in
other parts. It grew in little tussocks like bushes, each
plant composed of twenty or thirty stalks of a woody
toughness and about two and a half feet high. The
stems were thickly clothed with round leaves, soft as
velvet to the touch and so dark a green that at a little
distance they looked almost black against the bright
green of the moist turf. Their beauty was in the
blossoming season, when every stem produced its dozen
or more flowers growing singly among the leaves, in size
and shape like dog-roses, the petals of the purest,
loveliest yellow. As the flowers grew close to the stalk,
to gather them it was necessary to cut the stalk at the
root with all its leaves and flowers, and this I sometimes
did to take it to my mother, who had a great love of
wild flowers. But no sooner would I start with a bunch
of flowering stalks in my hand than the lovely delicate
petals would begin to drop off, and before I was half-
way home there would not be a petal left. This extreme
frailty or sensitiveness used to infect me with the
notion that this flower was something more than a mere
flower, something like a sentient being, and that it
had a feeling in it which caused it to drop its shining
petals and perish when removed from its parent root
and home.

One day in the plant's blossoming time, I was slowly
walking my pony through the dark bottle-green tufts,
when a big yellowish-tawny owl got up a yard or so
from the hoofs, and I instantly recognized it as the same
sort of bird as our mysterious pigeon-killer. And there
on the ground where it had been was its nest, just a
slight depression with a few dry bents by way of lining
and five round white eggs. From that time I was a
frequent visitor to the owls, and for three summers
they bred at the same spot in spite of the anxiety they
suffered on my account, and I saw and grew familiar

THE DOVECOTE   171

with their quaint-looking young, clothed in white
down and with long narrow pointed heads, more like
the heads of aquatic birds than of round-headed flat-
faced owls.

Later, I became even better acquainted with the short-
eared owl. A year or several years would sometimes
pass without one being seen, then all at once they
would come in numbers, and this was always when there
had been a great increase in field-mice and other small
rodents, and the owl population all over the country
had in some mysterious way become aware of the
abundance and had come to get their share of it. At
these times you could see the owls abroad in the late
afternoon, before sunset, in quest of prey, quartering
the ground like harriers, and dropping suddenly into the
grass at intervals, while at dark the air resounded with
their solemn hooting, a sound as of a deep-voiced mastiff
baying at a great distance.

As I have mentioned our famous pigeon-pies, when
describing the dovecote, I may as well conclude this
chapter with a fuller account of our way of living as
to food, a fascinating subject to most persons. The
psychologists tell us a sad truth when they say that
taste, being the lowest or least intellectual of our five
senses, is incapable of registering impressions on the
mind; consequently we cannot recall or recover vanished
flavours as we can recover, and mentally see and hear,
long-past sights and sounds. Smells, too, when we
cease smelling, vanish and return not, only we remember
that blossoming orange grove where we once walked,
and beds of wild thyme and pennyroyal when we sat
on the grass, also flowering bean and lucerne fields,
filled and fed us, body and soul, with delicious perfumes.
In like manner we can recollect the good things we
consumed long years ago—the things we cannot eat

172 FAR AWAY AND LONG AGO

now because we are no longer capable of digesting and assimilating them; it is like recalling past perilous adventures by land and water in the brave young days when we loved danger for its own sake. There was, for example, the salad of cold sliced potatoes and onions, drenched in oil and vinegar, a glorious dish with cold meat to go to bed on! Also hot maize-meal cakes eaten with syrup at breakfast, and other injudicious cakes. As a rule it was a hot breakfast and midday dinner; an afternoon tea, with hot bread and scones and peach preserve, and a late cold supper. For breakfast, mutton cutlets, coffee, and things made with maize. Eggs were plentiful—eggs of fowl, duck, goose, and wild-fowl's eggs—wild duck and plover in their season. In spring—August to October—we occasionally had an ostrich or rhea's egg in the form of a huge omelet at breakfast, and it was very good. The common native way of cooking it by thrusting a rod heated red through the egg, then burying it in the hot ashes to complete the cooking, did not commend itself to us. From the end of July to the end of September we feasted on plovers' eggs at breakfast. In appearance and taste they were precisely like our lapwings' eggs, only larger, the Argentine lapwing being a bigger bird than its European cousin. In those distant days the birds were excessively abundant all over the pampas where sheep were pastured, for at that time there were few to shoot wild birds and nobody ever thought of killing a lapwing for the table. The country had not then been overrun by bird-destroying immigrants from Europe, especially by Italians. Outside of the sheep zone in the exclusively cattle-raising country, where the rough pampas grasses and herbage had not been eaten down, the plover were sparsely distributed.

I remember that one day, when I was thirteen, I went out one morning after breakfast to look for plovers'

THE DOVECOTE 173

eggs, just at the beginning of the laying season when all the eggs one found were practically new-laid. My plan was that of the native boys, to go at a fast gallop over the plain and mark the spot far ahead where a lapwing was seen to rise and fly straight away to some distance. For this method some training is necessary to success, as in many cases more birds than one—sometimes as many as three or four—would be seen to rise at various points and distances, and one had to mark and keep in memory the exact spot to visit them successively and find the nests. The English method of going out and quartering the ground in search of a nest in likely places where the birds breed was too slow for us.

The nests I found that morning contained one or two and sometimes three eggs—very rarely the full clutch of four. Before midday I had got back with a bag of sixty-four eggs; and that was the largest number I ever gathered at one time.

Our dinner consisted of meat and pumpkin, boiled or baked, maize 'in the milk' in its season, and sweet potatoes, besides the other common vegetables and salads. Maize-meal puddings and pumpkin pies and tarts were common with us, but the sweet we loved best was a peach-pie, made like an apple-pie with a crust, and these came in about the middle of February and lasted until April or even May, when our late variety, which we called 'winter peach,' ripened.

My mother was a clever and thrifty housekeeper, and I think she made more of the peach than any other resident in the country who possessed an orchard. Her peach preserves, which lasted us the year round, were celebrated in our neighbourhood. Peach preserves were in most English houses, but our house was alone in making pickled peaches: I think this was an invention of her own; I do not know if it has taken on, but we

G 956

174 FAR AWAY AND LONG AGO

always had pickled peaches on the table and preferred them to all other kinds, and so did every person who tasted them.

I here recall an amusing incident with regard to our pickled peaches, and will relate it just because it serves to bring in yet another of our old native neighbours. I never thought of him when describing the others, as he was not so near us and we saw little of him and his people. His name was Ventura Gutierres, and he called himself an estanciero—a landowner and head of a cattle establishment; but there was very little land left and practically no cattle—only a few cows, a few sheep, a few horses. His estate had been long crumbling away and there was hardly anything left; but he was a brave spirit and had a genial, breezy manner, and dressed well in the European mode, with trousers and coat and waistcoat—this last garment being of satin and a very bright blue. And he talked incessantly of his possessions: his house, his trees, his animals, his wife and daughters. And he was immensely popular in the neighbourhood, no doubt because he was the father of four rather good-looking, marriageable girls; and as he kept open house his kitchen was always full of visitors, mostly young men, who sipped maté by the hour, and made themselves agreeable to the girls.

One of Don Ventura's most delightful traits—that is, to us young people—was his loud voice. I think it was a convention in those days for estancieros or cattlemen to raise their voices according to their importance in the community. When several gauchos are galloping over the plain, chasing horses, hunting or marking cattle, the one who is head of the gang shouts his directions at the top of his voice. Probably in this way the habit of shouting at all times by landowners and persons in authority had been acquired. And so it pleased us very much when Don Ventura came one evening to

THE DOVECOTE 175

see my father and consented to sit down to partake of supper with us. We loved to listen to his shouted conversation.

My parents apologized for having nothing but cold meats to put before him—cold shoulder of mutton, a bird, and pickles, cold pie, and so on. True, he replied, cold meat is never or rarely eaten by man on the plains. People do have cold meat in the house, but that as a rule is where there are children, for when a child is hungry, and cries for food, his mother gives him a bone of cold meat, just as in other countries where bread is common you give a child a piece of bread. However, he would try cold meat for once. It looked to him as if there were other things to eat on the table. 'And what is this?' he shouted, pointing dramatically at a dish of large, very green-looking pickled peaches. Peaches—peaches in winter! This is strange indeed!

It was explained to him that they were pickled peaches, and that it was the custom of the house to have them on the table at supper. He tried one with his cold mutton, and was presently assuring my parents that never in his life had he partaken of anything so good —so tasty, so appetizing, and whether or not it was because of the pickled peaches, or some quality in our mutton which made it unlike all other mutton, he had never enjoyed a meal as much. What he wanted to know was how the thing was done. He was told that large, sound fruit, just ripening, must be selected for pickling; when the finger dents a peach it is too ripe. The selected peaches are washed and dried and put into a cask, then boiling vinegar, with a handful of cloves, is poured in till it covers the fruit, the cask closed and left for a couple of months, by which time the fruit would be properly pickled. Two or three casks-full were prepared in this way each season and served us for the entire year.

176   FAR AWAY AND LONG AGO

It was a revelation, he said, and lamented that he and his people had not this secret before. He, too, had a peach orchard, and when the fruit ripened his family, assisted by all their neighbours, feasted from morning till night on peaches, and hardly left room in their stomachs for roast meat when it was dinner-time. The consequence was that in a very few weeks—he could almost say days—the fruit was all gone, and they had to say: 'No more peaches for another twelve months!' All that would now be changed. He would command his wife and daughters to pickle peaches—a cask-full, or two or three if one would not be enough. He would provide vinegar—many gallons of it, and cloves by the handful. And when they had got their pickled peaches he would have cold mutton for supper every day all the year round, and enjoy his life as he had never done before!

This amused us very much, as we knew that poor Don Ventura, notwithstanding his loud commanding voice, had little or no authority in his house; that it was ruled by his wife, assisted by a council of four marriageable daughters, whose present objects in life were little dances and other amusements, and lovers with courage enough to marry them or carry them off.

CHAPTER XV

SERPENT AND CHILD

My pleasure in bird life—Mammals at our new home—Snakes and how children are taught to regard them—A colony of snakes in the house—Their hissing confabulations—Finding serpent sloughs—A serpent's saviour—A brief history of our English neighbours, the Blakes.

IT is not an uncommon thing, I fancy, for a child or boy to be more deeply impressed and stirred at the sight of a snake than of any other creature. This at all events is my experience. Birds certainly gave me more pleasure than other animals, and this too is no doubt common with children, and I take the reason of it to be not only because birds exceed in beauty, but also on account of the intensity of life they exhibit— a life so vivid, so brilliant, as to make that of other beings, such as reptiles and mammals, seem a rather poor thing by comparison. But while birds were more than all other beings to me, mammals too had a great attraction. I have already spoken of rats, opossums, and armadillos; also of the *vizcacha*, the big burrowing rodent that made his villages all over the plain. One of my early experiences is of the tremendous outcry these animals would make at night when suddenly startled by a very loud noise, as by a clap of thunder. When we had visitors from town, especially persons new to the country who did not know the *vizcacha*, they would be taken out after supper, a little distance from the house, when the plain was all dark and profoundly silent, and after standing still for a few minutes to give them time to feel the silence, a gun would be discharged, and after two or three seconds the report would be

177

178 FAR AWAY AND LONG AGO

followed by an extraordinary hullabaloo, a wild outcry of hundreds and thousands of voices, from all over the plain for miles round, voices that seemed to come from hundreds of different species of animals, so varied they were, from the deepest booming sounds to the high shrieks and squeals of shrill-voiced birds. Our visitors used to be filled with astonishment.

Another animal that impressed us deeply and painfully was the skunk. They were fearless little beasts and in the evening would come quite boldly about the house, and if seen and attacked by a dog, they would defend themselves with the awful-smelling liquid they discharge at an adversary. When the wind brought a whiff of it into the house, when all the doors and windows stood open, it would create a panic, and people would get up from table feeling a little sea-sick, and go in search of some room where the smell was not. Another powerful-smelling but very beautiful creature was the common deer. I began to know it from the age of five, when we went to our new home, and where we children were sometimes driven with our parents to visit some neighbours several miles away. There were always herds of deer on the lands where the cardoon thistle flourished most, and it was a delight to come upon them and to see their yellow figures standing among the grey-green cardoon bushes, gazing motionless at us, then turning and rushing away with a whistling cry, and sending out gusts of their powerful musky smell, which the wind sometimes brought to our nostrils.

But there was a something in the serpent which produced a quite different and a stronger effect on the mind than bird or mammal or any other creature. The sight of it was always startling, and however often seen always produced a mixed sense of amazement and fear. The feeling was no doubt acquired from our elders. They regarded snakes as deadly creatures, and as a child I

SERPENT AND CHILD 179

did not know that they were mostly harmless, that it was just as senseless to kill them as to kill harmless and beautiful birds. I was told that when I saw a snake I must turn and run for my life until I was a little bigger, and then on seeing a snake I was to get a long stick and kill it; and it was furthermore impressed on me that snakes are exceedingly difficult to kill, that many persons believe that a snake never really dies until the sun sets, therefore when I killed a snake, in order to make it powerless to do any harm between the time of killing it and sunset, it was necessary to pound it to a pulp with the aforesaid long stick.

With such teaching it was not strange that even as a small boy I became a persecutor of snakes.

Snakes were common enough about us; snakes of seven or eight different kinds, green in the green grass, and yellow and dusky-mottled in dry and barren places and in withered herbage, so that it was difficult to detect them. Sometimes they intruded into the dwelling-rooms, and at all seasons a nest or colony of snakes existed in the thick old foundations of the house, and under the flooring. In winter they hibernated there, tangled together in a cluster no doubt; and in summer nights when they were at home, coiled at their ease or gliding ghost-like about their subterranean apartments, I would lie awake and listen to them by the hour. For although it may be news to some closet ophiologists, serpents are not all so mute as we think them. At all events this kind, the *Philodryas aestivus*—a beautiful and harmless colubrine snake, two and a half to three feet long, marked all over with inky black on a vivid green ground—not only emitted a sound when lying undisturbed in his den, but several individuals would hold a conversation together which seemed endless, for I generally fell asleep before it finished. A hissing conversation it is true, but not unmodulated or without

180 FAR AWAY AND LONG AGO

considerable variety in it; a long sibilation would be followed by distinctly heard ticking sounds, as of a husky-ticking clock, and after ten or twenty or thirty ticks another hiss, like a long expiring sigh, sometimes with a tremble in it as of a dry leaf swiftly vibrating in the wind. No sooner would one cease than another would begin; and so it would go on, demand and response, strophe and antistrophe; and at intervals several voices would unite in a kind of low mysterious chorus, death-watch and flutter and hiss; while I, lying awake in my bed, listened and trembled. It was dark in the room, and to my excited imagination the serpents were no longer under the floor, but out, gliding hither and thither over it, with uplifted heads, in a kind of mystic dance; and I often shivered to think what my bare feet might touch if I were to thrust a leg out and let it hang down over the bedside.

'I'm shut in a dark room with the candle blown out,' pathetically cried old Farmer Fleming, when he heard of his beautiful daughter Dahlia's clandestine departure to a distant land with a nameless lover. 'I've heard of a sort of fear you have in that dilemma, lest you should lay your fingers on edges of sharp knives, and if I think a step—if I go thinking a step, and feel my way, I do cut myself, and I bleed, I do.' Only in a comparatively snakeless country could such fancies be born and such metaphors used—snakeless and highly civilized, where the blades of Sheffield are cheap and abundant. In ruder lands, where ophidians abound, as in India and South America, in the dark one fears the cold living coil and deadly sudden fang.

Serpents were fearful things to me at that period; but whatsoever is terrible and dangerous, or so reported, has an irresistible attraction for the mind, whether of child or man; it was therefore always a pleasure to have seen a snake in the day's rambles, although the sight was a

SERPENT AND CHILD 181

startling one. Also in the warm season it was a keen
pleasure to find the cast slough of the feared and subtle
creature. Here was something not the serpent, yet so
much more than a mere picture of it; a dead and cast-off
part of it, but in its completeness, from the segmented
mask with the bright unseeing eyes, to the fine whip-
like tail end, so like the serpent itself; I could handle it,
handle the serpent as it were, yet be in no danger from
venomous tooth or stinging tongue. True, it was
colourless, but silvery bright, soft as satin to the touch,
crinkling when handled with a sound that to the startled
fancy recalled the dangerous living hiss from the dry
rustling grass! I would clutch my prize with a fearful
joy, as if I had picked up a strange feather dropped in
passing from the wing of one of the fallen but still
beautiful angels. And it always increased my satisfaction when, on exhibiting my treasure at home, the
first sight of it caused a visible start or an exclamation
of alarm.

When my courage and strength were sufficient I
naturally began to take an active part in the perse-
cution of serpents; for was not I also of the seed of
Eve? Nor can I say when my feelings towards our
bruised enemy began to change; but an incident which
I witnessed at this time, when I was about eight, had,
I think, a considerable influence on me. At all events
it caused me to reflect on a subject which had not previously seemed one for reflection. I was in the orchard,
following in the rear of a party of grown-up persons,
mostly visitors to the house, when among the foremost
there were sudden screams, gestures of alarm, and a
precipitate retreat: a snake had been discovered lying
in the path and almost trodden upon. One of the men,
the first to find a stick or perhaps the most courageous,
rushed to the front and was about to deal a killing blow
when his arm was seized by one of the ladies and the

*G 956

182   FAR AWAY AND LONG AGO

blow arrested. Then, stooping quickly, she took the creature up in her hands, and going away to some distance from the others, released it in the long green grass, green in colour as its glittering skin and as cool to the touch. Long ago as this happened it is just as vivid to my mind as if it had happened yesterday. I can see her coming back to us through the orchard trees, her face shining with joy because she had rescued the reptile from imminent death, her return greeted with loud expressions of horror and amazement, which she only answered with a little laugh and the question: 'Why should you kill it?' But why was she glad, so innocently glad as it seemed to me, as if she had done some meritorious and no evil thing? My young mind was troubled at the question, and there was no answer. Nevertheless, I think that this incident bore fruit later, and taught me to consider whether it might not be better to spare than to kill; better not only for the animal spared, but for the soul.

And the woman who did this unusual thing and in doing it unknowingly dropped a minute seed into a boy's mind, who was she? Perhaps it would be as well to give a brief account of her, although I thought that I had finished with the subject of our neighbours. She and her husband, a man named Matthew Blake, were our second nearest English neighbours, but they lived a good deal further than the Royds and were seldom visited by us. To me there was nothing interesting in them and their surroundings, as they had no family and no people but the native peons about them, and, above all, no plantation where birds could be seen. They were typical English people of the lower middle class, who read no books and conversed, with considerable misuse of the aspirate, about nothing but their own and their neighbours' affairs. Physically Mr Blake was a very big man, being six feet three in height and power-

SERPENT AND CHILD 183

fully built. He had a round ruddy face, clean-shaved except for a pair of side-whiskers, and pale-blue shallow eyes. He was invariably dressed in black cloth, his garments being home-made and too large for him, the baggy trousers thrust into his long boots. Mr Blake was nothing to us but a huge, serious, somewhat silent man who took no notice of small boys, and was clumsy and awkward and spoke very bad Spanish. He was well spoken of by his neighbours, and was regarded as a highly respectable and dignified person, but he had no intimates and was one of those unfortunate persons, not rare among the English, who appear to stand behind a high wall and, whether they desire it or not, have no power to approach and mix with their fellow-beings.

I think he was about forty-five to fifty years old when I was eight. His wife looked older and was a short ungraceful woman with a stoop, wearing a sun-bonnet and sack and a faded gown made by herself. Her thin hair was of a yellowish-grey tint, her eyes pale blue, and there was a sunburnt redness on her cheeks, but the face had a faded and weary look. But she was better than her giant husband and was glad to associate with her fellows, and was also a lover of animals—horses, dogs, cats, and any and every wild creature that came in her way.

The Blakes had been married a quarter of a century or longer and had spent at least twenty years of their childless solitary life in a mud-built ranch, sheep-farming on the pampas, and had slowly accumulated a small fortune, until now they were possessed of about a square league of land with twenty-five or thirty thousand sheep, and had built themselves a big ugly brick house to live in. They had thus secured the prize for which they had gone so many thousands of miles and had toiled for so many years, but they were certainly not happy. Poor Mr Blake, cut off from his fellow-creatures by that wall

184 FAR AWAY AND LONG AGO

that stood before him, had found companionship in the bottle, and was seen less and less of by his neighbours; and when his wife came to us to spend two or three days 'for a change,' although her home was only a couple of hours' ride away, the reason probably was that her husband was in one of his bouts and had made the place intolerable to her. I remember that she always came to us with a sad, depressed look on her face, but after a few hours she would recover her spirits and grow quite cheerful and talkative. And of an evening when there was music she would sometimes consent, after some persuasion, to give the company a song. That was a joy to us youngsters, as she had a thin cracked voice that always at the high notes went off into a falsetto. Her favourite air was *Home, sweet Home,* and her rendering in her wailing cracked voice was as great a feast to us as the strange laugh of our grotesque neighbour Gandara.

And that is all I can say about her. But now when I remember that episode of the snake in the orchard, she looks to me not unbeautiful in memory, and her voice in the choir invisible sounds sweet enough.

CHAPTER XVI

A SERPENT MYSTERY

A new feeling about snakes—Common snakes of the country—
A barren weedy patch—Discovery of a large black snake
—Watching for its reappearance—Seen going to its den—
The desire to see it again—A vain search—Watching a bat
—The black serpent reappears at my feet—Emotions and
conjectures—Melanism—My baby sister and a strange snake
—The mystery solved.

IT was not until after the episode related in the last
chapter and the discovery that a serpent was not neces-
sarily dangerous to human beings, therefore a creature
to be destroyed at sight and pounded to a pulp lest it
should survive and escape before sunset, that I began
to appreciate its unique beauty and singularity. Then,
somewhat later, I met with an adventure which produced another and a new feeling in me, that sense of
something supernatural in the serpent which appears to
have been universal among peoples in a primitive state
of culture and still survives in some barbarous or semi-
barbarous countries, and in others, like Hindustan,
which have inherited an ancient civilization.

The snakes I was familiar with as a boy up to this
time were all of comparatively small size, the largest
being the snake-with-a-cross, described in an early
chapter. The biggest specimen I have ever found of
this ophidian was under four feet in length; but the
body is thick, as in all the pit-vipers. Then, there was
the green-and-black snake described in the last chapter,
an inhabitant of the house, which seldom exceeded three
feet; and another of the same genus, the most common
snake in the country. One seldom took a walk or ride
on the plain without seeing it. It was in size and shape

185

186   FAR AWAY AND LONG AGO

like our common grass-snake, and was formerly classed
by naturalists in the same genus, *Coronella*. It is quite
beautiful, the pale greenish-grey body, mottled with
black, being decorated with two parallel bright red lines
extending from the neck to the tip of the fine-pointed
tail. Of the others the most interesting was a still
smaller snake, brightly coloured, the belly with alter-
nate bands of crimson and bright blue. This snake was
regarded by every one as exceedingly venomous and
most dangerous on account of its irascible temper and
habit of coming at you and hissing loudly, its head
and neck raised, and striking at your legs. But this was
all swagger on the snake's part: it was not venomous at
all, and could do no more harm by biting than a young
dove in its nest by puffing itself up and striking at an
intrusive hand with its soft beak.

Then one day I came upon a snake quite unknown to
me: I had never heard of the existence of such a snake
in our parts, and I imagine its appearance would have
strongly affected any one in any land, even in those
abounding in big snakes. The spot, too, in our plantation where I found it, served to make its singular
appearance more impressive.

There existed at that time a small piece of waste
ground about half an acre in extent, where there were
no trees and where nothing planted by man would
grow. It was at the far end of the plantation, adjoin-
ing the thicket of fennel and the big red willow tree
on the edge of the moat described in another chapter.
This ground had been ploughed and dug up again and
again, and planted with trees and shrubs of various
kinds which were supposed to grow on any soil, but
they had always languished and died, and no wonder,
since the soil was a hard white clay resembling china
clay. But although trees refused to grow there it was
always clothed in a vegetation of its own; all the hardiest

A SERPENT MYSTERY 187

weeds were there, and covered the entire barren area to the depth of a man's knees. These weeds had thin wiry stalks and small sickly leaves and flowers, and would die each summer long before their time. This barren piece of ground had a great attraction for me as a small boy, and I visited it daily and would roam about it among the miserable half-dead weeds with the sun-baked clay showing between the brown stalks, as if it delighted me as much as the alfalfa field, blue and fragrant in its flowering - time and swarming with butterflies.

One hot day in December I had been standing perfectly still for a few minutes among the dry weeds when a slight rustling sound came from near my feet, and glancing down I saw the head and neck of a large black serpent moving slowly past me. In a moment or two the flat head was lost to sight among the close-growing weeds, but the long body continued moving slowly by—so slowly that it hardly appeared to move, and as the creature must have been not less than six feet long, and probably more, it took a very long time, while I stood thrilled with terror, not daring to make the slightest movement, gazing down upon it. Although so long it was not a thick snake, and as it moved on over the white ground it had the appearance of a coal-black current flowing past me—a current not of water or other liquid but of some such element as quicksilver moving on in a rope-like stream. At last it vanished, and turning I fled from the ground, thinking that never again would I venture into or near that frightfully dangerous spot in spite of its fascination.

Nevertheless I did venture. The image of that black mysterious serpent was always in my mind from the moment of waking in the morning until I fell asleep at night. Yet I never said a word about the snake to any one: it was my secret, and I knew it was a dangerous

188   FAR AWAY AND LONG AGO

secret, but I did not want to be told not to visit that
spot again. And I simply could not keep away from
it; the desire to look again at that strange being was
too strong. I began to visit the place again, day after
day, and would hang about the borders of the barren
weedy ground watching and listening, and still no black
serpent appeared. Then one day I ventured, though
in fear and trembling, to go right in among the weeds,
and still finding nothing began to advance step by step
until I was right in the middle of the weedy ground
and stood there a long time, waiting and watching. All
I wanted was just to see it once more, and I had made
up my mind that immediately on its appearance, if it
did appear, I would take to my heels. It was when
standing in this central spot that once again that slight
rustling sound, like that of a few days before, reached
my straining sense and sent an icy chill down my back.
And there, within six inches of my toes, appeared the
black head and neck, followed by the long, seemingly
endless body. I dared not move, since to have attempted
flight might have been fatal. The weeds were thinnest
here, and the black head and slow-moving black coil
could be followed by the eye for a little distance. About
a yard from me there was a hole in the ground about the
circumference of a breakfast cup at the top, and into
this hole the serpent put his head and slowly, slowly
drew himself in, while I stood waiting until the whole
body to the tip of the tail had vanished and all danger
was over.

I had seen my wonderful creature, my black serpent
unlike any serpent in the land, and the excitement
following the first thrill of terror was still on me, but
I was conscious of an element of delight in it, and I
would not now resolve not to visit the spot again.
Still, I was in fear, and kept away three or four days.
Thinking about the snake I formed the conclusion that

A SERPENT MYSTERY   189

the hole he had taken refuge in was his den, where he
lived, that he was often out roaming about in search of
prey, and could hear footsteps at a considerable distance,
and that when I walked about at that spot my footsteps disturbed him and caused him to go straight to
his hole to hide himself from a possible danger. It
struck me that if I went to the middle of the ground
and stationed myself near the hole, I would be sure to
see him. It would indeed be difficult to see him any
other way, since one could never know in which direction
he had gone out to seek for food. But no, it was too
dangerous: the serpent might come upon me unawares
and would probably resent always finding a boy hanging
about his den. Still, I could not endure to think I had
seen the last of him, and day after day I continued to
haunt the spot, and going a few yards into the little
weedy wilderness would stand and peer, and at the
slightest rustling sound of an insect or falling leaf
would experience a thrill of fearful joy, and still the
black majestical creature failed to appear.

One day in my eagerness and impatience I pushed my
way through the crowded weeds right to the middle
of the ground and gazed with a mixed delight and fear
at the hole: would he find me there, as on a former
occasion? Would he come? I held my breath, I
strained my sight and hearing in vain, the hope and
fear of his appearance gradually died out, and I left the
place bitterly disappointed and walked to a spot about
fifty yards away, where the mulberry trees grew on the
slope of the mound inside the moat.

Looking up into the masses of big clustering leaves
over my head I spied a bat hanging suspended from a
twig. The bats, I must explain, in that part of the
world, that illimitable plain where there were no caverns
and old buildings and other dark places to hide in by
day, are not so intolerant of the bright light as in other

lands. They do not come forth until evening, but by day they are content to hitch themselves to the twig of a tree under a thick cluster of leaves and rest there until it is dark.

Gazing up at this bat suspended under a big green leaf, wrapped in his black and buff-coloured wings as in a mantle, I forgot my disappointment, forgot the serpent, and was so entirely taken up with the bat that I paid no attention to a sensation like a pressure or a dull pain on the instep of my right foot. Then the feeling of pressure increased and was very curious and was as if I had a heavy object like a crowbar lying across my foot, and at length I looked down at my feet, and to my amazement and horror spied the great black snake slowly drawing his long coil across my instep! I dared not move, but gazed down fascinated with the sight of that glistening black cylindrical body drawn so slowly over my foot. He had come out of the moat, which was riddled at the sides with rat-holes, and had most probably been there hunting for rats when my wandering footsteps disturbed him and sent him home to his den; and making straight for it, as his way was, he came to my foot, and instead of going round drew himself over it. After the first spasm of terror I knew I was perfectly safe, that he would not turn upon me so long as I remained quiescent, and would presently be gone from sight. And that was my last sight of him; in vain I watched and waited for him to appear on many subsequent days: but that last encounter had left in me a sense of a mysterious being, dangerous on occasion as when attacked or insulted, and able in some cases to inflict death with a sudden blow, but harmless and even friendly or beneficent towards those who regarded it with kindly and reverent feelings in place of hatred. It is in part the feeling of the Hindu with regard to the cobra which inhabits his house and may

A SERPENT MYSTERY

one day accidentally cause his death, but is not to be persecuted.

Possibly something of that feeling about serpents has survived in me; but in time, as my curiosity about all wild creatures grew, as I looked more on them with the naturalist's eyes, the mystery of the large black snake pressed for an answer. It seemed impossible to believe that any species of snake of large size and black as jet or anthracite coal in colour could exist in any inhabited country without being known, yet no person I interrogated on the subject had ever seen or heard of such an ophidian. The only conclusion appeared to be that this snake was the sole one of its kind in the land. Eventually I heard of the phenomenon of melanism in animals, less rare in snakes perhaps than in animals of other classes, and I was satisfied that the problem was partly solved. My serpent was a black individual of a species of some other colour. But it was not one of our common species —not one of those I knew. It was not a thick blunt-bodied serpent like our venomous pit-viper, our largest snake, and though in shape it conformed to our two common harmless species it was twice as big as the biggest specimens I had ever seen of them. Then I recalled that two years before my discovery of the black snake, our house had been visited by a large unknown snake which measured two or three inches over six feet and was similar in form to my black serpent. The colour of this strange and unwelcome visitor was a pale greenish-grey, with numerous dull black mottlings and small spots. The story of its appearance is perhaps worth giving.

It happened that I had a baby sister who could just toddle about on two legs, having previously gone on all-fours. One midsummer day she was taken up and put on a rug in the shade of a tree, twenty-five yards from the sitting-room door, and left alone there to amuse

192   FAR AWAY AND LONG AGO

herself with her dolls and toys. After half an hour or so she appeared at the door of the sitting-room where her mother was at work, and standing there with wide-open astonished eyes and moving her hand and arm as if to point to the place she came from, she uttered the mysterious word *kú-ku*. It is a wonderful word which the southern South American mother teaches her child from the moment it begins to toddle, and is useful in a desert and sparsely inhabited country where biting, stinging, and other injurious creatures are common. For babies when they learn to crawl and to walk are eager to investigate and have no natural sense of danger. Take as an illustration the case of the gigantic hairy brown spider, which is excessively abundant in summer and has the habit of wandering about as if always seeking something—'something it cannot find, it knows not what'; and in these wanderings it comes in at the open door and rambles about the room.   At the sight of such a creature the baby is snatched up with the cry of *kú-ku* and the intruder slain with a broom or other weapon and thrown out.   *Kú-ku* means dangerous, and the terrified gestures and the expression of the nurse or mother when using the word sink into the infant mind, and when that sound or word is heard there is an instant response, as in the case of a warning note or cry uttered by a parent bird which causes the young to fly away or crouch down and hide.

The child's gestures and the word it used caused her mother to run to the spot where it had been left in the shade, and to her horror she saw there a huge serpent coiled up in the middle of the rug.   Her cries brought my father on the scene, and seizing a big stick he promptly dispatched the snake.

The child, said everybody, had had a marvellous escape, and as she had never previously seen a snake and could not intuitively know it as dangerous, or *kú-ku*,

A SERPENT MYSTERY 193

It was conjectured that she had made some gesture or attempted to push the snake away when it came on to the rug, and that it had reared its head and struck viciously at her.

Recalling this incident I concluded that this unknown serpent, which had been killed because it wanted to share my baby sister's rug, and my black serpent were one and the same species—possibly they had been mates —and that they had strayed a distance away from their native place or else were the last survivors of a colony of their kind in our plantation. It was not until twelve or fourteen years later that I discovered that it was even as I had conjectured. At a distance of about forty miles from my home, or rather from the home of my boyhood where I no longer lived, I found a snake that was new to me, the *Philodryas scotti* of naturalists, a not uncommon Argentine snake, and recognized it as the same species as the one found coiled up on my little sister's rug and presumably as my mysterious black serpent. Some of the specimens which I measured exceeded six feet in length.

CHAPTER XVII

A BOY'S ANIMISM

The animistic faculty and its survival in us—A boy's animism
and its persistence—Impossibility of seeing our past exactly
as it was—Serge Aksakoff's history of his childhood—The
child's delight in nature purely physical—First intimations of
animism in the child—How it affected me—Feeling with
regard to flowers—A flower and my mother—History of a
flower—Animism with regard to trees—Locust trees by moonlight—Animism and nature-worship—Animistic emotion not
uncommon—Cowper and the Yardley oak—The religionist's
fear of nature—Pantheistic Christianity—Survival of nature-
worship in England—The feeling for nature—Wordsworth's
pantheism and animistic emotion in poetry.

THESE serpent memories, particularly the enduring image
of that black serpent which when recalled restores most
vividly the emotion experienced at the time, serve to
remind me of a subject not yet mentioned in my narrative; this is animism, or that sense of something in
nature which to the enlightened or civilized man is not
there, and in the civilized man's child, if it be admitted
that he has it at all, is but a faint survival of a phase
of the primitive mind. And by animism I do not mean
the theory of a soul in nature, but the tendency or
impulse or instinct, in which all myth originates, to
animate all things; the projection of ourselves into
nature; the sense and apprehension of an intelligence
like our own but more powerful in all visible things. It
persists and lives in many of us, I imagine, more than
we like to think, or more than we know, especially in
those born and bred amidst rural surroundings, where
there are hills and woods and rocks and streams and
waterfalls, these being the conditions which are most

A BOY'S ANIMISM 195

favourable to it—the scenes which have 'inherited associations' for us, as Herbert Spencer has said. In large towns and all populous places, where nature has been tamed until it appears like a part of man's work, almost as artificial as the buildings he inhabits, it withers and dies so early in life that its faint intimations are soon forgotten and we come to believe that we have never experienced them. That such a feeling can survive in any man, or that there was ever a time since his infancy when he could have regarded this visible world as anything but what it actually is—the stage to which he has been summoned to play his brief but important part, with painted blue and green scenery for background —becomes incredible. Nevertheless, I know that in me, old as I am, this same primitive faculty which manifested itself in my early boyhood, still persists, and in those early years was so powerful that I am almost afraid to say how deeply I was moved by it.

It is difficult, impossible I am told, for any one to recall his boyhood exactly as it was. It could not have been what it seems to the adult mind, since we cannot escape from what we are, however great our detachment may be; and in going back we must take our present selves with us: the mind has taken a different colour, and this is thrown back upon our past. The poet has reversed the order of things when he tells us that we come trailing clouds of glory, which melt away and are lost as we proceed on our journey. The truth is that unless we belong to the order of those who crystallize or lose their souls on their passage, the clouds gather about us as we proceed, and as cloud-compellers we travel on to the very end.

Another difficulty in the way of those who write of their childhood is that unconscious artistry will steal or sneak in to erase unseemly lines and blots, to retouch, and colour, and shade and falsify the picture. The poor,

196 FAR AWAY AND LONG AGO

miserable autobiographer naturally desires to make his personality as interesting to the reader as it appears to himself. I feel this strongly in reading other men's recollections of their early years. There are, however, a few notable exceptions, the best one I know being Serge Aksakoff's *History of My Childhood*; and in his case the picture was not falsified, simply because the temper, and tastes, and passions of his early boyhood —his intense love of his mother, of nature, of all wildness, and of sport—endured unchanged in him to the end and kept him a boy in heart, able after long years to revive the past mentally, and picture it in its true, fresh, original colours.

And I can say of myself with regard to this primitive faculty and emotion—this sense of the supernatural in natural things, as I have called it—that I am on safe ground for the same reason; the feeling has never been wholly outlived. And I will add, probably to the disgust of some rigidly orthodox reader, that these are childish things which I have no desire to put away.

The first intimations of the feeling are beyond recall; I only know that my memory takes me back to a time when I was unconscious of any such element in nature, when the delight I experienced in all natural things was purely physical. I rejoiced in colours, scents, sounds, in taste and touch: the blue of the sky, the verdure of earth, the sparkle of sunlight on water, the taste of milk, of fruit, of honey, the smell of dry or moist soil, of wind and rain, of herbs and flowers; the mere feel of a blade of grass made me happy; and there were certain sounds and perfumes, and above all certain colours in flowers, and in the plumage and eggs of birds, such as the purple polished shell of the tinamou's egg, which intoxicated me with delight. When, riding on the plain, I discovered a patch of scarlet verbenas in full bloom, the creeping plants covering an area of several yards,

A BOY'S ANIMISM 197

with a moist, green sward sprinkled abundantly with the shining flower-bosses, I would throw myself from my pony with a cry of joy to lie on the turf among them and feast my sight on their brilliant colour.

It was not, I think, till my eighth year that I began to be distinctly conscious of something more than this mere childish delight in nature. It may have been there all the time from infancy—I don't know; but when I began to know it consciously it was as if some hand had surreptitiously dropped something into the honeyed cup which gave it at certain times a new flavour. It gave me little thrills, often purely pleasurable, at other times startling, and there were occasions when it became so poignant as to frighten me. The sight of a magnificent sunset was sometimes almost more than I could endure and made me wish to hide myself away. But when the feeling was roused by the sight of a small and beautiful or singular object, such as a flower, its sole effect was to intensify the object's loveliness. There were many flowers which produced this effect in but a slight degree, and as I grew up and the animistic sense lost its intensity, these too lost their magic and were almost like other flowers which had never had it. There were others which never lost what for want of a better word I have just called their magic, and of these I will give an account of one.

I was about nine years old, perhaps a month or two more, when during one of my rambles on horseback I found at a distance of two or three miles from home, a flower that was new to me. The plant, a little over a foot in height, was growing in the shelter of some large cardoon thistle, or wild artichoke, bushes. It had three stalks clothed with long, narrow, sharply-pointed leaves, which were downy, soft to the feel like the leaves of our great mullein, and pale green in colour. All three stems were crowned with clusters of flowers, the single flower

198   FAR AWAY AND LONG AGO

a little larger than that of the red valerian, of a pale red hue and a peculiar shape, as each small pointed petal had a fold or twist at the end. Altogether it was slightly singular in appearance and pretty, though not to be compared with scores of other flowers of the plains for beauty. Nevertheless it had an extraordinary fascination for me, and from the moment of its discovery it became one of my sacred flowers. From that time onwards, when riding on the plain, I was always on the look-out for it, and as a rule I found three or four plants in a season, but never more than one at any spot. They were usually miles apart.

On first discovering it I took a spray to show to my mother, and was strangely disappointed that she admired it merely because it was a pretty flower, seen for the first time. I had actually hoped to hear from her some word which would have revealed to me why I thought so much of it: now it appeared as if it was no more to her than any other pretty flower, and even less than some she was peculiarly fond of, such as the fragrant little lily called Virgin's Tears, the scented pure white and the rose-coloured verbenas, and several others. Strange that she who alone seemed always to know what was in my mind, and who loved all beautiful things, especially flowers, should have failed to see what I had found in it!

Years later, when she had left us and when I had grown almost to manhood and we were living in another place, I found that we had as neighbour a Belgian gentleman who was a botanist. I could not find a specimen of my plant to show him, but gave him a minute description of it as an annual, with very large, tough, permanent roots, also that it exuded a thick milky juice when the stem was broken, and produced its yellow seeds in a long, cylindrical, sharply-pointed pod full of bright silvery down, and I gave him sketches of flower and leaf. He

A BOY'S ANIMISM

succeeded in finding it in his books: the species had been known upwards of thirty years, and the discoverer, who happened to be an Englishman, had sent seed and roots to the botanical societies abroad he corresponded with; the species had been named after him, and it was to be found now growing in some of the botanical gardens of Europe.

All this information was not enough to satisfy me; there was nothing about the man in his books. So I went to my father to ask him if he had ever known or heard of an Englishman of that name in the country. Yes, he said, he had known him well; he was a merchant in Buenos Ayres, a nice gentle-mannered man, a bachelor and something of a recluse in his private house, where he lived alone and spent all his week-ends and holidays roaming about the plains with his vasculum in search of rare plants. He had been long dead—oh, quite twenty or twenty-five years.

I was sorry that he was dead, and was haunted with a desire to find out his resting-place so as to plant the flower that bore his name on his grave. He, surely, when he discovered it, must have had that feeling which I had experienced when I first beheld it and could never describe. And perhaps the presence of those deep, ever-living roots near his bones, and of the flower in the sunshine above him, would bring him a beautiful memory in a dream, if ever a dream visited him, in his long unawakening sleep.

No doubt in cases of this kind, when a first impression and the emotions accompanying it endures through life, the feeling changes somewhat with time; imagination has worked on it and has had its effect; nevertheless the endurance of the image and emotion serves to show how powerfully the mind was moved in the first instance.

I have related this case because there were interesting

FAR AWAY AND LONG AGO

circumstances connected with it; but there were other flowers which produced a similar feeling, which, when recalled, bring back the original emotion; and I would gladly travel many miles any day to look again at any one of them. The feeling, however, was evoked more powerfully by trees than by even the most supernatural of my flowers; it varied in power according to time and place and the appearance of the tree or trees, and always affected me most on moonlight nights. Frequently, after I had first begun to experience it consciously, I would go out of my way to meet it, and I used to steal out of the house alone when the moon was at its full to stand, silent and motionless, near some group of large trees, gazing at the dusky green foliage silvered by the beams; and at such times the sense of mystery would grow until a sensation of delight would change to fear, and the fear increase until it was no longer to be borne, and I would hastily escape to recover the sense of reality and safety indoors, where there was light and company. Yet on the very next night I would steal out again and go to the spot where the effect was strongest, which was usually among the large locust or white acacia trees, which gave the name of Las Acacias to our place. The loose feathery foliage on moonlight nights had a peculiar hoary aspect that made this tree seem more intensely alive than others, more conscious of my presence and watchful of me.

I never spoke of these feelings to others, not even to my mother, notwithstanding that she was always in perfect sympathy with me with regard to my love of nature. The reason of my silence was, I think, my powerlessness to convey in words what I felt; but I imagine it would be correct to describe the sensation experienced on those moonlight nights among the trees as similar to the feeling a person would have if visited by a supernatural being, if he was perfectly convinced

A BOY'S ANIMISM

that it was there in his presence, albeit silent and unseen, intently regarding him, and divining every thought in his mind. He would be thrilled to the marrow, but not terrified if he knew that it would take no visible shape nor speak to him out of the silence.

This faculty or instinct of the dawning mind is or has always seemed to me essentially religious in character; undoubtedly it is the root of all nature-worship, from fetishism to the highest pantheistic development. It was more to me in those early days than all the religious teaching I received from my mother. Whatever she told me about our relations with the Supreme Being I believed implicitly, just as I believed everything else she told me, and as I believed that two and two make four and that the world is round in spite of its flat appearance; also that it is travelling through space and revolving round the sun instead of standing still, with the sun going round it, as one would imagine. But apart from the fact that the powers above would save me in the end from extinction, which was a great consolation, these teachings did not touch my heart as it was touched and thrilled by something nearer, more intimate, in nature, not only in moonlit trees or in a flower or serpent, but, in certain exquisite moments and moods and in certain aspects of nature, in 'every grass' and in all things, animate and inanimate.

It is not my wish to create the impression that I am a peculiar person in this matter; on the contrary, it is my belief that the animistic instinct, if a mental faculty can be so called, exists and persists in many persons, and that I differ from others only in looking steadily at it and taking it for what it is, also in exhibiting it to the reader naked and without a fig-leaf expressed, to use a Baconian phrase. When the religious Cowper confesses in the opening lines of his address to the famous Yardley oak, that the sense of awe and reverence

202 FAR AWAY AND LONG AGO

it inspired in him would have made him bow himself down and worship it but for the happy fact that his mind was illumined with the knowledge of the truth, he is but saying what many feel without it in most cases recognizing the emotion for what it is—the sense of the supernatural in nature. And if they have grown up, as was the case with Cowper, with the image of an implacable anthropomorphic deity in their minds, a being who is ever jealously watching them to note which way their wandering thoughts are tending, they rigorously repress the instinctive feeling as a temptation of the evil one, or as a lawless thought born of their own inherent sinfulness. Nevertheless it is not uncommon to meet with instances of persons who appear able to reconcile their faith in revealed religion with their animistic emotion. I will give an instance. One of the most treasured memories of an old lady friend of mine, recently deceased, was of her visits, some sixty years or more ago, to a great country house where she met many of the distinguished people of that time, and of her host, who was then old, the head of an ancient and distinguished family, and of his reverential feeling for his trees. His greatest pleasure was to sit out of doors of an evening in sight of the grand old trees in his park, and before going in he would walk round to visit them, one by one, and resting his hand on the bark he would whisper a good-night. He was convinced, he confided to his young guest, who often accompanied him in these evening walks, that they had intelligent souls and knew and encouraged his devotion.

There is nothing surprising to me in this; it is told here only because the one who cherished this feeling and belief was an orthodox Christian, a profoundly religious person; also because my informant herself, who was also deeply religious, loved the memory of this old friend of her early life mainly because of his feeling

A BOY'S ANIMISM 203

for trees, which she too cherished, believing, as she often told me, that trees and all living and growing things have souls. What has surprised me is that a form of tree-worship is still found existing among a few of the inhabitants in some of the small rustic villages in out-of-the-world districts in England. Not such survivals as the apple-tree folk-songs and ceremonies of the west, which have long become meaningless, but something living, which has a meaning for the mind, a survival such as our anthropologists go to the end of the earth to seek among barbarous and savage tribes.

The animism which persists in the adult in these scientific times has been so much acted on and changed by dry light that it is scarcely recognizable in what is somewhat loosely or vaguely called a 'feeling for nature': it has become intertwined with the aesthetic feeling and may be traced in a good deal of our poetic literature, particularly from the time of the first appearance of *Lyrical Ballads*, which put an end to the eighteenth-century poetic convention and made the poet free to express what he really felt. But the feeling, whether expressed or not, was always there. Before the classic period we find in Traherne a poetry which was distinctly animistic, with Christianity grafted on it. Wordsworth's pantheism is a subtilized animism, but there are moments when his feeling is like that of a child or savage when he is convinced that the flower enjoys the air it breathes.

I must apologize to the reader for having gone beyond my last, since I am not a student of literature, nor catholic in my literary tastes, and on such subjects can only say just what I feel. And this is, that the survival of the sense of mystery, or of the supernatural, in nature, is to me in our poetic literature like that ingredient of a salad which 'animates the whole'; that the absence of that emotion has made a great portion

204   FAR AWAY AND LONG AGO

of the eighteenth-century poetic literature almost intolerable to me, so that I wish the little big man who dominated his age (and till a few months ago still had in Mr Courthope one follower among us) had emigrated west when still young, leaving *Windsor Forest* as his only monument and sole and sufficient title to immortality.

CHAPTER XVIII

THE NEW SCHOOLMASTER

Mr Trigg recalled—His successor—Father O'Keefe—His mild rule and love of angling—My brother is assisted in his studies by the priest—Happy fishing afternoons—The priest leaves us—How he had been working out his own salvation—We run wild once more—My brother's plan for a journal to be called *The Tin Box*—Our imperious editor's exactions—My little brother revolts—*The Tin Box* smashed up—The loss it was to me.

THE account of our schooling days under Mr Trigg was given so far back in this history that the reader will have little recollection of it. Mr Trigg was in a small way a sort of Jekyll and Hyde, all pleasantness in one of his states and all black looks and truculence in the other; so that out of doors and at table we children would say to ourselves in astonishment: 'Is this our schoolmaster?' but when in school we would ask: 'Is this Mr Trigg?' But, as I have related, he had been forbidden to inflict corporal punishment on us, and was finally got rid of because in one of his demoniacal moods he thrashed us brutally with his horsewhip. When this occurred we, to our regret, were not permitted to go back to our aboriginal condition of young barbarians: some restraint, some teaching was still imposed upon us by our mother, who took, or rather tried to take, this additional burden on herself. Accordingly, we had to meet with our lesson-books and spend three or four hours every morning with her, or in the schoolroom without her, for she was constantly being called away, and when present a portion of the time was spent in a little talk which was not concerned with our lessons. For we moved and breathed and had our being in a

206 FAR AWAY AND LONG AGO

strange moral atmosphere, where lawless acts were common and evil and good were scarcely distinguishable, and all this made her more anxious about our spiritual than our mental needs.

My two elder brothers did not attend, as they had long discovered that their only safe plan was to be their own schoolmasters, and it was even more than she could manage very well to keep the four smaller ones to their tasks. She sympathized too much with our impatience at confinement when sun and wind and the cries of wild birds called insistently to us to come out and be alive and enjoy ourselves in our own way.

At this stage a successor to Mr Trigg, a real schoolmaster, was unexpectedly found for us in the person of Father O'Keefe, an Irish priest without a cure and with nothing to do. Some friends of my father, on one of his periodical visits to Buenos Ayres, mentioned this person to him—this priest who in his wanderings about the world had drifted hither and was anxious to find some place to stay at out on the plains while waiting for something to turn up. As he was without means he said he would be glad of the position of schoolmaster in the house for a time, that it would exactly suit him.

Father O'Keefe, who now appeared on the scene, was very unlike Mr Trigg; he was a very big man in black but rusty clerical garments. He also had an extraordinarily big head and face, all of a dull, reddish colour, usually covered with a three or four days' growth of grizzly hair. Although his large face was unmistakably, intensely Irish, it was not the gorilla-like countenance so common in the Irish peasant-priest—the priest one sees every day in the streets of Dublin. He was, perhaps, of a better class, as his features were all good. A heavy man as well as a big one, he was not so amusing and so fluent a talker out of school as his predecessor, nor, as we were delighted

THE NEW SCHOOLMASTER 207

to discover, so exacting and tyrannical in school. On the contrary, in and out of school he was always the same, mild and placid in temper, with a gentle sort of humour, and he was also very absent-minded. He would forget all about school hours, roam about the gardens and plantations, get into long conversations with the workmen, and eventually, when he found that he was somewhat too casual to please his employer, he enjoined us to 'look him up' and let him know when it was school-time. Looking him up usually took a good deal of time. His teaching was not very effective. He could not be severe nor even passably strict, and never punished us in any way. When lessons were not learned he would sympathize with and comfort us by saying we had done our best and more could not be expected. He was also glad of any excuse to let us off for half a day. We found out that he was exceedingly fond of fishing—that with a rod and line in his hand he would spend hours of perfect happiness, even without a bite to cheer him, and on any fine day that called us to the plain we would tell him that it was a perfect day for fishing, and ask him to let us off for the afternoon. At dinner-time he would broach the subject and say the children had been very hard at their studies all the morning, and that it would be a mistake to force their young minds too much, that all work and no play makes Jack a dull boy, and so on and so forth, and that he considered it would be best for them, instead of going back to take more lessons in the afternoon, to go for a ride. He always gained his point, and dinner over we would rush out to catch and saddle our horses, and one for Father O'Keefe.

The younger of our two elder brothers, the sportsman and fighter, and our leader and master in all our outdoor pastimes and peregrinations, had taken to the study of mathematics with tremendous enthusiasm, the same

208   FAR AWAY AND LONG AGO

temper which he displayed in every subject and exercise
that engaged him—fencing, boxing, shooting, hunting,
and so on; and on Father O'Keefe's engagement he was
anxious to know if the new master would be any use to
him. The priest had sent a most satisfactory reply;
he would be delighted to assist the young gentleman
with his mathematics, and to help him over all his
difficulties; it was accordingly arranged that my brother
was to have an early hour each morning with the
master before school hours, and an hour or two in the
evening. Very soon it began to appear that the studies
were not progressing smoothly; the priest would come
forth as usual with a smiling, placid countenance, my
brother with a black scowl on his face, and gaining his
room, he would hurl his books down and protest in
violent language that the O'Keefe was a perfect fraud,
that he knew as much of the infinitesimal calculus as a
gaucho on horseback or a wild Indian. Then, beginning
to see it in a humorous light, he would shout with
laughter at the priest's pretensions to know anything,
and would say he was only fit to teach babies just out
of the cradle to say their A B C. He only wished the
priest had also pretended to some acquaintance with
the manly art, so that they could have a few bouts
with the gloves on, as it would have been a great pleasure
to bruise that big humbugging face black and blue.

The mathematical lessons soon ceased altogether,
but whenever an afternoon outing was arranged my
brother would throw aside his books to join us and take
the lead. The ride to the river, he would say, would
give us the opportunity for a little cavalry training and
lance-throwing exercise. In the cane-brake he would
cut long, straight canes for lances, which at the fishing-
ground would be cut down to a proper length for rods.
Then, mounting, we would set off, O'Keefe ahead,
absorbed as usual in his own thoughts, while we at a

THE NEW SCHOOLMASTER 209

distance of a hundred yards or so would form in line
and go through our evolutions, chasing the flying enemy,
O'Keefe; and at intervals our commander would give
the order to charge, whereupon we would dash forward
with a shout, and when about forty yards from him
we would all hurl our lances so as to make them fall
just at the feet of his horse. In this way we would
charge him a dozen or twenty times before getting to
our destination, but never once would he turn his head
or have any inkling of our carryings-on in the rear, even
when his horse lashed out viciously with his hind legs
at the lances when they fell too near his feet.

We enjoyed the advantage of the O'Keefe régime
for about a year, then one day, in his usual casual
manner, without a hint as to how his private affairs
were going, he said that he had to go somewhere to see
someone about something, and we saw him no more.
However, news of his movements and a good deal of
information about him reached us incidentally, from
all which it appeared that during his time with us, and
for some months previously, Father O'Keefe had been
working out his own salvation in a quiet way in accord-
ance with a rather elaborate plan which he had devised.
Before he became our teacher he had lived in some
priestly establishment in the capital, and had been a
hanger-on at the Bishop's palace, waiting for a benefice
or for some office, and at length, tired of waiting in
vain, he had quietly withdrawn himself from this society
and had got into communication with one of the Protestant clergymen of the town. He intimated or insinuated
that he had long been troubled with certain scruples,
that his conscience demanded a little more liberty than
his Church would allow its followers, and this had
caused him to cast a wistful eye on that other Church
whose followers were, alas! accorded a little more
liberty than was perhaps good for their souls. But

210   FAR AWAY AND LONG AGO

he didn't know, and in any case he would like to correspond on these important matters with one on the other side. This letter met with a warm response, and there was much correspondence and meetings with other clerics — Anglican or Episcopalian, I forget which. But there were also Presbyterians, Lutherans, and Methodist ministers, all with churches of their own in the town, and he may have flirted a little with all of them. Then he came for his year of waiting to us, during which he amused himself by teaching the little ones, smoothing the way for my mathematical brother, and fishing. But the authorities of the Church had not got rid of him; they heard not infrequently from him, and it was not pleasant hearing. He had come, he told them, a Roman Catholic priest to a Roman Catholic country, and had found himself a stranger in a strange land. He had waited patiently for months, and had been put off with idle promises or thrust aside, while every greedy, pushing priest that arrived from Spain and Italy was received with open arms and a place provided for him. Then, when his patience and private means had been exhausted, he had accidentally been thrown among those who were not of the Faith, yet had received him with open arms. He had been humiliated and pained at the disinterested hospitality and Christian charity shown to him by those outside the pale, after the treatment he had received from his fellow-priests.

Probably he said more than this: for it is a fact that he had been warmly invited to preach in one or two of the Protestant churches in the town. He did not go so far as to accept that offer: he was wise in his generation, and eventually got his reward.

Our schoolmaster gone, we were once more back in the old way; we did just what we liked. Our parents probably thought that our life would be on the plains, with sheep- and cattle-breeding for only vocations,

THE NEW SCHOOLMASTER   211

and that should any one of us, like my mathematical-
minded brother, take some line of his own, he would
find out the way of it for himself: his own sense, the
light of nature, would be his guide.   I had no inclination to do anything with books myself: books were
lessons, therefore repellent, and that any one should
read a book for pleasure was inconceivable.   The only
attempt to improve our minds at this period came,
oddly enough, from my masterful brother who despised
our babyish intellects—especially mine.   However, one
day he announced that he had a grand scheme to put
before us.   He had heard or read of a family of boys
living just like us in some wild isolated land where there
were no schools or teachers and no newspapers, who
amused themselves by writing a journal of their own,
which was issued once a week.   There was a blue pitcher
on a shelf in the house, and into this pitcher every boy
dropped his contribution, and one of them—of course
the most intelligent one—carefully went through them,
selected the best, and copied them all out in one large
sheet, and this was their weekly journal called *The Blue
Pitcher*, and it was read and enjoyed by the whole house,
He proposed that we should do the same; he, of course,
would edit the paper and write a large portion of it; it
would occupy two or four sheets of quarto paper, all in
his beautiful handwriting, which resembled copperplate,
and it would be issued for us all to read every Saturday.
We all agreed joyfully, and as the title had taken our
fancy we started hunting for a blue pitcher all over the
house, but couldn't find such a thing, and finally had
to put up with a tin box with a wooden lid and a lock
and key.   The contributions were to be dropped in
through a slit in the lid which the carpenter made for
us, and my brother took possession of the key.   The
title of the paper was to be *The Tin Box*, and we were
instructed to write about the happenings of the week

212 FAR AWAY AND LONG AGO

and anything in fact which had interested us, and not
to be such little asses as to try to deal with subjects
we knew nothing about. I was to say something
about birds: there was never a week went by in which
I didn't tell them a wonderful story of a strange bird
I had seen for the first time: well, I could write about
that strange bird and make it just as wonderful as I
liked.

We set about our task at once with great enthusiasm,
trying for the first time in our lives to put our thoughts
into writing. All went well for a few days. Then our
editor called us together to hear an important communication he wished to make. First he showed us, but
would not allow us to read or handle, a fair copy of the
paper, or of the portion he had done, just to enable us
to appreciate the care he was taking over it. He then
went on to say that he could not give so much time to
the task and pay for stationery as well without a small
weekly contribution from us. This would only be about
three-halfpence or twopence from our pocket-money,
and would not be much missed. To this we all agreed
at once except my younger brother, aged about seven
at that time. Then, he was told, he would not be
allowed to contribute to the paper. Very well, he
wouldn't contribute to it, he said. In vain we all tried
to coax him out of his stubborn resolve; he would not
part with a copper of his money and would have nothing
to do with *The Tin Box*. Then the editor's wrath broke
out, and he said he had already written his editorial,
but would now, as a concluding article, write a second
one in order to show up the person who had tried to
wreck the paper in his true colours. He would exhibit
him as the meanest, most contemptible insect that ever
crawled on the surface of the earth.

In the middle of this furious tirade my poor little
brother burst out crying. 'Keep your miserable tears

THE NEW SCHOOLMASTER 213

till the paper is out,' shouted the other, 'as you will have good reason to shed them then. You will be a marked being, every one will then point the finger of scorn at you and wonder how he could ever have thought well of such a pitiful little wretch.'

This was more than the little fellow could stand, and he suddenly fled from the room, still crying; then we all laughed, and the angry editor laughed too, proud of the effect his words had produced.

Our little brother did not join us at play that afternoon: he was in hiding somewhere, keeping watch on the movements of his enemy, who was no doubt engaged already in writing that dreadful article which would make him a marked being for the rest of his life.

In due time the editor, his task finished, came forth, and mounting his horse, galloped off; and the little watcher came out and stealing into the room where the Tin Box was kept, carried it off to the carpenter's shop. There, with chisel and hammer he broke the lid to pieces, and taking out all the papers, set to work to tear them up into the minutest fragments, which were carried out and scattered all over the place.

When the big brother came home and discovered what had been done he was in a mighty rage, and went off in search of the avaricious little rebel who had dared to destroy his work. But the little rebel was not to be caught; at the right moment he fled from the coming tempest to his parents and claimed their protection. Then the whole matter had to be inquired into, and the big boy was told that he was not to thrash his little brother, that he himself was to blame for everything on account of the extravagant language he had used, which the poor little fellow had taken quite seriously. If he actually believed *The Tin Box* article was going to have that disastrous effect on him, who could blame him for destroying it?

*H 956

214 FAR AWAY AND LONG AGO

That was the end of *The Tin Box*; not a word about starting it afresh was said, and from that day my elder brother never mentioned it. But years later I came to think it a great pity that the scheme had miscarried. I believe, from later experience, that even if it had lasted but a few weeks it would have given me the habit of recording my observations, and that is a habit without which the keenest observation and the most faithful memory are not sufficient for the field naturalist. Thus, through the destruction of the Tin Box, I believe I lost a great part of the result of six years of life with wild nature, since it was not until six years after my little brother's rebellious act that I discovered the necessity of making a note of every interesting thing I witnessed.

CHAPTER XIX

BROTHERS

Our third and last schoolmaster—His many accomplishments
—His weakness and final breakdown—My important brother
—Four brothers, unlike in everything except the voice—
A strange meeting—Jack the Killer, his life and character
—A terrible fight—My brother seeks instructions from Jack
—The gaucho's way of fighting and Jack's contrasted—Our
sham fight with knives—A wound and the result—My feeling
about Jack and his eyes—Bird-lore—My two elder brothers'
practical joke.

THE vanishing of the unholy priest from our ken left
us just about where we had been before his large red
face had lifted itself above our horizon. At all events
the illumination had not been great. And thereafter
it was holiday once more for a goodish time until yet a
third tutor came upon the scene—yet another stranger
in a strange land who had fallen into low (and hot)
water and was willing to fill a vacant time in educating
us. Just as in the case of the O'Keefe, he was thrust
upon my good-natured and credulous father by his
friends in the capital, who had this gentleman with
them and were anxious to get him off their hands.
He was, they assured my father, just the man he wanted,
a fine fellow of good family, highly educated and all
that; but he had been a bit wild, and all that was
wanted to bring him round was to get him out a good
distance from the capital and its temptations and
into a quiet, peaceful home like ours. Strange to say,
he actually turned out to be all they had said, and
more. He had studied hard at college and when
reading for a profession; he was a linguist, a musician,
he had literary tastes, and was well read in science, and

215

216   FAR AWAY AND LONG AGO

above all he was a first-rate mathematician. Naturally,
to my studious brother he came as an angel beautiful
and bright, with no suggestion of the fiend in him;
for not only was he a mathematician, but he was also
an accomplished fencer and boxer. And so the two
were soon fast friends, and worked hard together over
their books, and would then repair for an hour or two
every day to the plantation to fence and box and
practise with pistol and rifle at the target. He also
took to the humbler task of teaching the rest of us with
considerable zeal, and succeeded in rousing a certain
enthusiasm in us. We were, he told us, grossly ignorant
—simply young barbarians; but he had penetrated
beneath the thick crust that covered our minds, and was
pleased to find that there were possibilities of better
things; that if we would but second his efforts and throw
ourselves, heart and soul, into our studies, we should
eventually develop from the grub condition to that
of purple-winged butterflies.

Our new teacher was tremendously eloquent, and it
looked as if he had succeeded in conquering that wildness
or weakness or whatever it was which had been his
undoing in the past. Then came a time when he would
ask for a horse and go for a long ride. He would make
a call at some English estancia, and drink freely of the
wine and spirits hospitably set on the table. And the
result would be that he would come home raving like
a lunatic—a very little alcohol would drive him mad.
Then would follow a day or two of repentance and
black melancholy; then recovery and a fresh fair start.

All this was somewhat upsetting to all of us: to my
mother it was peculiarly distressing, and became more
so when, in one of his repentent fits and touched by her
words, he gave her a packet of his mother's letters to
read—the pathetic letters of a broken-hearted woman
to her son, her only and adored child, lost to her for ever

BROTHERS

in a distant country, thousands of miles from home. These sad appeals only made my mother more anxious to save him, and it was no doubt her influence that for a while did save and make him able to succeed in his efforts to overcome his fatal weakness. But he was of too sanguine a temper, and by-and-by began to think that he had conquered, that he was safe, that it was time for him to do something great; and with some brilliant scheme he had hatched in his mind, he left us and went back to the capital to work it out. But alas! before many months, when he was getting seriously to work, with friends and money to help him and every prospect of success, he broke down once more, so hopelessly that once more he had to be got rid of, and he was sent out of the country, but whether back to his own people or to some other remote district in Argentina I do not remember, nor do I know what became of him.

Thus disastrously ended the third and last attempt my father made to have us instructed at home. Nor could he send us to town, where there was but one English school for boys, run by a weak, sickly gentleman, whose house was a nest of fevers and every sort of ailment incidental to boys herded together in an unhealthy boarding-school. Prosperous English people sent their children home to be educated at that time, but it was enormously expensive and we were not well off enough. A little later an exception had to be made in the case of my elder brother, who would not settle down to sheep-farming or any other occupation out on the pampas, but had set his heart on pursuing his studies abroad.

At this period of my life this brother was so important a person to me that I shall have to give even more space to him in this chapter than he had in the last one. Yet of my brothers he was not the one nearest to my heart. He was five full years my senior, and

218   FAR AWAY AND LONG AGO

naturally associated with an elder brother, while we two
smaller ones were left to amuse ourselves together in
our own childish way.   With a younger brother for only
playmate, I prolonged my childhood, and when I was
ten my brother of fifteen appeared a young man to me.
We were all four extremely unlike in character as well
as appearance, and alike in one thing only—the voice,
inherited from our father; but just as our relationship
appeared in that one physical character, so I think that
under all the diversions in our minds and temperaments
there was a hidden quality, a something of the spirit,
which made us one; and this, I believe, came from the
mother's side.

That family likeness in the voice was brought home
to us in a curious way just about this time, when I was
in my tenth year.   My brother went one day to Buenos
Ayres, and arriving at the stable where our horses were
always put up, long after dark, he left his horse, and on
going out called to the stableman, giving him some direction.   As soon as he had spoken a feeble voice was heard
from the open door of a dark room near the gate, calling:
'That's a Hudson that spoke!   Father or son—who
is it?'

My brother turned back and groped his way into the
dark room, and replied: 'Yes, I'm a Hudson—Edwin's
my name.   Who are you?'

'Oh, I'm glad you're here!   I'm your old friend
Jack,' returned the other, and it was a happy meeting
between the boy in his sixteenth year and the grey-
headed old battered vagabond and fighter, known far
and wide in our part of the country as Jack the Killer,
and by other dreadful nicknames, both English and
Spanish.   Now he was lying there alone, friendless,
penniless, ill, on a rough bed the stableman had given
him in his room.   My brother came home full of the
subject, sad at poor old Jack's broken-down condition

BROTHERS 219

and rejoicing that he had by chance found him there and had been able to give him help.

Jack the Killer was one of those strange Englishmen frequently to be met with in those days, who had taken to the gaucho's manner of life, when the gaucho had more liberty and was a more lawless being than he is now or can ever be again, unless that vast level area of the pampas should at some future time become dispeopled and go back to what it was down to half a century ago. He had drifted into that outlandish place when young, and finding the native system of life congenial had made himself as much of a native as he could, and dressed like them and talked their language, and was horse-breaker, cattle-drover, and many other things by turn, and like any other gaucho he could make his own bridle and whip and horse-gear and lasso and *bolas* out of raw hide. And when not working he could gamble and drink like any gaucho to the manner born—and fight too. But here there was a difference. Jack could affiliate with the natives, yet could never be just like them. The stamp of the foreigner, of the Englishman, was never wholly eradicated. He retained a certain dignity, a reserve, almost a stiffness, in his manner which made him a marked man among them, and would have made him a butt to the wits and bullies among his comrades but for his pride and deadly power. To be mocked as a foreigner, a gringo, an inferior being, was what he could not stand, and the result was that he had to fight, and it then came as a disagreeable revelation that when Jack fought he fought to kill. This was considered bad form; for though men were often killed when fighting, the gaucho's idea is that you do not fight with that intention, but rather to set your mark upon and conquer your adversary, and so give yourself fame and glory. Naturally, they were angry with Jack and became anxious to get rid of him, and by-and-by he gave

220 FAR AWAY AND LONG AGO

them an excuse. He fought with and killed a man, a famous young fighter, who had many relations and friends, and some of these determined to avenge his death. And one night a band of nine men came to the rancho where Jack was sleeping, and leaving two of their number at the door to kill him if he attempted to escape that way, the others burst into his room, their long knives in their hands. As the door was thrown open Jack woke, and instantly divining the cause of the intrusion, he snatched up the knife near his pillow and sprang like a cat out of his bed; and then began a strange and bloody fight, one man, stark naked, with a short-bladed knife in his hand, against seven men with their long *facons*, in a small, pitch-dark room. The advantage Jack had was that his bare feet made no sound on the clay floor, and that he knew the exact position of a few pieces of furniture in the room. He had, too, a marvellous agility, and the intense darkness was all in his favour, as the attackers could hardly avoid wounding one another. At all events, the result was that three of them were killed and the other four wounded, all more or less seriously. And from that time Jack was allowed to live among them as a harmless, peaceful member of the community, so long as no person twitted him with being a gringo.

Quite naturally, my brother regarded Jack as one of his greatest heroes, and whenever he heard of his being in our neighbourhood he would mount his horse and go off in search of him, to spend long hours in his company and persuade him to talk about that awful fight in a dark room with so many against him. One result of his intimacy with Jack was that he became dissatisfied with his own progress in the manly art of self-defence. It was all very well to make himself proficient with the foils and as a boxer, and to be a good shot, but he was living among people who had the knife

BROTHERS

for sole weapon, and if by chance he were attacked by a man with a knife, and had no pistol or other weapon, he would find himself in an exceedingly awkward position. There was then nothing to do but to practise with the knife, and he wanted Jack, who had been so successful with that weapon, to give him some lessons in its use.

Jack shook his head. If his boy friend wanted to learn the gaucho way of fighting he could easily do so. The gaucho wrapped his poncho on his left arm to use it as a shield, and flourished his *facon*, or knife with a sword-like blade and a guard to the handle. This whirling about of the knife was quite an art, and had a fine look when two accomplished fighters stood up to each other and made their weapons look like shining wheels or revolving mirrors in the sun. Meanwhile, the object of each man was to find his opportunity for a sweeping blow which would lay his opponent's face open. Now all that was pretty to look at, but it was mere playing at fighting and he never wanted to practise it. He was not a fighter by inclination; he wanted to live with and be one with the gauchos, but not to fight. There were numbers of men among them who never fought and were never challenged to fight, and he would be of those if they would let him. He never had a pistol, he wore a knife like everybody else, but a short knife for use and not to fight. But when he found that, after all, he had to fight or else exist on sufferance as a despised creature among them, the butt of every fool and bully, he did fight in a way which he had never been taught and could not teach to another. It was nature: it was in him. When the dangerous moment came and knives flashed out, he was instantly transformed into a different being. He was on springs, he couldn't keep still or in one place for a second, or a fraction of a second; he was like a cat, like indiarubber, like steel—like anything you like, but something that flew

222   FAR AWAY AND LONG AGO

round and about his opponent and was within striking distance one second and a dozen yards away the next, and when an onset was looked for it never came where it was expected but from another side, and in two minutes his opponent became confused, and struck blindly at him, and his opportunity came, not to slash and cut, but to drive his knife with all his power to the heart in the other's body and finish him for ever. That was how he had fought and had killed, and because of that way of fighting he had got his desire and had been permitted to live in peace and quiet until he had grown grey and no fighter or swashbuckler had said to him: 'Do you still count yourself a killer of men? Then kill me and prove your right to the title,' and no one had jeered at or called him 'gringo.'

In spite of this discouragement my brother was quite determined to learn the art of defending himself with a knife, and he would often go out into the plantation and practise for an hour with a tree for an opponent, and try to capture Jack's unpremeditated art of darting hither and thither about his enemy and making his deadly strokes. But as the tree stood still and had no knife to oppose him, it was unsatisfactory, and one day he proposed to me and my younger brother to have a fight with knives, just to find out if he was making any progress. He took us out to the far end of the plantation, where no one could see us, and produced three very big knives, with blades like butchers' knives, and asked us to attack him with all our might and try our best to wound him, while he would act solely on the defensive. At first we declined, and reminded him that he had punished us terribly with gloves and foils and singlestick, and that it would be even worse with knives—he would cut us in pieces! No, he said, he would not dream of hurting us: it would be absolutely safe for us, and for him too, as he didn't for a moment

BROTHERS   223

believe that we could touch him with our weapons,
no matter how hard we tried. And at last we were
persuaded, and taking off our jackets and wrapping
them, gaucho fashion, on our left arms as a protection,
we attacked him with the big knives, and getting excited,
we slashed and lunged at him with all our power, while
he danced and jumped and flew about *à la* Jack the
Killer, using his knife only to guard himself and to try
and knock ours out of our hands; but in one such attempt at disarming me his weapon went too far and
wounded my right arm about three inches below the
shoulder. The blood rushed out and dyed my sleeve
red, and the fight came to an end. He was greatly
distressed, and running off to the house, quickly returned with a jug of water, sponge, towel, and linen to
bind the wounded arm. It was a deep, long cut, and the
scar has remained to this day, so that I can never wash
in the morning without seeing it and remembering that
old fight with knives. Eventually he succeeded in
stopping the flow of blood and binding my arm tightly
round; and then he made the desponding remark:
'Of course they will have to know all about it now.'

'Oh no,' I returned, 'why should they? My arm
has stopped bleeding, and they won't find out. If
they notice that I can't use it—well, I can just say I
had a knock.'

He was immensely relieved, and so pleased that he
patted me on the back—the first time he had ever
done so—and praised me for my manliness in taking
it that way; and to be praised by him was such a rare
and precious thing that I felt very proud, and began
to think I was almost as good as a fighter myself. And
when all traces of blood had been removed and we were
back in the house and at the supper-table, I was unusually talkative and hilarious, not only to prevent
any one from suspecting that I had just been seriously

224 FAR AWAY AND LONG AGO

wounded in a fight with knives, but also to prove to
my brother that I could take these knocks with proper
fortitude. No doubt he was amused; but he didn't
laugh at me, he was too delighted to escape being
found out.

There were no more fights with knives, although
when my wound was healed he did broach the subject
again on two or three occasions, and was anxious to
convince me that it would be greatly to our advantage
to know how to defend ourselves with a knife while
living among people who were always as ready on any
slight provocation to draw a knife on you as a cat was
to unsheathe its claws. Nor could all he told us about
the bloody and glorious deeds of Jack *el Matador* arouse
any enthusiasm in me; and though in his speech and
manner Jack was as quiet and gentle a being as one
could meet, I could never overcome a curious shrinking,
an almost uncanny feeling, in his presence, particularly
when he looked straight at me with those fine eyes of
his. They were light grey in colour, clear and bright
as in a young man, but the expression pained me; it
was too piercing, too concentrated, and it reminded
me of the look in a cat's eyes when it crouches motionless just before making its dash at a bird.

Nevertheless, the fight and wound had one good
result for me; my brother had all at once become less
masterful, or tyrannical, towards me, and even began
to show some interest in my solitary disposition and
tastes. A little bird incident brought out this feeling
in a way that was very agreeable to me. One evening
I told him and our eldest brother that I had seen a
strange thing in a bird which had led me to find out
something new. Our commonest species was the
parasitic cow-bird, which laid its eggs anywhere in
the nests of all the other small birds. Its colour was
a deep glossy purple, almost black; and seeing two

BROTHERS

of these birds flying over my head, I noticed that they had a small chestnut-coloured spot beneath the wing, which showed that they were not the common species. It had then occurred to me that I had heard a peculiar note or cry uttered by what I took to be the cow-bird, which was unlike any note of that bird; and following this clue, I had discovered that we had a bird in our plantation which was like the cow-bird in size, colour, and general appearance, but was a different species. They appeared amused by my story, and a few days later they closely interrogated me on three consecutive evenings as to what I had seen that was remarkable that day, in birds especially, and were disappointed because I had nothing interesting to tell them.

The next day my brother said he had a confession to make to me. He and the elder brother had agreed to play a practical joke on me, and had snared a common cow-bird and dyed or painted its tail a brilliant scarlet, then liberated it, expecting that I should meet with it in my day's rambles and bird-watching in the plantation and would be greatly excited at the discovery of yet a third purple cow-bird, with a scarlet tail, but otherwise not distinguishable from the common one. Now, on reflection, he was glad I had not found their bird and given them their laugh, and he was ashamed at having tried to play such a mean trick on me!

CHAPTER XX

BIRDING IN THE MARSHES

Visiting the marshes—*Pajonales* and *juncales*—Abundant bird
life—A coots' metropolis—Frightening the coots—Grebe and
painted snipe colonies—The haunt of the social marsh-hawk
—The beautiful jacana and its eggs—The colony of marsh-
troupials—The bird's music—The aquatic plant *durasmillo*—
The troupial's nest and eggs—Recalling a beauty that has
vanished—Our games with gaucho boys—I am injured by a
bad boy—The shepherd's advice—Getting my revenge in a
treacherous manner—Was it right or wrong?—The game of
hunting the ostrich.

AT this time of my boy-life most of the daylight hours
were spent out of doors, as when not watching the birds
in our plantation or asked to go and look at the flock
grazing somewhere a mile or so from home, in the absence of the shepherd or his boy, I was always away
somewhere on the plain with my small brother on egg-
hunting or other expeditions. In the spring and summer
we often visited the lagoons or marshes, the most fascinating places I knew on account of their abundant
wild-bird life. There were four of these lagoons, all in
different directions and all within two or three miles
from home. They were shallow lakelets, called *lagunas*,
each occupying an area of three or four hundred acres,
with some open water and the rest overgrown with
bright green sedges in dense beds, called *pajonales*, and
immense beds of bulrushes, called *juncales*. These
last were always the best to explore when the water
was not deeper than the saddle-girth, and where the
round dark polished stems, crowned with their bright
brown tufts, were higher than our heads when we urged
our horses through them. These were the breeding

226

BIRDING IN THE MARSHES 227

places of some small birds that had their beautifully-made nests a couple of feet or so above the water, attached in some cases to single, in others to two or three, rush-stems. And here, too, we found the nests of several large species — egret, night-heron, cormorant, and occasionally a hawk—birds which build on trees in forest districts, but here on the treeless region of the pampas they made their nests among the rushes. The fourth lakelet had no rush- or sedge-beds and no reeds, and was almost covered with a luxuriant growth of the floating *camaloté*, a plant which at a distance resembles the wild musk or mimulus in its masses of bright green leaves and brilliant yellow blossoms. This, too, was a fascinating spot, as it swarmed with birds, some of them being kinds which did not breed in the reeds and rushes. It was a sort of metropolis of the coots, and before and after the breeding season they would congregate in flocks of many hundreds on the low wet shore, where their black forms had a singular appearance on the moist green turf. It looked to me like a reproduction in small size of a scene I had witnessed —the vast level green pampa with a scattered herd of two or three thousand black cattle grazing on it, on a large cattle estate where only black beasts were bred. We always thought it great fun when we found a big assembly of coots at some distance from the margin. Whipping up our horses, we would suddenly charge the flock to see them run and fly in a panic to the lake and rush over the open water, striking the surface with their feet and raising a perfect cloud of spray behind them.

Coots, however, were common everywhere, but this water was the only breeding-place of the grebe in our neighbourhood; yet here we could find scores of nests any day—scores with eggs and a still greater number of false nests, and we could never tell which had eggs in it before pulling off the covering of wet weeds. Another bird rarely seen at any other spot than this was the painted snipe, a prettily-marked species with a green curved bill. It has curiously sluggish habits, rising only when almost trodden upon, and going off in a wild scared manner like a nocturnal species, then dropping again into hiding at a short distance. The natives call it *dormilón*—sleepy-head. On one side of the lagoon, where the ground was swampy and wet, there was always a breeding-colony of these quaint birds; at every few yards one would spring up close to the hoofs, and dismounting we would find the little nest on the wet ground under the grass, always with two eggs so thickly blotched all over with black as to appear almost entirely black.

There were other rushy lagoons at a greater distance which we visited only at long intervals, and one of these I must describe, as it was almost more attractive than any one of the others on account of its bird life. Here, too, there were some kinds which we never found breeding elsewhere.

It was smaller than the other lagoons I have described and much shallower, so that the big birds, such as the stork, wood-ibis, crested screamer, and the great blue ibis, called *vanduria*, and the roseate spoonbill, could wade almost all over it without wetting their feathers. It was one of those lakes which appear to be drying up, and was pretty well covered with a growth of *camaloté* plant, mixed with reed, sedge, and bulrush patches. It was the only water in our part of the country where the large water-snail was found, and the snails had brought the bird that feeds on them—the large social marsh-hawk, a slate-coloured bird resembling a buzzard in its size and manner of flight. But being exclusively a feeder on snails, it lives in peace and harmony with the other bird inhabitants of the marsh. There was

BIRDING IN THE MARSHES   229

always a colony of forty or fifty of these big hawks to be seen at this spot. A still more interesting bird was the jacana, as it is spelt in books; but pronounced *yä-sä-nä* by the Indians of Paraguay, a quaint rail-like bird supposed to be related to the plover family: black and maroon-red in colour, the wing quills a shining greenish-yellow, it has enormously long toes, spurs on its wings, and yellow wattles on its face. Here I first saw this strange beautiful fowl, and here to my delight I found its nest in three consecutive summers, with three or four clay-coloured eggs spotted with chestnut-red.

Here, too, was the breeding-place of the beautiful black-and-white stilt, and of other species too many to mention. But my greatest delight was in finding breeding in this place a bird I loved more than all the others I have named—a species of marsh-troupial, a bird about the size of the common cow-bird, and, like it, of a uniform deep purple, but with a cap of chestnut-coloured feathers on its head. I loved this bird for its song—the peculiar delicate tender opening notes and trills. In spring and autumn large flocks would occasionally visit our plantation, and the birds in hundreds would settle on a tree and all sing together, producing a marvellous and beautiful noise, as of hundreds of small bells all ringing at one time. It was by the water I first found their breeding-place, where about three or four hundred birds had their nests quite near together, and nests and eggs and the plants on which they were placed, with the solicitous purple birds flying round me, made a scene of enchanting beauty. The nesting-site was on a low swampy piece of ground grown over with a semi-aquatic plant called *durasmillo* in the vernacular. It has a single white stalk, woody in appearance, two to three feet high, and little thicker than a man's middle finger, with a palm-like crown of large loose lanceolate leaves, so that it looks like a miniature

230 FAR AWAY AND LONG AGO

palm, or rather an ailanthus tree, which has a slender perfectly white bole. The solanaceous flowers are purple, and it bears fruit the size of cherries, black as jet, in clusters of three to five or six. In this forest of tiny palms the nests were hanging, attached to the boles, where two or three grew close together; it was a long and deep nest, skilfully made of dry sedge leaves woven together, and the eggs were white or skim-milk blue spotted with black at the large end.

That enchanting part of the marsh, with its forest of graceful miniature trees, where the social troupials sang and wove their nests and reared their young in company—that very spot is now, I dare say, one immense field of corn, lucerne, or flax, and the people who now live and labour there know nothing of its former beautiful inhabitants, nor have they ever seen or even heard of the purple-plumaged troupial, with its chestnut cap and its delicate trilling song. And when I recall these vanished scenes, those rushy and flowery meres, with their varied and multitudinous wild-bird life—the cloud of shining wings, the heart-enlivening wild cries, the joy unspeakable it was to me in those early years—I am glad to think I shall never revisit them, that I shall finish my life thousands of miles removed from them, cherishing to the end in my heart the image of a beauty which has vanished from earth.

My elder brother occasionally accompanied us on our egg-hunting visits to the lagoons, and he also joined us in our rides to the two or three streams where we used to go to bathe and fish; but he took no part in our games and pastimes with the gaucho boys: they were beneath him. We ran races on our ponies, and when there were race-meetings in our neighbourhood my father would give us a little money to go and enter our ponies in a boys' race. We rarely won when there

BIRDING IN THE MARSHES   231

were any stakes, as the native boys were too clever
on horseback for us, and had all sorts of tricks to prevent us from winning, even when our ponies were better
than theirs. We also went tinamou, or partridge,
catching, and sometimes we had sham fights with lances,
or long canes with which we supplied the others. These
games were very rough, and one day when we were
armed, not with canes but long straight pliant green
poplar boughs we had cut for that purpose, we were
having a running fight, when one of the boys got in a
rage with me for some reason and, dropping behind,
then coming quietly up, gave me a blow on the face
and head with his stick which sent me flying off my
pony. They all dashed on, leaving me there to pick
myself up, and mounting my pony I went home crying
with pain and rage. The blow had fallen on my head,
but the pliant stick had come down over my face from
the forehead to the chin, taking the skin off. On my
way back I met our shepherd and told him my story,
and said I would go to the boy's parents to tell them.
He advised me not to do so; he said I must learn to
take my own part, and if any one injured me and I
wanted him punished I must do the punishing myself.
If I made any fuss and complaint about it I should only
get laughed at, and he would go scot free. What, then,
was I to do? I asked, seeing that he was older and
stronger than myself, and had his heavy whip and
knife to defend himself against attack.

'Oh, don't be in a hurry to do it,' he returned. 'Wait
for an opportunity, even if you have to wait for days;
and when it comes, do to him just what he did to you.
Don't warn him, but simply knock him off his horse,
and then you will be quits.'

Now this shepherd was a good man, much respected
by every one, and I was glad that in his wisdom and
sympathy he had put such a simple, easy plan into my

232   FAR AWAY AND LONG AGO

head, and I dried my tears and went home and washed
the blood from my face, and when asked how I had got
that awful wound that disfigured me I made light of it.
Two days later my enemy appeared on the scene. I
heard his voice outside the gate calling to someone,
and peering out I saw him sitting on his horse. His
guilty conscience made him afraid to dismount, but he
was anxious to find out what was going to be done
about his treatment of me, also, if he could see me, to
discover my state of mind after two days.

I went out to the timber pile and selected a bamboo
cane about twenty feet long, not too heavy to be handled
easily, and holding it up like a lance I marched to the
gate and started swinging it round as I approached him,
and showing a cheerful countenance. 'What are you
going to do with that cane?' he shouted, a little apprehensively. 'Wait and see,' I returned. 'Something to
make you laugh.' Then, after whirling it round half a
dozen times more, I suddenly brought it down on his
head with all my force, and did exactly what I had been
counselled to do by the wise shepherd—knocked him
clean off his horse. But he was not stunned, and
starting up in a screeching fury, he pulled out his knife
to kill me. And I, for strategic reasons, retreated,
rather hastily. But his wild cries quickly brought
several persons on the scene, and, recovering courage,
I went back and said triumphantly: 'Now we are
quits!' Then my father was called and asked to judge
between us, and after hearing both sides he smiled and
said his judgment was not needed, that we had already
settled it all ourselves, and there was nothing now
between us. I laughed, and he glared at me, and mounting his horse, rode off without another word. It was,
however, only because he was suffering from the blow
on his head; when I next met him we were good friends
again.

BIRDING IN THE MARSHES   233

More than once during my life, when recalling that
episode, I have asked myself if I did right in taking the
shepherd's advice. Would it have been better, when
I went out to him with the bamboo cane, and he asked
me what I was going to do with it, if I had gone up to
him and shown him my face with that broad band
across it from the chin to the temple, where the skin
had come off and a black crust had formed, and had
said to him: 'This is the mark of the blow you gave me
the day before yesterday, when you knocked me off
my horse; you see it is on the right side of my face and
head; now take the cane and give me another blow
on the left side'? Tolstoy (my favourite author,
by the way) would have answered: 'Yes, certainly it
would have been better for you—better for your soul.'
Nevertheless, I still ask myself: 'Would it?' and if this
incident should come before me half a second before
my final disappearance from earth, I should still be in
doubt.

One of our favourite games at this period—the
only game on foot we ever played with the gaucho
boys—was hunting the ostrich. To play this game
we had *bolas*, only the balls at the end of the thong
were not of lead like those with which the grown-up
gaucho hunter captures the real ostrich or rhea. We
used light wood to make balls, so as not to injure each
other. The fastest boy was chosen to play the ostrich,
and would be sent off to roam ostrich fashion on the
plain, pretending to pick clover from the ground as
he walked in a stooping attitude, or making little
runs and waving his arms about like wings, then
standing erect and mimicking the hollow booming
sounds the cock bird emits when calling the flock
together.

The hunters would then come on the scene and the
chase begin, the ostrich putting forth all his speed,

234   FAR AWAY AND LONG AGO

doubling to this side and that, and occasionally thinking to escape by hiding, dropping upon the ground in the shelter of a cardoon thistle, only to jump up again when the shouts of the hunters drew near, to rush on as before. At intervals the *bolas* would come whirling through the air, and he would dodge or avoid them by a quick turn, but eventually he would be hit and the thong would wind itself about his legs and down he would come.

Then the hunters would gather round him, and pulling out their knives begin operations by cutting off his head; then the body would be cut up, the wings and breast removed, these being the best parts for eating, and there would be much talk about the condition and age of the bird, and so on. Then would come the most exciting part of the proceedings—the cutting the gizzard open and the examination of its varied contents; and by-and-by there would be an exultant shout, and one of the boys would pretend to come on a valuable find —a big silver coin perhaps, a *patacon*, and there would be a great gabble over it and perhaps a fight for its possession, and they would wrestle and roll on the grass, struggling for the imaginary coin. That finished, the dead ostrich would get up and place himself among the hunters, while the boy who had captured him with his *bolas* would then play ostrich, and the chase would begin anew.

When this game was played I was always chosen as first ostrich, as at that time I could easily outrun and out-jump any of my gaucho playmates, even those who were three or four years older than myself. Nevertheless, these games—horse-racing, sham fights, and ostrich-hunting, and the like—gave me no abiding satisfaction; they were no sooner over than I would go back, almost with a sense of relief, to my solitary rambles and bird-watching, and to wishing that the

BIRDING IN THE MARSHES 235

day would come when my masterful brother would allow me to use a gun and practise the one sport of wild duck shooting I desired.

That was soon to come, and will form the subject of the ensuing chapter.

CHAPTER XXI

WILD-FOWLING ADVENTURES

My sporting brother and the armoury—I attend him on his
shooting expeditions—Adventure with golden plover—A
morning after wild duck—Our punishment—I learn to shoot
—My first gun—My first wild duck—My ducking tactics—
My gun's infirmities—Duck-shooting with a blunderbuss—
Ammunition runs out—An adventure with rosy-bill duck
—Coarse gunpowder and home-made shot—The war danger
comes our way—We prepare to defend the house—The
danger over and my brother leaves home.

I HAVE said I was not allowed to shoot before the age
of ten, but the desire had come long before that; I was
no more than seven when I used to wish to be a big, or
at all events a bigger, boy, so that, like my brother, I
too might carry a gun and shoot big wild birds. But
he said 'No' very emphatically, and there was an end
to it.

He had virtually made himself the owner of all the
guns and weapons generally in the house. These
included three fowling-pieces, a rifle, an ancient Tower
musket with a flint-lock—doubtless dropped from the
dead hands of a slain British soldier in one of the fights
in Buenos Ayres in 1807 or 1808—a pair of heavy horse-
pistols, and a ponderous, formidable-looking old blunderbuss, wide at the mouth as a tea-cup saucer. His, too,
were the swords. To our native neighbours this appeared an astonishingly large collection of weapons,
for in those days they possessed no fire-arm except, in
some rare instances, a carbine, brought home by a
runaway soldier and kept concealed lest the authorities
should get wind of it.

As the next best thing to doing the shooting myself,

236

I attended my brother on his expeditions, to hold his horse or to pick up and carry the birds, and was deeply grateful to him for allowing me to serve him in this humble capacity. We had some exciting adventures together. One summer day he came rushing home to get his gun, having just seen an immense flock of golden plover come down at a spot a mile or so from home. With his gun and a sack to put the birds in, he mounted his pony, I with him, as our ponies were accustomed to carry two and even three at a pinch. We found the flock where he had seen it alight—thousands of birds evenly scattered, running about busily feeding on the wet, level ground.

The bird I speak of is the *Charadrius dominicana,* which breeds in Arctic America and migrates in August and September to the plains of La Plata and Patagonia, so that it travels about sixteen thousand miles every year. In appearance it is so like our golden plover, *Charadrius pluvialis,* as to be hardly distinguishable from it. The birds were quite tame: all our wild birds were if anything too tame, although not *shockingly* so as Alexander Selkirk found them on his island—the poet's, not the real Selkirk. The birds being so scattered, all he could do was to lie flat down and fire with the barrel of his fowling-piece level with the flock, and the result was that the shot cut through the loose flock to a distance of thirty or forty yards, dropping thirty-nine birds, which we put into the sack, and remounting our pony set off home at a fast gallop. We were riding barebacked, and as our pony's back had a forward slope we slipped further and further forward until we were almost on his neck, and I, sitting behind my brother, shouted for him to stop. But he had his gun in one hand and the sack in the other, and had lost the reins; the pony, however, appeared to have understood, as he came to a dead stop of his own accord on the edge of a rain-pool, into which we were pitched headlong. When I raised my head I saw the bag of birds at my side, and the gun lying under water at a little distance; about three yards further on my brother was just sitting up, with the water streaming from his long hair, and a look of astonishment on his face. But the pool was quite clean, with the soft grass for bottom, and we were not hurt.

However, we did sometimes get into serious trouble. On one occasion he persuaded me and the little brother to accompany him on a secret shooting expedition he had planned. We were to start on horseback before daybreak, ride to one of the marshes about two miles from home, shoot a lot of duck, and get back about breakfast-time. The main thing was to keep the plan secret, then it would be all right, since the sight of the number of wild duck we should have to show on our return would cause our escapade to be overlooked.

In the evening, instead of liberating our ponies as usual, we took and tethered them in the plantation, and next morning about three o'clock we crept cautiously out of the house and set off on our adventure. It was a winter morning, misty and cold when the light came, and the birds were excessively wild at that hour. In vain we followed the flocks, my brother stalking them through the sedges, above his knees in the water; not a bird could he get, and at last we were obliged to go back empty-handed to face the music. At half-past ten we rode to the door, wet and hungry and miserable, to find the whole house in a state of commotion at our disappearance. When we were first missed in the morning, one of the workmen reported that he had seen us taking our horses to conceal them in the plantation at a little after dark, and it was assumed that we had run away—that we had gone south where the country was more thinly settled and wild animals more abun-

WILD-FOWLING ADVENTURES 239

dant, in quest of new and more stirring adventures. They were greatly relieved to see us back, but as we had no ducks to placate them we could not be forgiven, and as a punishment we had to go breakfastless that day, and our leader was in addition sternly lectured and forbidden to use a gun for the future.

We thought this a very hard thing, and for the following days were inclined to look at life as a rather tame, insipid business; but soon, to our joy, the ban was removed. In forbidding us the use of the guns my father had punished himself as well as us, since he never thoroughly enjoyed a meal—breakfast, dinner, or supper —unless he had a bird on the table, wild duck, plover, or snipe. A cold roast duck was his favourite breakfast dish, and he was never quite happy when he didn't get it.

Still, I was not happy, and could not be so long as I was not allowed to shoot. It was a privilege to be allowed to attend, but it seemed to me that at the age of ten I was quite old enough to have a gun. I had been a rider on horseback since the age of six, and in some exercises I was not much behind my brother, although when we practised with the foils or with the gloves he punished me in rather a barbarous manner. He was my guide and philosopher, and had also been a better friend ever since our fight with knives and the cow-bird episode; nevertheless he still managed to dissemble his love, and when I revolted against his tyranny I generally got well punished for it.

About that time an old friend of the family, who took an interest in me and wished to do something to encourage me in my natural history tastes, made me a present of a set of pen-an-ink drawings. There was, however, nothing in these pictures to help me in the line I had taken: they were mostly architectural drawings made by himself of buildings—houses,

240 FAR AWAY AND LONG AGO

churches, castles, and so on; but my brother fell in love with them and began to try to get them from me. He could not rest without them, and was continually offering me something of his own in exchange for them; but though I soon grew tired of looking at them I refused to part with them, either because his anxiety to have them gave them a fictitious value in my sight, or because it was pleasing to be able to inflict a little pain on him in return for the many smarts I had suffered at his hands. At length one day, finding me still unmoved, he all at once offered to teach me to shoot and to allow me the use of one of the guns in exchange for the pictures. I could hardly believe my good fortune; it would have surprised me less if he had offered to give me his horse with 'saddle and bridle also.'

As soon as the drawings were in his hand he took me to our gun-room and gave me a quite unneeded lesson in the art of loading a gun—first so much powder, then a wad well rammed down with the old obsolete ramrod; then so much shot and a second wad and ramming down; then a percussion cap on the nipple. He then led the way to the plantation, and finding two wild pigeons sitting together in a tree, he ordered me to fire. I fired, and one fell, quite dead, and that completed my education, for now he declared he was not going to waste any more time on my instruction.

The gun he had told me to use was a single-barrel fowling-piece, an ancient converted flint-lock, the stock made of an iron-hard black wood with silver mountings. When I stood it up and measured myself by it I found it was nearly two inches taller than I was, but it was light to carry and served me well: I became as much attached to it as to any living thing, and it was like a living thing to me, and I had great faith in its intelligence.

My chief ambition was to shoot wild duck. My

WILD-FOWLING ADVENTURES 241

brother shot them in preference to anything else: they
were so much esteemed and he was so much commended
when he came in with a few in his bag that I looked on
duck-shooting as the greatest thing I could go in for.
Ducks were common enough with us and in great variety;
I know not in what country morê kinds are to be found.
There were no fewer than five species of teal, the commonest a dark brown bird with black mottlings; another,
very common, was pale grey, the plumage beautifully
barred and pencilled with brown and black; then we
had the blue-winged teal, a maroon-red duck which
ranges from Patagonia to California; the ringed teal,
with salmon-coloured breast and velvet-black collar;
the Brazilian teal, a lovely olive-brown and velvet-
black duck, with crimson beak and legs. There were
two pintails, one of which was the most abundant
species in the country; also a widgeon, a lake duck, a
shoveller duck, with red plumage, grey head and neck,
and blue wings; and two species of the long-legged
whistling or tree duck. Another common species was
the rosy-billed duck, now to be seen on ornamental
waters in England; and occasionally we saw the wild
Muscovy duck, called Royal duck by the natives, but
it was a rare visitor so far south. We also had geese
and swans: the upland geese from the Magellanic Straits
that came to us in winter—that is to say, our winter
from May to August. And there were two swans, the
black-necked, which has black flesh and is unfit to eat,
and the white or Coscoroba swan, as good a table bird
as there is in the world. And oddly enough this bird
has been known to the natives as a 'goose' since the
discovery of America, and now after three centuries
our scientific ornithologists have made the discovery
that it is a link between the geese and swans, but is
more goose than swan. It is a beautiful white bird,
with bright red bill and legs, the wings tipped with

242   FAR AWAY AND LONG AGO

black; and has a loud musical cry of three notes, the last prolonged note with a falling inflection.

These were the birds we sought after in winter; but we could shoot for the table all the year round, for no sooner was it the ducks' pairing and breeding season than another bird-population from their breeding-grounds in the arctic and sub-arctic regions came on the scene—plover, sandpiper, godwit, curlew, whimbrel —a host of northern species that made the summer-dried pampas their winter abode.

My first attempt at duck-shooting was made at a pond not many minutes' walk from the house, where I found a pair of shoveller ducks, feeding in their usual way in the shallow water with head and neck immersed. Anxious not to fail in this first trial, I got down flat on the ground and crawled snake fashion for a distance of fifty or sixty yards, until I was less than twenty yards from the birds, when I fired and killed one.

That first duck was a great joy, and having succeeded so well with my careful tactics, I continued in the same way, confining my attention to pairs or small parties of three or four birds, when by patiently creeping a long distance through the grass I could get very close to them. In this way I shot teal, widgeon, pintail, shovellers, and finally the noble rosy-bill, which was esteemed for the table above all the others.

My brother, ambitious of a big bag, invariably went a distance from home in quest of the large flocks, and despised my way of duck-shooting; but it sometimes vexed him to find on his return from a day's expedition that I had succeeded in getting as many birds as himself without having gone much more than a mile from home.

Some months after I had started shooting I began to have trouble with my beloved gun, owing to a weakness it had developed in its lock—one of the infirmities incidental to age which the gunsmiths of

WILD-FOWLING ADVENTURES 243

Buenos Ayres were never able to cure effectively. Whenever it got bad I was permitted to put it into the cart sent to town periodically, to have it repaired, and would then go gunless for a week or ten days. On one of these occasions I one day saw a party of shoveller duck dibbling in a small rain-pool at the side of the plantation, within a dozen yards of the old moat which surrounded it. Ducks always appeared to be exceptionally tame and bold when I was without a gun, but the boldness of those shovellers was more than I could stand, and running to the house I got out the old blunderbuss, which I had never been forbidden to use, since no one had ever thought it possible that I should want to use such a monster of a gun. But I was desperate, and loading it for the first (and last) time, I went after those shovellers.

I had once been told that it would be impossible to shoot wild duck or anything with the blunderbuss unless one could get within a dozen yards of them, on account of its tremendous scattering power. Well, by going along the bottom of the moat, which was luckily without water just then, I could get as near the birds as I liked and kill the whole flock. When I arrived abreast of the pool I crept up the grassy crumbling outside bank, and resting the ponderous barrel on the top of the bank, fired at the shovellers at a distance of about fifteen yards, and killed nothing, but received a kick which sent me flying to the bottom of the fosse. It was several days before I got over that pain in my shoulder.

Later on there was a period of trouble and scarcity in the land. There was war, and the city from which we obtained our supplies was besieged by an army from the 'upper provinces' which had come down to break the power and humble the pride of Buenos Ayres. Our elders missed their tea and coffee most

244 FAR AWAY AND LONG AGO

but our anxiety was that we should soon be without powder and shot. My brother constantly warned me not to be wasteful, although he fired half a dozen shots to my one without getting more birds for the table. At length there came a day when there was little shot left—just about enough to fill one shot-pouch—and knowing it was his intention to have a day out, I sneaked into the gun-room and loaded my fowling-piece just to have one shot more. He was going to try for upland geese that day, and, as I had expected, carried off all the shot.

After he had gone I took my gun, and being determined to make the most of my one shot, refused to be tempted by any of the small parties of duck I found in the pools near home, even when they appeared quite tame. At length I encountered a good-sized flock of rosy-bills by the side of a marshy stream about two miles from home. It was a still, warm day in mid-winter, and the ducks were dozing on the green bank in a beautiful crowd, and as the land near them was covered with long grass, I saw it would be possible to get quite close to them. Leaving my pony at a good distance, I got down flat on the ground and began my long laborious crawl, and got within twenty-five yards of the flock. Never had I had such a chance before! As I peeped through the grass and herbage I imagined all sorts of delightful things—my brother far away vainly firing long shots at the wary geese, and his return and disgust at the sight of my heap of noble rosy-bills, all obtained near home at one shot!

Then I fired just as the birds, catching sight of my cap, raised their long necks in alarm. Bang! Up they rose with a noise of wings, leaving not one behind! Vainly I watched the flock, thinking that some of the birds I must have hit would soon be seen to waver in their course and then drop to earth. But none wavered

WILD-FOWLING ADVENTURES 245

or fell. I went home as much puzzled as disappointed. Late in the day my brother returned with one upland goose and three or four ducks, and inquired if I had had any luck. I told him my sad story, whereupon he burst out laughing and informed me that he had taken care to draw the shot from my gun before going out. He was up to my little tricks, he said; he had seen what I had done, and was not going to allow me to waste the little shot we had left!

Our duck-shooting was carried on under difficulties during those days. We searched for ammunition at all the houses for some leagues around, and at one house we found and purchased a quantity of exceedingly coarse gunpowder, with grain almost the size of canary-seed. They told us it was cannon-powder, and to make it fit for use in our fowling-pieces we ground it fine with glass and stone bottles for rollers on a tin plate. Shot we could not find, so had to make it for ourselves by cutting up plates of lead into small square bits with a knife and hammer.

Eventually the civil war, which had dragged on for a long time, brought an unexpected danger to our house and caused us to turn our minds to more important things than ducks. I have said that the city was besieged by an army from the provinces, but away on the southern frontier of the province of Buenos Ayres the besieged party, or faction, had a powerful friend in an estanciero in those parts who was friendly with the Indians, and who collected an army of Indians hungry for loot, and gauchos, mostly criminals and deserters, who in those days were accustomed to come from all parts of the country to put themselves under the protection of this good man.

This horde of robbers and enthusiasts was now advancing upon the capital to raise the siege, and each day brought us alarming reports—whether true

*I 956

246 FAR AWAY AND LONG AGO

or false we could not know — of depredations they were committing on their march. The good man, their commander, was not a soldier, and there was no pretence of discipline of any kind; the men, it was said, did what they liked, swarming over the country on the line of march in bands, sacking and burning houses, killing or driving off the cattle, and so on. Our house was unfortunately on the main road running south from the capital, and directly in the way of the coming rabble. That the danger was a real and very great one we could see in the anxious faces of our elders; besides, nothing was now talked of but the coming army and of all we had to fear.

At this juncture my brother took it upon himself to make preparations for the defence of the house. Our oldest brother was away, shut up in the besieged city, but the three of us at home determined to make a good fight, and we set to work cleaning and polishing up our firearms—the Tower musket, the awful blunderbuss, the three fowling-pieces, double- and single-barrelled, and the two big horse-pistols and an old revolver. We collected all the old lead we could find about the place and made bullets in a couple of bullet-moulds we had found—one for ounce and one for small bullets, three to the ounce. The fire to melt the lead was in a shelter we had made behind an outhouse, and here one day, in spite of all our precautions, we were discovered at work, with rows and pyramids of shining bullets round us, and our secret was out. We were laughed at as a set of young fools for our pains. 'Never mind,' said my brother. 'Let them mock now; by-and-by when it comes to choosing between having our throats cut and defending ourselves, they will probably be glad the bullets were made.'

But though they laughed, our work was not inter-

WILD-FOWLING ADVENTURES 247

fered with, and some hundreds of bullets were turned out and made quite a pretty show.

Meanwhile the besiegers were not idle; they had in their army a cavalry officer who had had a long experience of frontier warfare and had always been successful in his fights with the pampas Indians; and this man, with a picked force composed of veteran fighters, was dispatched against the barbarians. They had already crossed the Salado river and were within two or three easy marches of us, when the small disciplined force met and gave them battle and utterly routed them. Indians and gauchos were sent flying south like thistle-down before the wind; but all being well mounted, not many were killed.

So ended that danger, and I think we boys were all a little disappointed that no use had been made of our bright beautiful bullets. I am sure my brother was; but soon after that he left home for a distant country, and our shooting and other adventures together were ended for ever.

CHAPTER XXII

BOYHOOD'S END

The book—The Saladero, or killing-grounds, and their smell—
Walls built of bullocks' skulls—A pestilential city—River
water and *aljibe* water—Days of lassitude—Novel scenes—
Home again—Typhus—My first day out—Birthday reflections—What I asked of life—A boy's mind—A brother's resolution—End of our thousand and one nights—A reading
spell—My boyhood ends in disaster.

THIS book has already run to a greater length than was
intended; nevertheless there must be yet another chapter or two to bring it to a proper ending, which I can only
find by skipping over three years of my life, and so getting at once to the age of fifteen. For that was a time
of great events and serious changes, bodily and mental,
which practically brought the happy time of my boyhood
to an end.

On looking back over the book, I find that on three
or four occasions I have placed some incident in the
wrong chapter or group, thus making it take place a
year or so too soon or too late. These small errors of
memory are, however, not worth altering now: so
long as the scene or event is rightly remembered and
pictured it doesn't matter much whether I was six or
seven or eight years old at the time. I find, too, that
I have omitted many things which perhaps deserved a
place in the book—scenes and events which are vividly
remembered, but which unfortunately did not come
up at the right moment, and so were left out.

Of these scenes unconsciously omitted, I will now
give one which should have appeared in the chapter
describing my first visit to Buenos Ayres city: placed

248

BOYHOOD'S END 249

here it will serve very well as an introduction to this chapter.

In those days, and indeed down to the seventies of last century, the south side of the capital was the site of the famous Saladero, or killing-grounds, where the fat cattle, horses, and sheep brought in from all over the country were slaughtered every day, some to supply the town with beef and mutton and to make *charque*, or sun-dried beef, for exportation to Brazil, where it was used to feed the slaves, but the greater number of the animals, including all the horses, were killed solely for their hides and tallow. The grounds covered a space of three or four square miles, where there were cattle enclosures made of upright posts placed close together, and some low buildings scattered about. To this spot were driven endless flocks of sheep, half or wholly wild horses, and dangerous-looking, long-horned cattle in herds of a hundred or so to a thousand, each moving in its cloud of dust, with noise of bellowings and bleatings and furious shouting of the drovers as they galloped up and down, urging the doomed animals on. When the beasts arrived in too great numbers to be dealt with in the buildings, you could see hundreds of cattle being killed in the open all over the grounds in the old barbarous way the gauchos use, every animal being first lassoed, then hamstrung, then its throat cut—a hideous and horrible spectacle, with a suitable accompaniment of sounds in the wild shouts of the slaughterers and the awful bellowings of the tortured beasts. Just where the animal was knocked down and killed, it was stripped of its hide and the carcass cut up, a portion of the flesh and the fat being removed and all the rest left on the ground to be devoured by the pariah dogs, the carrion-hawks, and a multitude of screaming black-headed gulls always in attendance. The blood so abundantly shed from day to day, mixing

250   FAR AWAY AND LONG AGO

with the dust, had formed a crust half a foot thick all
over the open space: let the reader try to imagine the
smell of this crust and of tons of offal and flesh and
bones lying everywhere in heaps. But no, it cannot
be imagined. The most dreadful scenes, the worst in
Dante's *Inferno*, for example, can be visualized by the
inner eye; and sounds, too, are conveyed to us in a
description so that they can be heard mentally; but it
is not so with smells. The reader can only take my
word for it that *this* smell was probably the worst ever
known on the earth, unless he accepts as true the story
of Tobit and the 'fishy fumes' by means of which that
ancient hero defended himself in his retreat from the
pursuing devil.

It was the smell of carrion, of putrefying flesh, and
of that old and ever-newly moistened crust of dust
and coagulated blood. It was, or seemed, a curiously
substantial and stationary smell; travellers approaching or leaving the capital by the great south road,
which skirted the killing-grounds, would hold their
noses and ride a mile or so at a furious gallop until
they got out of the abominable stench.

One extraordinary feature of the private *quintas*
or orchards and plantations in the vicinity of the
Saladero was the walls or hedges. These were built
entirely of cows' skulls, seven, eight, or nine deep,
placed evenly like stones, the horns projecting. Hundreds of thousands of skulls had been thus used, and
some of the old, very long walls, crowned with green
grass and with creepers and wild flowers growing from
the cavities in the bones, had a strangely picturesque
but somewhat uncanny appearance. As a rule there
were rows of old Lombardy poplars behind these strange
walls or fences.

In those days bones were not utilized: they were
thrown away, and those who wanted walls in a stone-

BOYHOOD'S END 251

.ess land, where bricks and wood for palings were dear
to buy, found in the skulls a useful substitute.

The abomination I have described was but one of
many—the principal and sublime stench in a city of
evil smells, a populous city built on a plain without
drainage and without water-supply beyond that which
was sold by watermen in buckets, each bucketful
containing about half a pound of red clay in solution.
It is true that the best houses had *aljibes*, or cisterns,
under the courtyard, where the rain-water from the
flat roofs was deposited. I remember that water well:
you always had one or two to half a dozen scarlet
wrigglers, the larvae of mosquitoes, in a tumblerful,
and you drank your water, quite calmly, wrigglers and
all!

All this will serve to give an idea of the condition
of the city at that time from the sanitary point of
view, and this state of things lasted down to the seventies of the last century, when Buenos Ayres came to be
the chief pestilential city of the globe and was obliged
to call in engineers from England to do something to
save the inhabitants from extinction.

When I was in my fifteenth year, before any changes
had taken place and the great outbreaks of cholera and
yellow fever were yet to come, I spent four or five weeks
in the city, greatly enjoying the novel scenes and new
life. After about ten or twelve days I began to feel
tired and languid, and this feeling grew on me day by
day until it became almost painful to exert myself to
visit even my most favoured haunts—the great South
Market, where cage-birds were to be seen in hundreds,
green paroquets, cardinals, and bishop-birds predomin-
ating; or to the river front, where I spent much time
fishing for little silvery king-fishes from the rocks; or
further away to the *quintas* and gardens on the cliff,
where I first feasted my eyes on the sight of orange

252   FAR AWAY AND LONG AGO

groves laden with golden fruit amidst the vivid green
polished foliage, and old olive-trees with black egg-shaped
fruit showing among the grey leaves.

And through it all the feeling of lassitude continued,
and was, I thought, due to the fact that I was on foot
instead of on horseback, and walking on a stony pavement instead of on a green turf.   It never occurred to
me that there might be another cause, that I was
breathing in a pestilential atmosphere and that the
poison was working in me.

Leaving town I travelled by some conveyance to
spend a night at a friend's house, and next morning
set out for home on horseback.   I had about twenty-
seven miles across country to ride and never touched
a road, and I was no sooner on my way than my spirits
revived; I was well and unspeakably happy again, on
horseback on the wide green plain, drinking in the pure
air like a draught of eternal life.   It was autumn, and
the plain as far as one could see on every side a moist
brilliant green, with a crystal blue sky above, over which
floated shining white clouds.   The healthy glad feeling
lasted through my ride and for a day or two after,
during which I revisited my favourite haunts in the
grounds, rejoicing to be with my beloved birds and trees
once more.

Then the hateful town feeling of lassitude returned
on me and all my vigour was gone, all pleasure in
life ended.   Thereafter for a fortnight I spent the
time moping about the house; then there was a spell
of frosty weather with a bleak, cutting wind to tell
us that it was winter, which even in those latitudes
can be very cold.   One day after early dinner my mother
and sisters went in the carriage to pay a visit to a neigh-
bouring estancia, and my brothers being out or absent
from home I was left alone.   The veranda appeared
to me the warmest place I could find, as the sun shone on

BOYHOOD'S END   253

it warm and bright, and there I settled down on a chair
placed against the wall at the side of a heap of sacks of
meal or something which had been left there, and
formed a nice shelter from the wind.

The house was strangely quiet, and the westering
sun shining full on me made me feel quite comfortable,
and in a little while I fell asleep. The sun set and it
grew bitterly cold, but I did not wake, and when my
mother returned and inquired for me I could not be .
found. Finally the whole household turned out with
lanterns and searched for me up and down through the
plantation, and the hunt was still going on when, about
ten o'clock at night, someone hurrying along the
veranda stumbled on me in my sheltered corner by
the sacks, still in my chair but unconscious and in a
burning fever. It was the dread typhus, an almost
obsolete malady in Europe, and in fact in all civilized
countries, but not uncommon at that date in the pestilential city. It was wonderful that I lived through
it in a place where we were out of reach of doctors and
apothecaries, with only my mother's skill in nursing
and her knowledge of such drugs as were kept in the
house to save me. She nursed me day and night for
the three weeks during which the fever lasted, and when
it left me, a mere shadow of my former self, I was
dumb—not even a little Yes or No could I articulate
however hard I tried, and it was at last concluded that
I would never speak again. However, after about a
fortnight, the lost faculty came back, to my mother's
inexpressible joy.

Winter was nearing its end when one morning in
late July I ventured out of doors for the first time,
though still but a skeleton, a shadow of my former
self. It was a windy day of brilliant sunshine, a day
I shall never forget, and the effect of the air and the sun
and smell of earth and early flowers, and the sounds of

254 FAR AWAY AND LONG AGO

wild birds, with the sight of the intensely green young
grass and the vast crystal dome of heaven above, was
like deep draughts of some potent liquor that made the
blood dance in my veins. Oh, what an inexpressible,
immeasurable joy to be alive and not dead, to have my
feet still on the earth, and drink in the wind and sunshine
once more! But the pleasure was more than I could
endure in that feeble state; the chilly wind pierced me
like needles of ice, my senses swam, and I would have
fallen to the ground if my elder brother had not caught
me in his arms and taken me back to the house.

In spite of that fainting fit I was happy again with
the old happiness, and from day to day I regained
strength, until one day in early August I was suddenly
reminded that it was my anniversary by my brothers
and sisters all coming to me with birthday presents,
which they had been careful to provide beforehand,
and congratulations on my recovery.

Fifteen years old! This was indeed the most memorable day of my life, for on that evening I began to think
about myself, and my thoughts were strange and unhappy thoughts to me—what I was, what I was in the
world for, what I wanted, what destiny was going to
make of me! Or was it for me to do just what I wished,
to shape my own destiny, as my elder brothers had done?
It was the first time such questions had come to me, and
I was startled at them. It was as though I had only
just become conscious; I doubt that I have ever been
fully conscious before. I had lived till now in a paradise
of vivid sense-impressions in which all thoughts came
to me saturated with emotion, and in that mental state
reflection is well-nigh impossible. Even the idea of
death, which had come as a surprise, had not made me
reflect. Death was a person, a monstrous being who
had sprung upon me in my flowery paradise and had
inflicted a wound with a poisoned dagger in my flesh.

BOYHOOD'S END   255

Then had come the knowledge of immortality for the soul, and the wound was healed, or partly so, for a time at all events; after which the one thought that seriously troubled me was that I could not always remain a boy. To pass from boyhood to manhood was not so bad as dying; nevertheless it was a change painful to contemplate. That everlasting delight and wonder, rising to rapture, which was in the child and boy would wither away and vanish, and in its place there would be that dull low kind of satisfaction which men have in the set task, the daily and hourly intercourse with others of a like condition, and in eating and drinking and sleeping. I could not, for example, think of so advanced an age as fifteen without the keenest apprehension. And now I was actually at that age—at that parting of the ways, as it seemed to me.

What, then, did I want?—what did I ask to have? If the question had been put to me then, and if I had been capable of expressing what was in me, I should have replied: I want only to keep what I have; to rise each morning and look out on the sky and the grassy dew-wet earth from day to day, from year to year. To watch each June and July for spring, to feel the same old sweet surprise and delight at the appearance of each familiar flower, every new-born insect, every bird returned once more from the north. To listen in a trance of delight to the wild notes of the golden plover coming once more to the great plain, flying, flying south, flock succeeding flock the whole day long. Oh, those wild beautiful cries of the golden plover! I could exclaim with Hafiz, with but one word changed: 'If after a thousand years that sound should float o'er my tomb, my bones uprising in their gladness would dance in the sepulchre!' To climb trees and put my hand down in the deep hot nest of the Bien-te-veo and feel the hot eggs—the five long-pointed cream-coloured eggs with

256 FAR AWAY AND LONG AGO

chocolate spots and splashes at the larger end. To lie on a grassy bank with the blue water between me and beds of tall bulrushes, listening to the mysterious sounds of the wind and of hidden rails and coots and courlans conversing together in strange human-like tones; to let my sight dwell and feast on the *camaloté* flower amid its floating masses of moist vivid green leaves —the large alamanda-like flower of a purest divine yellow that when plucked sheds its lovely petals, to leave you with nothing but a green stem in your hand. To ride at noon on the hottest days, when the whole earth is a-glitter with illusory water, and see the cattle and horses in thousands, covering the plain at their watering-places, to visit some haunt of large birds at that still, hot hour and see storks, ibises, grey herons, egrets of a dazzling whiteness, and rose-coloured spoonbills and flamingoes, standing in the shallow water in which their motionless forms are reflected. To lie on my back on the rust-brown grass in January and gaze up at the wide hot whity-blue sky, peopled with millions and myriads of glistening balls of thistledown, ever, ever floating by; to gaze and gaze until they are to me living things and I, in an ecstasy, am with them, floating in that immense shining void!

And now it seemed that I was about to lose it— this glad emotion which had made the world what it was to me, an enchanted realm, a nature at once natural and supernatural; it would fade and lessen imperceptibly day by day, year by year, as I became more and more absorbed in the dull business of life, until it would be lost as effectually as if I had ceased to see and hear and palpitate, and my warm body had grown cold and stiff in death, and, like the dead and the living, I should be unconscious of my loss.

It was not a unique nor a singular feeling: it is known to other boys, as I have read and heard; also

BOYHOOD'S END 257

I have occasionally met with one who, in a rare moment of confidence, has confessed that he had been troubled at times at the thought of all he would lose. But I doubt that it was ever more keenly felt than in my case; I doubt, too, that it is common or strong in English boys, considering the conditions in which they exist. For restraint is irksome to all beings, from a black-beetle or an earthworm to an eagle, or, to go higher still in the scale, to an orang-utan or a man; it is felt most keenly by the young, in our species at all events, and the British boy suffers the greatest restraint during the period when the call of nature, the instincts of play and adventure, are most urgent. Naturally, he looks eagerly forward to the time of escape, which he fondly imagines will be when his boyhood is over and he is free of masters.

To come back to my own case: I did not and could not know that it was an exceptional case, that my feeling for nature was something more than the sense of pleasure in sun and rain and wind and earth and water and in liberty of motion, which is universal in children, but was in part due to a faculty which is not universal or common. The fear, then, was an idle one, but I had good reason for it when I considered how it had been with my elder brothers, who had been as little restrained as myself, especially that masterful adventurous one, now in a distant country thousands of miles from home, who, at about the age at which I had now arrived, had made himself his own master, to do what he liked with his own life. I had seen him at *his* parting of the ways, how resolutely he had abandoned his open-air habits, everything in fact that had been his delight, to settle down to sheer hard mental work, and this at our home on the pampas where there were no masters, and even the books and instruments required for his studies could only be procured with great difficulty and after

258 FAR AWAY AND LONG AGO

long delays. I remember one afternoon when we were gathered in the dining-room for tea, he was reading, and my mother coming in looked over his shoulder and said: 'You are reading a novel: don't you think all that romantic stuff will take your mind off your studies?'

Now he 'll flare up, said I to myself; he 's so confoundly independent and touchy no one can say a word to him. It surprised me when he answered quietly: 'Yes, mother, I know, but I must finish this book now; it will be the last novel I shall read for some years.' And so it was, I believe.

His resolution impressed us even more in another matter. He had an extraordinary talent for inventing stories, mostly of wars and wild adventures with plenty of fighting in them, and whenever we boys were all together, which was usually after we had gone to bed and put the candle out, he would begin one of his wonderful tales and go on for hours, we all wide awake, listening in breathless silence. At length towards midnight the flow of the narrative would suddenly stop, and after an interval we would all begin to cry out to him to go on. 'Oh, you *are* awake!' he would exclaim, with a chuckle of laughter. 'Very well, then, you know just where we are in our history, to be resumed another day. Now you can go to sleep.' On the following evening he would take up the tale, which would often last an entire week, to be followed by another just as long, then another, and so on—our thousand and one nights. And this delightful yarn-spinning was also dropped as he became more and more absorbed in his mathematical and other studies.

To this day I can recall portions of those tales, especially those in which birds and beasts instead of men were the actors, and so much did we miss them that sometimes when we were all assembled of an afternoon we would start begging him for a story—'just one

BOYHOOD'S END   259

more, and the longer the better,' we would say to tempt
him.   And he, a little flattered at our keen appreciation
of his talent as a yarn-spinner, would appear inclined
to yield.   'Well, now, what story shall I tell you?' he
would say; and then, just when we were settling down
to listen, he would shout: 'No, no, no more stories,' and
to put the matter from him he would snatch up a book
and order us to hold our tongues or clear out of the
room!

It was not for me to follow his lead; I had not the
intellect or strength of will for such tasks, and not only
on that memorable evening of my anniversary, but for
days afterwards I continued in a troubled state of mind,
ashamed of my ignorance, my indolence, my disinclination to any kind of mental work—ashamed
even to think that my delight in nature and wish for
no other thing in life was merely due to the fact that
while the others were putting away childish things as
they grew up, I alone refused to part with them.

The result of all these deliberations was that I tem-
porized: I would not, I could not, give up the rides and
rambles that took up most of my time, but I would try
to overcome my disinclination to serious reading.
There were plenty of books in the house—it was always
a puzzle to me how we came to have so many.   I was
familiar with their appearance on the shelves—they
had been before me since I first opened my eyes—their
shape, size, colour, even their titles, and that was all
I knew about them.   A general Natural History and
two little works by James Rennie on the habits and
faculties of birds was all the literature suited to my
wants in the entire collection of three or four hundred
volumes.   For the rest, I had read a few story-books
and novels: but we had no novels; when one came into
the house it would be read and lent to our next neighbour
five or six miles away, and he in turn would lend to

260   FAR AWAY AND LONG AGO

another, twenty miles further on, and so on until it disappeared in space.

I made a beginning with Rollin's *Ancient History* in two huge quarto volumes; I fancy it was the large clear type and numerous plates which illustrated it that determined my choice. Rollin, the good old priest, opened a new wonderful world to me, and instead of the tedious task I had feared the reading would prove, it was as delightful as it had formerly been to listen to my brother's endless histories of imaginary heroes and their wars and adventures.

Still athirst for history, after finishing Rollin I began fingering other works of that kind: there was Whiston's *Josephus*, too ponderous a book to be held in the hands when read out of doors; and there was Gibbon in six stately volumes. I was not yet able to appreciate the lofty artificial style, and soon fell on something better suited to my boyish taste in letters—a *History of Christianity* in, I think, sixteen or eighteen volumes of a convenient size. The simple natural diction attracted me, and I was soon convinced that I could not have stumbled on more fascinating reading than the lives of the Fathers of the Church included in some of the earlier volumes, especially that of Augustine, the greatest of all: how beautiful and marvellous his life was, and his mother Monica's! what wonderful books he wrote! —his *Confessions* and *City of God*, from which long excerpts were given in this volume.

These biographies sent me to another old book, *Leland on Revelation*, which told me much I was curious to know about the mythologies and systems of philosophy of the ancients—the innumerable false cults which had flourished in a darkened world before the dawn of the true religion.

Next came Carlyle's *French Revolution* and at last Gibbon, and I was still deep in the *Decline and Fall*

BOYHOOD'S END

when disaster came to us: my father was practically ruined, owing, as I have said in a former chapter, to his childlike trust in his fellow-men, and we quitted the home he had counted as a permanent one, which in due time would have become his property had he but made his position secure by a proper deed on first consenting to take over the place in its then ruinous condition.

Thus ended, sadly enough, the enchanting years of my boyhood; and here, too, the book should finish: but having gone so far, I will venture a little further and give a brief account of what followed and the life which, for several succeeding years, was to be mine—the life, that is to say, of the mind and spirit.

CHAPTER XXIII

A DARKENED LIFE

A severe illness—Case pronounced hopeless—How it affected me
—Religious doubts and a mind distressed—Lawless thoughts
—Conversation with an old gaucho about religion—George
Combe and the desire for immortality.

AFTER we had gone back impoverished to our old home
where I first saw the light—which was still my father's
property and all he had left—I continued my reading,
and was so taken up with the affairs of the universe,
seen and unseen, that I did not feel the change in our
position and comforts too greatly. I took my share
in the rough work and was much out of doors on horseback looking after the animals, and not unhappy. I
was already very tall and thin at that time, in my
sixteenth year, still growing rapidly, and though ath-
letic, it was probable that some weakness had been left
in me by the fever. At all events, I had scarcely
settled down to the new way of life before a fresh blow
fell upon me, a malady which, though it failed to kill
me, yet made shipwreck of all my new-born earthly
hopes and dreams, and a dismal failure of my after life.

One day I undertook, unaided, to drive home a
small troop of cattle we had purchased at a distance
of a good many leagues, and was in the saddle from
morning till after dark in a continuous flooding rain
and violent wind. The wind was against me, and the
beasts were incessantly trying to turn and rush back
to the place they had been taken from, and the fight
with wind and cattle went wearily on, the driving rain
gradually soaking through my woollen poncho, then
through my clothes to my skin, and trickling down

262

A DARKENED LIFE 263

until my long boots were full and slopping over at the knees. For the last half of that mid-winter day my feet and legs were devoid of feeling. The result of it was rheumatic fever and years of bad health, with constant attacks of acute pain and violent palpitation of the heart which would last for hours at a stretch. From time to time I was sent or taken to consult a doctor in the city, and in that way from first to last I was in the hands of pretty well all the English doctors in the place, but they did me no permanent good, nor did they say anything to give me a hope of complete recovery. Eventually we were told that it was a practically hopeless case, that I had 'outgrown my strength,' and had a permanently bad heart and might drop down at any moment.

Naturally this pronouncement had a most disastrous effect on me. That their diagnosis proved in the end to be wrong mattered nothing, since the injury had been done and could not be undone if I lived a century. For the blow had fallen at the most critical period in life, the period of transition when the newly-awakened mind is in its freshest, most receptive stage, and is most curious, most eager, when knowledge is most readily assimilated, and, above everything, when the foundations of character and the entire life of the man are laid.

I speak, it will be understood, of a mind that had not been trained or pressed into a mould or groove by schoolmasters and schools—of a mind that was a forest wilding rather than a plant, one in ten thousand like it, grown under glass in a prepared soil, in a nursery.

That I had to say good-bye to all thoughts of a career, all bright dreams of the future which recent readings had put into my mind, was not felt as the chief loss, it was in fact a small matter compared with the dreadful thought that I must soon resign this earthly

264   FAR AWAY AND LONG AGO

life which was so much more to me, as I could not help
thinking, than to most others. I was like that young
man with a ghastly face I had seen bound to a post in
our barn; or like any wretched captive, tied hand and
foot and left to lie there until it suited his captor to
come back and cut his throat or thrust him through
with a spear, or cut him into strips with a sword, in a
leisurely manner so as to get all the satisfaction possible
out of the exercise of his skill and the spectacle of
gushing blood and his victim's agony.

Nor was this all nor even the worst which had befallen
me; I now discovered that in spite of all my strivings
after the religious mind, that old dread of annihilation
which I had first experienced as a small child was not
dead as I had fondly imagined, but still lived and worked
in me. This visible world—this paradise of which I
had had so far but a fleeting glimpse—the sun and moon
and other worlds peopling all space with their brilliant
constellations, and still other suns and systems, so utterly
remote, in such inconceivable numbers as to appear
to our vision as a faint luminous mist in the sky—all
this universe which had existed for millions and billions
of ages, or from eternity, would have existed in vain,
since now it was doomed with my last breath, my last
gleam of consciousness, to come to nothing. For that
was how the thought of death presented itself to me.

Against this appalling thought I struggled with all
my power, and prayed and prayed again, morning,
noon, and night, wrestling with God, as the phrase was,
trying as it were to wring something from His hands
which would save me, and which He, for no reason that
I could discover, withheld from me.

It was not strange in these circumstances that I
became more and more absorbed in the religious literature of which we had a good amount on our book-
shelves—theology, sermons, meditations for every day

A DARKENED LIFE 265

in the year, *The Whole Duty of Man, A Call to the Unconverted*, and many other old works of a similar character.

Among these I found one entitled, if I remember rightly, *An Answer to the Infidel*, and this work, which I took up eagerly in the expectation that it would allay those maddening doubts perpetually rising in my mind and be a help and comfort to me, only served to make matters worse, at all events for a time. For in this book I was first made acquainted with many of the arguments of the free-thinkers, both of the Deists who were opposed to the Christian creed, and of those who denied the truth of all supernatural religion. And the answers to the arguments were not always convincing. It was idle, then, to seek for proofs in the books. The books themselves, after all their arguments, told me as much when they said that only by faith could a man be saved. And to the sad question: 'How was it to be attained?' the only answer was, by striving and striving until it came. And as there was nothing else to do I continued striving, with the result that I believed and did not believe, and my soul, or rather my hope of immortality, trembled in the balance.

This, from first to last, was the one thing that mattered; so much was it to me that in reading one of the religious books entitled *The Saints' Everlasting Rest*, in which the pious author, Richard Baxter, expatiates on and labours to make his readers realize the condition of the eternally damned, I have said to myself: 'If an angel, or one returned from the dead, could come to assure me that life does not end with death, that we mortals are destined to live for ever, but that for me there can be no blessed hereafter on account of my want of faith, and because I loved or worshipped Nature rather than the Author of my being, it would be, not a message of despair, but of consolation; for in that

266 FAR AWAY AND LONG AGO

dreadful place to which I should be sent, I should be alive and not dead, and have my memories of earth, and perhaps meet and have communion there with others of like mind with myself, and with recollections like mine.'

This was but one of many lawless thoughts which assailed me at this time. Another, very persistent, was the view I took of the sufferings of the Saviour of mankind. Why, I asked, were they made so much of?—why was it said that He suffered as no man had suffered? It was nothing but the physical pain which thousands and millions have had to endure! And if I could be as sure of immortality as Jesus, death would be no more to me than the prick of a thorn. What would it matter to be nailed to a cross and perish in a slow agony if I believed that, the agony over, I should sit down refreshed to sup in paradise? The worst of it was that when I tried to banish these bitter, rebellious ideas, taking them to be the whisperings of the Evil One, as the books taught, the quick reply would come that the supposed Evil One was nothing but the voice of my own reason striving to make itself heard.

But the contest could not be abandoned; devil or reason, or whatever it was, must be overcome, else there was no hope for me; and such is the powerful effect of fixing all one's thoughts on one object, assisted no doubt by the reflex effect on the mind of prayer, that in due time I did succeed in making myself believe all I wished to believe, and had my reward, since after many days or weeks of mental misery there would come beautiful intervals of peace and of more than peace, a new and surprising experience, a state of exaltation, when it would seem to me that I was lifted or translated into a purely spiritual atmosphere and was in communion and one with the unseen world.

It was wonderful. At last and for ever my Dark

A DARKENED LIFE 267

Night of the Soul was over; no more bitter broodings
and mocking whispers and shrinkings from the awful
phantom of death continually hovering near me; and,
above all, no more 'difficulties'—the rocky barriers
I had vainly beat and bruised myself against. For I
had been miraculously lifted over them and set safely
down on the other side, where it was all plain walking.

Unhappily, these blissful intervals would not last
long. A recollection of something I had heard or
read would come back to startle me out of the confident happy mood; reason would revive as from a
benumbed or hypnotized condition, and the mocking
voice would be heard telling me that I had been under
a delusion. Once more I would abhor and shudder
at the black phantom, and when the thought of annihilation was most insistent, I would often recall the
bitter, poignant words about death and immortality
spoken to me about two years before by an old gaucho
landowner who had been our neighbour in my former
home.

He was a rough, rather stern-looking man, with a
mass of silver-white hair and grey eyes; a gaucho in
his dress and primitive way of life, the owner of a little
land and a few animals—the small remnant of the
estancia which had once belonged to his people. But
he was a vigorous old man, who spent half of his day
on horseback, looking after the animals, his only living.
One day he was at our house, and coming out to where
I was doing something in the grounds, he sat down on a
bench and called me to him. I went gladly enough,
thinking that he had some interesting bird news to give
me. He remained silent for some time, smoking a
cigar, and staring at the sky as if watching the smoke
vanish in the air. At length he opened fire.

'Look,' he said, 'you are only a boy, but you can
tell me something I don't know. Your parents read

268   FAR AWAY AND LONG AGO

books, and you listen to their conversation and learn things. We are Roman Catholics, and you are Protestants. We call you heretics and say that for such there is no salvation. Now I want you to tell me what is the difference between our religion and yours.'

I explained the matter as well as I knew how, and added, somewhat maliciously, that the main difference was his religion was a corrupt form of Christianity and ours a pure one.

This had no effect on him; he went on smoking and staring at the sky as if he hadn't heard me. Then he began again: 'Now I know. These differences are nothing to me, and though I was curious to know what they were, they are not worth talking about, because, as I know, all religions are false.'

'What did he mean—how did he know?' I asked, very much surprised.

'The priests tell us,' he replied, 'that we must believe and live a religious life in this world to be saved. Your priests tell you the same, and as there is no other world and we have no souls, all they say must be false. You see all this with your eyes,' he continued, waving his hands to indicate the whole visible world. 'And when you shut them or go blind you see no more. It is the same with our brains. We think of a thousand things and remember, and when the brain decays we forget everything, and we die, and everything dies with us. Have not the cattle eyes to see and brains to think and remember too? And when they die no priest tells us that they have a soul and have to go to purgatory, or wherever he likes to send them. Now, in return for what you told me, I 've told you something you didn't know.'

It came as a great shock to me to hear this. Hitherto I had thought that what was wrong with our native friends was that they believed too much, and this

A DARKENED LIFE 269

man—this good honest old gaucho we all respected —believed nothing; I tried to argue with him and told him he had said a dreadful thing, since every one knew in his heart that he had an immortal soul and had to be judged after death. He had distressed and even frightened me, but he went on calmly smoking and appeared not to be listening to me, and as he refused to speak I at last burst out: 'How do you know? Why do you say you know?'

At last he spoke. 'Listen. I was once a boy too, and I know that a boy of fourteen can understand things as well as a man. I was an only child, and my mother was a widow, and I was more than all the world to her, and she was more than everything else to me. We were alone together in the world—we two. Then she died, and what her loss was to me —how can I say it?—how could you understand? And after she was taken away and buried, I said: "She is not dead, and wherever she now is, in heaven or in purgatory, or in the sun, she will remember and come to me and comfort me." When it was dark I went out alone and sat at the end of the house, and spent hours waiting for her. "She will surely come," I said, "but I don't know whether I shall see her or not. Perhaps it will be just a whisper in my ear, perhaps a touch of her hand on mine, but I shall know that she is with me." And at last, worn out with waiting and watching, I went to my bed and said she will come to-morrow. And the next night and the next it was the same. Sometimes I would go up the ladder, always standing against the gable so that one could go up, and standing on the roof, look out over the plain and see where our horses were grazing. There I would sit or lie on the thatch for hours. And I would cry: "Come to me, my mother! I cannot live without you! Come soon—come soon, before I die of a broken heart!"

K 956

270   FAR AWAY AND LONG AGO

That was my cry every night, until worn out with my vigil I would go back to my room. And she never came, and at last I knew that she was dead and that we were separated for ever—that there is no life after death.'

His story pierced me to the heart, and without another word I left him, but I succeeded in making myself believe that his grief for his mother had made him mad, that as a boy he had got these delusions in his mind and had kept them all his life. Now this recollection haunted me. Then one day, with my mind in this troubled state, in reading George Combe's *Physiology* I came on a passage in which the question of the desire for immortality is discussed, his contention being that it is not universal, and as a proof of this he affirms that he himself had no such desire.

This came as a great shock to me, since up to the moment of reading it I had in my ignorance taken it for granted that the desire is inherent in every human being from the dawn of consciousness to the end of life, that it is our chief desire, and is an instinct of the soul like that physical instinct of the migratory bird which calls it annually from the most distant regions back to its natal home. I had also taken it for granted that our hope of immortality, or rather our belief in it, was founded on this same passion in us and in its universality. The fact that there were those who had no such desire was sufficient to show that it was no spiritual instinct or not of divine origin.

There were many more shocks of this kind—when I go back in memory to that sad time, it seems almost incredible to me that that poor doubtful faith in revealed religion still survived, and that the struggle still went on, but go on it certainly did.

To many of my readers, to all who have interested themselves in the history of religion and its effect on individual minds—its psychology—all I have written

A DARKENED LIFE

concerning my mental condition at that period will come as a twice-told tale, since thousands and millions of men have undergone similar experiences and have related them in numberless books. And here I must beg my reader to bear in mind that in the days of my youth we had not yet fallen into the indifference and scepticism which now infect the entire Christian world. In those days people still believed; and here in England, in the very centre and mind of the world, many thousands of miles from my rude wilderness, the champions of the Church were in deadly conflict with the Evolutionists. I knew nothing about all that: I had no modern books—those we had were mostly about a hundred years old. My fight up to this period was all on the old lines, and on this account I have related it as briefly as possible; but it had to be told, since it comes into the story of the development of my mind at that period. I have no doubt that my sufferings through these religious experiences were far greater than in the majority of cases, and this for the special reason which I have already intimated.

CHAPTER XXIV

LOSS AND GAIN

The soul's loneliness—My mother and her death—A mother's
love for her son—Her character—Anecdotes—A mystery and
a revelation—The autumnal migration of birds—Moonlight
vigils—My absent brother's return—He introduces me to
Darwin's works—A new philosophy of life—Conclusion.

THE mournful truth that a man—every man—must die
alone had been thrust sharply into my mind and kept
there by the frequent violent attacks of my malady I
suffered at that time, every one of which threatened to
be the last. And this sense and apprehension of loneliness at the moment of the severance of all earthly
ties and parting with light and life, was perhaps the
cause of the idea or notion which possessed me, that in
all our most intimate thoughts and reflections concerning our destiny and our deepest emotions, we are and
must be alone. Anyhow, in so far as these matters
are concerned, I never had nor desired a confidant.
In this connection I recall the last words spoken to me
by my younger brother, the being I loved best on earth
at that time and the one I had been more intimate with
than any other person I have ever known. This was
after the dark days and years had been overpast, when
I had had long periods of fairly good health and had
known happiness in the solitary places I loved to haunt,
communing with wild nature, with wild birds for
company.

He was with me in the ship in which I had taken
my passage 'home,' as I insisted on calling England,
to his amusement, and when we had grasped hands
for the last time and had said our last good-bye, he

LOSS AND GAIN 273

added this one more last word: 'Of all the people I have ever known you are the only one I don't know.'

It was a word, I imagine, never spoken by a mother of a loved son, her insight, born of her exceeding love, being so much greater than that of the closest friend and brother. I never breathed a word of my doubts and mental agonizings to my mother; I spoke to her only of my bodily sufferings; yet she knew it all, and I knew that she knew. And because she knew and understood the temper of my mind as well, she never questioned, never probed, but invariably when alone with me she would with infinite tenderness in her manner touch on spiritual things and tell me of her own state, the consolations of her faith which gave her peace and strength in all our reverses and anxieties.

I knew, too, that her concern at my state was the greater because it was not her first experience of a trouble of this kind. My elder long-absent brother had scarcely ceased to be a boy before throwing off all belief in the Christian creed and congratulating himself on having got rid of old wives' fables, as he scornfully expressed it. But never a word did he say to her of this change, and without a word she knew it, and when she spoke to us on the subject nearest to her heart and he listened in respectful silence, she knew the thought and feeling that was in him—that he loved her above everybody but was free of her creed.

He had been able to cast it off with a light heart because of his perfect health, since in that condition death is not in the mind—the mind refuses to admit the thought of it, so remote is it in that state that we regard ourselves as practically immortal. And, untroubled by that thought, the mind is clear and vigorous and unfettered. What, I have asked myself, even when striving after faith, would faith in another world have

274 FAR AWAY AND LONG AGO

mattered to me if I had not been suddenly sentenced to an early death, when the whole desire of my soul was life, nothing but life—to live for ever!

Then my mother died. Her perfect health failed her suddenly, and her decline was not long. But she suffered much, and on the last occasion of my being with her at her bedside she told me that she was very tired and had no fear of death, and would be glad to go but for the thought of leaving me in such a precarious state of health and with a mind distressed. Even then she put no questions to me, but only expressed the hope that her prayers for me would be answered and that at the last we should be together again.

I cannot say, as I might say in the case of any other relation or friend, that I had lost her. A mother's love for the child of her body differs essentially from all other affections, and burns with so clear and steady a flame that it appears like the one unchangeable thing in this earthly mutable life, so that when she is no longer present it is still a light to our steps and a consolation.

It came to me as a great surprise a few years ago to have my secret and most cherished feelings about my own mother expressed to me as I had never heard them expressed before by a friend who, albeit still young, has made himself a name in the world, one who had never known a mother, she having died during his infancy. He lamented that it had been so, not only on account of the motherless childhood and boyhood he had known, but chiefly because in after life it was borne in on him that he had been deprived of something infinitely precious which others have—the enduring and sustaining memory of a love which is unlike any other love known to mortals, and is almost a sense and prescience of immortality.

In reading, nothing goes to my heart like any true account of a mother and son's love for one another,

LOSS AND GAIN 275

such as we find in that true book I have already spoken of in a former chapter, Serge Aksakoff's *History of My Childhood*. Of other books I may cite Leigh Hunt's *Autobiography* in the early chapters. Reading the incidents he records of his mother's love and pity for all in trouble and her self-sacrificing acts, I have exclaimed: 'How like my mother! It is just how she would have acted!' I will give an instance here of her loving-kindness.

Some days after her death I had occasion to go to the house of one of our native neighbours—the humble rancho of poor people. It was not in my mind at the moment that I had not seen these people since my mother died, and on coming into the living-room the old mother of the family, who had grandchildren of my age, rose from her seat with tottering steps to meet me, and taking my hand in hers, with tears streaming from her eyes, cried: 'She has left us! She who called me mother on account of my years and her loving heart. It was she who was my mother and the mother of us all. What shall we do without her?'

Only after going out and getting on my horse it occurred to me that the old woman's memory went back to the time when she first knew my mother, a girl-wife, many years before I was born. She could remember numerous acts of love and compassion: that when one of her daughters died in childbirth in that very house, my mother, who was just then nursing me, went to give them whatever aid and comfort she could, and finding the child alive, took it home and nursed it, with me, at her own breasts for several days until a nurse was found.

From the time when I began to think for myself I used to wonder at her tolerance; for she was a saint in her life, spiritually-minded in the highest degree. To her, a child of New England parents and ancestors,

276 FAR AWAY AND LONG AGO

reared in an intensely religious atmosphere, the people
of the pampas among whom her lot was cast must have
appeared almost like the inhabitants of another world.
They were as strange to her soul, morally and spiritually,
as they were unlike her own people outwardly in language, dress, and customs. Yet she was able to affiliate
with them, to visit and sit at ease with them in their
lowliest ranchos, interesting herself as much in their
affairs as if she belonged to them. This sympathy and
freedom endeared her to them, and it was a grief to
some who were much attached to her that she was not
of their faith. She was a Protestant, and what that
exactly meant they didn't know, but they supposed
it was something very bad. Protestants, some of them
held, had been concerned in the crucifixion of the
Saviour; at all events, they would not go to mass or
confessional, and despised the saints, those glorified
beings who, under the Queen of Heaven, and with the
angels, were the guardians of Christian souls in this
life and their intercessors in the next. They were
anxious to save her, and when I was born, the same old
dame I have told about a page or two back, finding
that I had come into the world on St Dominic's Day,
set herself to persuade my mother to name me after
that saint, that being the religious custom of the country.
For if they should succeed in this it would be taken
as a sign of grace, that she was not a despiser of the
saints and her case hopeless. But my mother had
already fixed on a name for me and would not change
it for another, even to please her poor neighbours—
certainly not for such a name as Dominic; perhaps
there is not one in the calendar more obnoxious to
heretics of all denominations.

They were much hurt—it was the only hurt she
ever caused them—and the old dame and some of
her people, who had thought the scheme too good

LOSS AND GAIN 277

to be dropped altogether, insisted always on calling me Dominic!

My mother's sympathy and love for everybody appeared, too, in the hospitality she delighted to exercise. That, indeed, was the common virtue of the country, especially in the native population; but from all my experience during my wanderings on these great plains in subsequent years, when every night would find me a guest in a different establishment, I never saw anything quite on a par with my parents' hospitality. Nothing seemed to make them happier than having strangers and travellers taking their rest with us; there were also a good number of persons who were accustomed to make periodical visits to the city from the southern part of the province who, after a night with us, with perhaps half a day's rest to follow, would make our house a regular resting-place. But no distinctions were made. The poorest, even men who would be labelled tramps in England, travellers on foot perhaps where cattle made it dangerous to be on foot, would be made as welcome as those of a better class. Our delight as children, loving fun too well, was when we had a guest of this humble description at the supper-table. Settling down in our places at the long table laden with good things, a stern admonitory glance from our father would let us into the secret of the new guest's status—his unsuitability to his surroundings. It was great fun to watch him furtively and listen to his blundering conversational efforts, but we knew that the least sound of a titter on our part would have been an unpardonable offence. The poorer and more uncouth, or ridiculous, from our childish point of view they appeared, the more anxious my mother would be to put them at their ease. And she would sometimes say to us afterwards that she could not laugh with us because she remembered the poor fellow

*K 956

278 FAR AWAY AND LONG AGO

probably had a mother somewhere in a distant country who was perhaps thinking of him at the very time he was at the table with us, and hoping and praying that in his wanderings he would meet with some who would be kind to him.

I remember many of these chance guests, and will give a particular account of one—the guest and the evening we passed in his company—as this survives with a peculiar freshness in my memory, and it was also a cherished recollection of my mother's.

I was then nine or ten years old, and our guest was a young Spanish gentleman, singularly handsome, with a most engaging expression and manner. He was on a journey from Buenos Ayres to a part in our province some sixty or seventy leagues further south, and after asking permission to pass the night at our house, he explained that he had only one horse, as he liked that way of travelling rather than the native way of driving a *tropilla* before him, going at a furious gallop from dawn to dark, and changing horses every three or four leagues. Having but one horse, he had to go in a leisurely way with many rests, and he liked to call at many houses every day just to talk with the people.

After supper, during which he charmed us with his conversation and pure Castilian, which was like music as he spoke it, we formed a circle before a wood fire in the dining-room and made him take the middle seat. For he had confessed that he performed on the guitar, and we all wanted to sit where we could see as well as listen. He tuned the instrument in a leisurely way, pausing often to continue the conversation with my parents, until at last, seeing how eager we all were, he began to play, and his music and style were strange to us, for he had no jigging tunes with fantastic flights and flourishes so much affected by our native guitarists. It was beautiful but serious music.

LOSS AND GAIN 279

Then came another long pause and he talked again, and said the pieces he had been playing were composed by his chief favourite, Sarasate. He said that Sarasate had been one of the most famous guitarists in Spain, and had composed a good deal of music for the guitar before he had given it up for the violin. As a violinist he would win a European reputation, but in Spain they were sorry that he had abandoned the national instrument.

All he said was interesting, but we wanted more and more of his music, and he played less and less and at longer intervals, and at last he put the guitar down, and turning to my parents, said with a smile that he begged to be excused—that he could play no more for thinking. He owed it to them, he said, to tell them what he was thinking about; they would then know how much they had done for his pleasure that evening and how he appreciated it. He was, he continued, one of a large family, very united, all living with their parents at home; and in winter which was cold in his part of Spain, their happiest time was in the evening when they would gather before a big fire of oak logs in their *sala* and pass the time with books and conversation and a little music and singing. Naturally, since he had left his country years ago, the thought of that time and those evenings had occasionally been in his mind—a passing thought and memory. On this evening it had come in a different way, less like a memory than a revival of the past, so that as he sat there among us, he was a boy back in Spain once more, sitting by the fire with his brothers and sisters and parents. With that feeling in him he could not go on playing. And he thought it most strange that such an experience should have come to him for the first time in that place out on that great naked pampa, sparsely inhabited, where life was so rough, so primitive.

280 FAR AWAY AND LONG AGO

And while he talked we all listened—how eagerly!
—drinking in his words, especially my mother, her
eyes bright with the moisture rising in them; and she
often afterwards recalled that evening guest, who was
seen no more by us but had left an enduring image
in our hearts.

This is a picture of my mother as she appeared to
all who knew her. In my individual case there was
more, a secret bond of union between us, since she
best understood my feeling for Nature and sense of
beauty, and recognized that in this I was nearest
to her. Thus, besides and above the love of mother
and son, we had a spiritual kinship, and this was so
much to me that everything beautiful in sight or
sound that affected me came associated with her to
my mind. I have found this feeling most perfectly
expressed in some lines to the Snowdrop by our lost
poet, Dolben. I am in doubt, he wrote,

> If summer brings a flower so lovable,
> Of such a meditative restfulness
> As this, with all her roses and carnations.
> The morning hardly stirs their noiseless bells;
> Yet could I fancy that they whispered 'Home,'
> For all things gentle, all things beautiful,
> I hold, my mother, for a part of thee.

So have I held. All things beautiful, but chiefly
flowers. Her feeling for them was little short of
adoration. Her religious mind appeared to regard
them as little voiceless messengers from the Author
of our beings and of Nature, or as divine symbols of a
place and a beauty beyond our power to imagine.

I think it is likely that when Dolben penned those
lines to the Snowdrop it was in his mind that this was
one of his mother's favourites. My mother had her
favourites too; not the roses and carnations in our
gardens, but mostly among the wild flowers growing

LOSS AND GAIN 281

on the pampas—flowers which I never see in England.
But I remember them, and if by some strange chance
I should find myself once more in that distant region,
I should go out in search of them, and seeing them
again, feel that I was communing with her spirit.

These memories of my mother are a relief to me
in recalling that melancholy time, the years of my
youth that were wasted and worse, considering their
effect and that the very thought of that period
which is to others the fullest, richest, and happiest
in life, has always been painful to me. Yet to it I am
now obliged to return for the space of two or three
pages to relate how I eventually came out of it.
My case was not precisely like that of Cowper's
Castaway, but rather like that of a fugitive from his
ship on some tropical coast who, on swimming to
the shore, finds himself in a mangrove swamp, waist-
deep in mire, tangled in rope-like roots, straining
frantically to escape his doom.
I have told how after my fifteenth anniversary,
when I first began to reflect seriously on my future
life, the idea still persisted that my perpetual delight
in Nature was nothing more than a condition or phase
of my child's and boy's mind, and would inevitably
fade out in time. I might have guessed at an earlier
date that this was a delusion, since the feeling had
grown in strength with the years, but it was only
after I took to reading at the beginning of my sixteenth year that I discovered its true character. One
of the books I read then for the first time was White's
Selborne, given to me by an old friend of our family,
a merchant in Buenos Ayres, who had been accustomed to stay a week or two with us once a year when
he took his holiday. He had been on a visit to Europe,
and one day, he told me, when in London on the eve

282 FAR AWAY AND LONG AGO

of his departure, he was in a bookshop, and seeing this book on the counter and glancing at a page or two, it occurred to him that it was just the right thing to get for that bird-loving boy out on the pampas. I read and re-read it many times, for nothing so good of its kind had ever come to me, but it did not reveal to me the secret of my own feeling for Nature—the feeling of which I was becoming more and more conscious, which was a mystery to me, especially at certain moments, when it would come upon me with a sudden rush. So powerful it was, so unaccountable, I was actually afraid of it, yet I would go out of my way to seek it. At the hour of sunset I would go out half a mile or so from the house, and sitting on the dry grass with hands clasped round my knees, gaze at the western sky, waiting for it to take me. And I would ask myself: What does it mean? But there was no answer to that in any book concerning the 'life and conversation of animals.' I found it in other works: in Brown's *Philosophy*—another of the ancient tomes on our shelves—and in an old volume containing appreciations of the early nineteenth-century poets; also in other works. They did not tell me in so many words that it was the mystical faculty in me which produced those strange rushes or bursts of feeling and lifted me out of myself at moments; but what I found in their words was sufficient to show me that the feeling of delight in Nature was an enduring one, that others had known it, and that it had been a secret source of happiness throughout their lives.

This revelation, which in other circumstances would have made me exceedingly happy, only added to my misery when, as it appeared, I had only a short time to live. Nature could charm, she could enchant me, and her wordless messages to my soul were to me sweeter than honey and the honeycomb, but she

LOSS AND GAIN 283

could not take the sting and victory from death, and I had perforce to go elsewhere for consolation. Yet even so, in my worst days, my darkest years, when occupied with the laborious business of working out my own salvation with fear and trembling, with that spectre of death always following me, even so I could not rid my mind of its old passion and delight. The rising and setting sun, the sight of a lucid blue sky after cloud and rain, the long unheard familiar call-note of some newly-returned migrant, the first sight of some flower in spring, would bring back the old emotion and would be like a sudden ray of sunlight in a dark place—a momentary intense joy, to be succeeded by ineffable pain. Then there were times when these two opposite feelings mingled and would be together in my mind for hours at a time, and this occurred oftenest during the autumnal migration, when the great wave of bird-life set northwards, and all through March and April the birds were visible in flock succeeding flock from dawn to dark, until the summer visitants were all gone, to be succeeded in May by the birds from the far south, flying from the antarctic winter.

This annual spectacle had always been a moving one, but the feeling it now produced—this mingled feeling—was most powerful on still moonlight nights, when I would sit or lie on my bed gazing out on the prospect, earth and sky, in its changed mysterious aspect. And, lying there, I would listen by the hour to the three-syllable call-note of the upland or solitary plover, as the birds went past, each bird alone far up in the dim sky, winging his way to the north. It was a strange vigil I kept, stirred by strange thoughts and feelings, in that moonlit earth that was strange too, albeit familiar, for never before had the sense of the supernatural in Nature been stronger. And the bird

284 FAR AWAY AND LONG AGO

I listened to, that same solitary plover I had known and admired from my earliest years, the most graceful of birds, beautiful to see and hear when it would spring up before my horse with its prolonged wild bubbling cry of alarm and go away with swift, swallow-like flight—what intensity and gladness of life was in it, what a wonderful inherited knowledge in its brain, and what an inexhaustible vigour in its slender frame to enable it to perform that annual double journey of upwards of ten thousand miles! What a joy it would be to live for ages in a world of such fascinating phenomena! If some great physician, wise beyond all others, infallible, had said to me that all my doctors had been wrong, that, barring accidents, I had yet fifty years to live, or forty, or even thirty, I should have worshipped him and would have counted myself the happiest being on the globe, with so many autumns and winters and springs and summers to see yet.

With these supernatural moonlight nights I finish the story of that dark time, albeit the darkness had not yet gone; to have recalled it and related it briefly as I could once in my life is enough. Let me now go back to the simile of the lost wretch struggling for life in the mangrove swamp. The first sense of having set my foot on a firmer place in that slough of fetid slime, of a wholesome breath of air blown to me from outside the shadow of the black abhorred forest, was when I began to experience intervals of relief from physical pain, when these grew more and more frequent and would extend to entire days, then to weeks, and for a time I would become oblivious of my precarious state. I was still and for a long time subject to attacks, when the pain was intolerable and was like steel driven into my heart, always followed by violent palpitations, which would last for hours. But I found that exercise on foot or horseback made me no worse, and I became

LOSS AND GAIN 285

more and more venturesome, spending most of my
time out of doors, although often troubled with the
thought that my passion for Nature was a hindrance
to me, a turning aside from the difficult way I had
been striving to keep.

Then my elder brother returned, an event of the
greatest importance in my life; and as he had not
been expected so soon, I was for a minute in doubt
that this strange visitor could be my brother, so
greatly had he altered in appearance in those five
long years of absence, which had seemed like an age
to me. He had left us as a smooth-faced youth,
with skin tanned to such a deep colour that with his
dark piercing eyes and long black hair he had looked
to me more like an Indian than a white man. Now
his skin was white, and he had grown a brown beard
and moustache. In disposition, too, he had grown
more genial and tolerant, but I soon discovered that
in character he had not changed.

As soon as an opportunity came he began to inter-
rogate and cross-question me as to my mind—life
and where I stood, and expressed himself surprised
to hear that I still held to the creed in which we had
been reared. How, he demanded, did I reconcile
these ancient fabulous notions with the doctrine of
evolution? What effect had Darwin produced on me?
I had to confess that I had not read a line of his work,
that with the exception of Draper's *History of Civilization*,
which had come by chance in my way, I had during all
those five years read nothing but the old books which
had always been on our shelves. He said he knew
Draper's *History*, and it was not the sort of book for
me to read at present. I wanted a different history,
with animals as well as men in it. He had a store of
books with him, and would lend me the *Origin of Species*
to begin with.

286 FAR AWAY AND LONG AGO

When I had read and returned the book, and he was eager to hear my opinion, I said it had not hurt me in the least, since Darwin had to my mind only succeeded in disproving his own theory with his argument from artificial selection. He himself confessed that no new species had .ever been produced in that way.

That, he said in reply, was the easy criticism that any one who came to the reading in a hostile spirit would make. They would fasten on that apparently weak point and not pay much attention to the fact that it is fairly met and answered in the book. When he first read the book it convinced him; but he had come to it with an open mind and I with a prejudiced mind on account of my religious ideas. He advised me to read it again, to read and consider it carefully with the sole purpose of getting at the truth. 'Take it,' he said, 'and read it again in the right way for you to read it—as a naturalist.'

He had been surprised that I, an ignorant boy or youth on the pampas, had ventured to criticize such a work. I, on my side, had been equally surprised at his quiet way of reasoning with me, with none of the old scornful spirit flaming out. He was gentle with me, knowing that I had suffered much and was not free yet.

I read it again in the way he had counselled, and then refused to think any more on the subject. I was sick of thinking. Like the wretch who long has tossed upon the thorny bed of pain, I only wanted to repair my vigour lost and breathe and walk again; to be on horseback, galloping over the green pampas, in sun and wind. For after all it was only a reprieve, not a commutation of sentence—though one of a kind unknown in the Courts, in which the condemned man is allowed out on bail. My pardon was not

LOSS AND GAIN

received until a few years later. I returned with a new wonderful zest to my old sports, shooting and fishing, and would spend days and weeks from home, sometimes staying with old gaucho friends and former neighbours at their ranchos, attending cattle markings and partings, dances, and other gatherings, and also made longer expeditions to the southern and western frontiers of the province, living out of doors for months at a time.

Despite my determination to put the question off, my mind, or subconscious mind, like a dog with a bone which it refuses to drop in defiance of its master's command, went on revolving it. It went to bed and got up with me, and was with me the day long, and whenever I had a still interval, when I would pull up my horse to sit motionless watching some creature, bird or beast or snake, or sat on the ground poring over some insect occupied with the business of its little life, I would become conscious of the discussion and argument going on. And every creature I watched, from the great soaring bird circling in the sky at a vast altitude to the little life at my feet, was brought into the argument, and was a type, representing a group marked by a family likeness not only in figure and colouring and language, but in mind as well, in habits and the most trivial traits and tricks of gesture and so on; the entire group in its turn related to another group, and to others still further and further away, the likeness growing less and less. What explanation was possible but that of community of descent? How incredible it appeared that this had not been seen years ago—yes, even before it was discovered that the world was round and was one of a system of planets revolving round the sun! All this starry knowledge was of little or no importance compared to that of our relationship with all the infinitely various forms of life

288   FAR AWAY AND LONG AGO

that share the earth with us. Yet it was not till the
second half of the nineteenth century that this great,
almost self-evident truth had won a hearing in the
world!

No doubt this is a common experience: no sooner
has the inquirer been driven to accept a new doctrine
than it takes complete possession of his mind, and
has not then the appearance of a strange and unwelcome guest, but rather that of a familiar friendly
one, and is like a long-established house-mate. I
suppose the explanation is that when we throw open
the doors to the new importunate visitor, it is virtually a ceremony, since the real event has been already
accomplished, the guest having stolen in by some
other way and made himself at home in the subconscious mind. Insensibly and inevitably I had become
an evolutionist, albeit never wholly satisfied with
natural selection as the only and sufficient explanation
of the change in the forms of life. And again, insensibly
and inevitably, the new doctrine has led to modifications
of the old religious ideas and eventually to a new and
simplified philosophy of life. A good enough one so
far as this life is concerned, but unhappily it takes no
account of another, a second and perdurable life without
change of personality.

This subject has been much in men's minds during
the past two or three dreadful years, often reminding
me of that shock I received as a boy of fourteen at
the old gaucho's bitter story of his soul; I have also
again been reminded of the theory in which that younger
and greatly-loved brother of mine was able to find
comfort. He had become deeply religious, and after
much reading in Herbert Spencer and other modern
philosophers and evolutionists, he told me he thought
it was idle for Christians to fight against the argument
of the materialists that the mind is a function of the

LOSS AND GAIN 289

brain. Undoubtedly it was that, and our mental faculties perished with the brain; but we had a soul that was imperishable as well. *He knew it*, which meant that he too was a mystic, and being wholly pre-occupied with religion, his mystical faculty found its use and exercise there. At all events, his notion served to lift him over *his* difficulties and to get him out of *his* mangrove swamp—a way perhaps less impossible than the one recently pointed out by William James.

Thus I came out of the contest a loser, but as a compensation had the knowledge that my physicians were false prophets; that, barring accidents, I could count on thirty, forty, even fifty years with their summers and autumns and winters. And that was the life I desired—the life the heart can conceive—the earth life. When I hear people say they have not found the world and life so agreeable or interesting as to be in love with it, or that they look with equanimity to its end, I am apt to think they have never been properly alive nor seen with clear vision the world they think so meanly of, or anything in it—not a blade of grass. Only I know that mine is an exceptional case, that the visible world is to me more beautiful and interesting than to most persons, that the delight I experienced in my communings with Nature did not pass away, leaving nothing but a recollection of vanished happiness to intensify a present pain. The happiness was never lost, but owing to that faculty I have spoken of, had a cumulative affect on the mind and was mine again, so that in my worst times, when I was compelled to exist shut out from Nature in London for long periods, sick and poor and friendless, I could yet always feel that it was infinitely better to be than not to be.

INDEX

INDEX

ACACIA, black, 41–2; white, or
false, 43, 200
Ailanthus, 43
Aksakoff, Serge, his *History of
My Childhood* referred to,
196, 275
Alfalfa, its attraction for butterflies, 45–6
Animism, survival of, in civilized man, 194–5; first childish intimations of, 196–7;
personal experiences of, with
flowers, 196–8; with trees,
200; its religious character,
201–3; its persistence in
adults, 202–3
Armadillo, adventure with an,
44; eaten by gauchos, 147
Aros con leche, 121
Avalos, Don Amáro, 98–9

Barboza, Basilio, fighter and
singer, 119–20, 121, 123; his
niece Anjelita, 124–5, 126
Barn, a murderer confined in a,
17–18
Bats, habits of, on the pampas,
189–90
Baxter, Richard, his *Saints'
Everlasting Rest*, 265
Beggar on horseback, a, 20–1
Beggars, Buenos Ayrean, 85–6
Bien-te-veo tyrant-bird, 109,
255–6; a forgotten ballad of,
110–11
Blake, Matthew, 182–4
Blake, Mrs, a snake rescued by,
182; portrait of, 183; her
singing, 184
Blue ibis, 228
Blunderbuss, adventure with a,
243

Bolas, hunting golden plover
with, 150, 151
Books, first acquaintance with,
259, 260
Brown's *Philosophy*, 282
Buenavida, Don Anastacio, 144,
145–6; his devotion to pigs,
147
Buenos Ayres, first visit to, 79;
sights and adventures in,
80–91;threatened siege of,243,
245; the Saladero at, 249–50;
insanitary condition of, 251

Camaloté, 227, 228, 256
Cañada Seca estancia, 144, 145
Cane-brake, a, 46
Carancho (Polyborus tharus), 70,
169; nest of, 71, 73; preda-
ceous habits of, 71, 72
Cardoon thistle, used as fire-
wood, 17, 128; its abundance,
54, 94; thickets of, frequented
by deer, 75, 76
Carlyle's *French Revolution*, 260
Carriage, a home-built, 133
Carrion-hawk. *See Carancho*
Casa Antigua estancia, 127–8
Cattle, home - returning, 9;
native method of slaughter-
ing, 35–6
Ceratophrys ornata, 152; con-
certs of, 152, 154; an expedi-
tion against, 153
Cervus campestris, 76
Cheeses made of sheep's milk,
129, 130
Childhood, difficulty of recalling, 1, 195, 196; nature of
mentality in, 31–2
Chimango hawk, 41

293

INDEX

Chrysomitris magellanica. See Siskin, Argentine
Combe, George, his *Physiology* referred to, 270
Conarus patagonicus, 73-4
Conrad, Joseph, his *Mirror of the Sea* referred to, 62
Coots, 227-8
Courthope, W. J., referred to, 204
Cow-bird, purple, 51, 229; its concert-singing, 51; a practical joke played with one, 224-5
Cowper, William, animism in, 201-2
Crested screamer, flight of, 164-5; wading habits of, 228
Cuckoo, Guira, 42; yellow-billed, 53

Dardo, a native boy, 96, 97, 98, 99, 100
Darwin, Charles, his *Voyage of a Naturalist*, 107; his *Origin of Species*, 285-6; effect of his doctrine on the author, 287-8
Death, a child's thoughts and experiences of, 30-1, 34-8; a youth's attitude towards, 254-5, 263-4
Deer, fighting, 75-6; their powerful odour, 178
Diet of pampas-dwellers, 57
Ditch, an immense, 43-4
Dogs, portraits of: Pechicho, 7-9; Caesar, 28-30; a shad-fisher, 86-7
Dolben, D. M., quoted, 280
Dormilon, native name of painted snipe, 228
Doves, an attempt to catch them with salt, 68-9
Draper, J. W., his *History of Civilization*, 285
Duck, shooting wild, 240-1, 242, 243, 244-5; species enumerated, 241

Duellists, gaucho, 117, 119, 120; their method of fighting, 221-2, 223
Durasmillo, a semi-aquatic solanaceous plant, 229-30

Earth, smell of moist, 6
Encarnacion, Doña, 93
English inn-keeper, an, 159, 160
Escuerzo, native name of *Ceratophrys ornata*, 152
Estanislao the ostrich-hunter, 132-3
Eusebio, Don, Rosas' court jester, 90-1

Fashions, masculine, in Buenos Ayres, 82
Father, the author's, his disregard of danger, 100, 101, 102, 104; his trustfulness 103, 104
Fences made of cows' skulls, 250-1
Fennel, the solitary, 46-7
Finch, a field (*Sycalis luteola*), concert-singing by, 49, 50; its effect on a stolid Englishman, 50-1
Fires on the pampas, 59-60
Firewood-gatherer (*Anumbius acuticaudatus*), 41
Flamingo, first sight of, 67; beauty of, 67
Fleming, Marjorie, quoted, 167

Gandara, Don Gregorio, 135-6; his family, 137; his fancy for piebalds, 138, 139-40; his daughter's wedding, 142-3
Giant thistle, 55; abundance of in 'thistle-years,' 58; danger of fire from, 59, 60; as fodder, 61, 62
Gibbon's *Decline and Fall*, 260
Glossy ibis, musky odour of, 115
God, a small child's conception of, 33-4
Goldfinch, 41, 89

INDEX 295

Golondrina domestica (*Progne chalybea*), 53
Grebe, 227
Guitar-player, a refined, 278–80
Gun, author's first use of a, 240
Gutierres, Ventura, 174; his first taste of pickled peaches, 175, 176

Hafiz quoted, 255
Hailstones, destruction caused by, 63, 64–5
Hermit, the, 11–12; his death, 14
Horse, story of a, 63–4
Houses on the pampas, 56–7
Hudson, Edwin, his armoury, 153, 236; his mathematical studies, 207, 208; his journalistic venture, 211–14; his meeting with Jack the Killer, 218–19; his knife-practice, 222; his resolute spirit, 257–8; his gift of story-telling, 258–9; his rejection of Christianity, 273; his home-coming, 285
Humming-bird, 52–3
Hunt, Leigh, his *Autobiography* quoted, 275

Immortality, the desire for, 270, 288

Jacana, 229
Jack the Killer, 218, 219–20
James, William, referred to, 289
Jefferies, Richard, his *Story of My Heart* referred to, 106–7
John, the 'Cumberland boor,' 50–1

Killing-ground at Buenos Ayres, 249–50
Kowe-kowe, native name of yellow-billed cuckoo, 53
Kú-ku, the meaning of, 192

La Paja Brava estancia, 160, 162–3
La Tapera estancia, 135, 137–8

Lagrimas de la Virgen (Virgin's Tears), 169–70, 198
Lapwing, Argentine or spurwing, 47; its eggs a delicacy, 172; hunting for its eggs, 173
Laugh, an extraordinary, 136
Leland on Revelation, 260
Lombardy poplars, 18, 39, 41, 55, 127; leafing of, 52
Loro barranquero, native name of Patagonian parrot, 73–4
Los Alamos estancia, 114, 115, 116
Los Veinte-cinco Ombues estancia, the author's birthplace, 4; a ghost at, 6–7; farewell.to, 16; return to, 262
Lower, Mark Anthony, the Sussex antiquary, 140
Lucía del Ombú, Doña, 120
Lyrical Ballads referred to, 203

Mácachina, flowering of the, 149–50
Marcos, called *El Rengo*, 121–2, 123
Marshes, the, 226–35
Marsh-troupial (*Agelaeus ruficapillus*), 229, 230
Martins, 53
Melanism, 191
Meredith, George, his *Rhoda Fleming* quoted, 180
Minister of War, Rosas', 94; his mania for peacocks, 94
Mirage on the pampas, 57–8
Misto, native name of *Sycalis luteola*, 49
Mother, death of author's, 274; her character, 275–81
Mulberry trees, 43

Nata, Doña, 96–7, 98, 99–100
Nature, a boy's feeling for, 255–6, 281, 282–4, 285
Newhaven, the miller of, 140–1
Night-watchmen at Buenos Ayres, 84–5; wresting trophies from, 85, 95

296 INDEX

O'Keefe, Father, 206–7, 208;
his toyings with Protestantism, 209–10
Ombú tree, described, 4; a solitary, 120
Opossums, snake in a nest of, 45
Oribe, General, 94
Ostrich, hunting the, a boys' game, 233–4
Owl, short-eared, a pigeon-killing, 168; range of, 169; discovery of its nest, 170; intermittent abundance of, 171

Painted snipe, 228
Pampero, the, 60, 61, 62
Parental attitude, the proper, 9–10
Paroquet, green, 48, 73, 75; social habits of, 74
Parrot, Patagonian or cliff, 73; migrating flocks of, 73; its partiality for pumpkin-seeds, 74
Pascuala, Doña, 115–16; her cavalier treatment of St Anthony, 116
Peach trees, 42; blossoming, 48, 49
Peaches, pickled, 173–4, 175, 176
Peacocks, a war-minister's, 94
Peñalva, Cipriana, 161–2
Peñalva, Don Evaristo, the Patriarch, 156–63; his six wives, 158; his cure for shingles, 158
Peregrine falcon, 165; its method of capturing pigeons, 166
Philodryas aestivus, a conversational snake, 179–80
Philodryas scotti, 193
Piebalds, a breeder of, 138, 139, 140, 141–2
Pigeons at author's home, 165–6, 167, 168

Pigs, a breed of wild, 147; an adventure with, 148, 149
Pintails, 241
Plover, golden (*Charadrius dominicana*), killed by hail-stones, 65; at Cañada Seca, 150; a great flock of, 237
Polyborus tharus, see *Carancho*
Pope, Alexander, his *Windsor Forest* referred to, 204
Pumpkin, wild, 74

Quince trees, 42

Race-meetings, 230
Ramsdale, Mr, 74–5
Rats, a great congregation of, 19; method of killing, 44
Religious difficulties, 264–71
Religious literature, 265
Rennie, James, books by, 259
Rhea, first sight of, 77; its tricky instinct, 77–8; a tame, 138; eaten by gauchos, 147; omelettes of its eggs, 172
Rollin's *Ancient History*, 260
Rosas, the Dictator, 90, 91, 92; a portrait of him, 92, 93; his defeat, 100; light on his character, 108–13
Roseate spoonbill, 228
Rosy-billed duck, 241, 242
Royd, George, 128, 129; his family, 129–32; his enthusiasm for cookery, 132; his home-built carriage, 133; his tragic end, 134

St Anthony, cavalier treatment of, 116
St Augustine, 260
Saladero, the, at Buenos Ayres, 249–50
Sandpiper, buff-coloured (*Tringites rufescens*), 151
Sarasate, Pablo, as composer for the guitar, 279
Scarlet tyrant-bird, 52
Scissor-tail tyrant-bird, 40–1

INDEX

297

Scott, Captain, 10–11
Shad in the Plata river, 87
Sham fights, 231
Shingles, a cure for, 158
Shoveller duck, 241, 242, 243
Siskin, Argentine, 41, 88–9
Skunk, 178
Snakes, childish impressions of, 177, 178–9, 180, 181; species found about author's home, 179, 185–6; finding their sloughs, 181; a new feeling about them, 185; adventures with, 185–93
Snipe, solitary or summer, 44
Social marsh-hawk, 228–9
Spencer, Herbert, quoted, 195
Stilt, 229
Stork, 228
Storm, a great, 63, 64–5
Swallows, 47, 53
Swans, 241–2

Taste-impressions, evanescence of, 171
Teal, 241, 242
'Thistle-years,' 58–9, 61–2
Throat-cutting, primitive satisfaction in, 106, 107–8
Tinamou, 231
Toad, shingles cured by application of a, 158
Tolstoy referred to, 233
Torcasa, native name of Zenaida maculata, 70
Traherne, Thomas, animism in, 203
Tree, a wonderful flowering, 5

Tree of heaven, 43
Tree-planting by early colonists, 55–6
Trees, animistic attitude towards, 200–3
Trigg, Mr, 22–4, 25–7, 205, 206,
Typhus, author attacked by, 253

Upland duck, 241
Upland geese, 241
Upland plover, 283–4
Urquiza, Captain-General, 93; his successful rebellion, 100

Vanduria, native name of blue ibis, 228
Violets, 39–40
Vivora de la cruz, 45, 185
Vizcachas, 55; effect of loud noises on, 177–8

Washerwomen at Buenos Ayres, 83; their word-battles with young bloods, 84
Water-snail, 228
Weeds, thickets of, 46–7
Whiston's Josephus, 260
White's Selborne, 281, 282
Willows, two great red, 40, 41, 164, 165
Wordsworth, William, on childhood, 195; his subtilized animism, 203

Zango, the riding-horse, 63–4
Zenaida doves, 68–9

Printed in the USA
CPSIA information can be obtained
at www.ICGtesting.com
LVHW041310160424
777527LV00001B/14